## THE ALBIGENSIAN CRUSADE

Languedoc is among the most varied and beautiful parts of France. But eight centuries ago it was far from certain that it would become part of France at all. The semi-independent Mediterranean principality, ruled by the house of Toulouse, seemed far apart from the world of the feudal north. In this rich region a persuasive heresy of eastern origin implanted itself. For more than fifty years the Catholic Church retreated in the face of a rival whose teaching appeared to question the very foundations of Christian thought; until in 1208 the Church proclaimed a crusade against the 'infidels' who had taken possession of one of Christendom's oldest provinces. Languedoc was conquered by the armies, and ultimately by the manners and civilisation, of northern France.

This book is far more than the history of one of the most savage of all medieval wars. It reconstructs a world in which every French province had its own cultural tradition, a tradition which in Languedoc created the *troubadours*, the basilica of St. Sernin, and the castles of Cabaret and Carcassonne.

Jonathan Sumption was a history fellow of Magdalene College, Oxford, until 1975. He is a QC practising at the commerical bar and is the author of *Pilgrimage: An Image of Medieval Religion*, and *Trial by Battle* and *Trial by Fire*, the first two volumes of his history of the Hundred Years War.

# THE
# ALBIGENSIAN CRUSADE

✤

Jonathan Sumption

*faber and faber*
LONDON·NEW YORK

First published in 1978
by Faber and Faber Limited
3 Queen Square London WC1N 3AU
This paperback edition first published in 1999

Printed in England by Clays Ltd, St Ives plc

A CIP record for this book
is available from the British Library

ISBN 0–571–20002–8

4 6 8 10 9 7 5 3

'If thou shalt hear say in one of thy cities . . . , Let us go and serve other Gods . . . ; then shalt thou surely smite the inhabitants of that city with the edge of the sword, destroying it utterly and all that is therein. . . . And thou shalt burn with fire the city and all the spoil thereof every whit for the Lord thy God. . . . And it shall be an heap for ever; and it shall not be built again.'

(DEUTERONOMY XIII. 12–16.)

TO TERESA

# Contents

| | | | |
|---|---|---|---:|
| I. | Languedoc | *page* | 15 |
| II. | The dualist tradition | | 32 |
| III. | The Cathar church | | 43 |
| IV. | 1194–1208: Raymond VI | | 63 |
| V. | 1208–1209: The launching of the crusade | | 77 |
| VI. | 1209: Béziers and Carcassonne | | 88 |
| VII. | 1209–1211: The breach with Raymond VI | | 104 |
| VIII. | 1211: Triumph and disaster | | 128 |
| IX. | 1211–1212: The conquest of the south | | 143 |
| X. | 1212–1213: Muret | | 156 |
| XI. | 1213–1216: Judgement in Rome | | 171 |
| XII. | 1216–1218: The turning of the tide | | 183 |
| XIII. | 1218–1224: The liberation | | 199 |
| XIV. | 1224–1229: The crusade of Louis VIII | | 212 |
| XV. | The Inquisition | | 226 |
| XVI. | Epilogue: France and Languedoc | | 244 |
| | Notes | | 253 |
| | Select bibliography | | 256 |
| | Index | | 261 |

# Maps

| | | |
|---|---|---|
| I. | Languedoc in 1204: territorial divisions | *page* 26–7 |
| II. | Carcasses–Minervois–Narbonnais | 91 |
| III. | Carcassonne in 1209 | 95 |
| IV. | Minerve in 1210 | 115 |
| V. | Toulouse–Laurageais–Carcasses | 132 |
| VI. | Albigeois–southern Quercy | 147 |
| VII. | Muret in 1213 | 165 |
| VIII. | Battle of Muret | 168 |
| IX. | Beaucaire in 1216 | 185 |
| X. | Toulouse in 1218 | 194 |
| XI. | Languedoc in the time of the crusade | 270–1 |

✠ I ✠

# Languedoc

'A land of wheat and barley, vines and fig trees.'
DEUTERONOMY VIII.8

North of Arles, where the river Rhône divides, a papal legate was assassinated on a January morning in 1208. The legate, Peter of Castelnau, had left the abbey of St.-Gilles with a small bodyguard on the previous day and reached the west bank of the Rhône after nightfall. Since it was too late to cross the fast-flowing river by boat, the party spent the night near the river. Before dawn on 14th January they rose, said Mass, and set out towards the river bank. As they did so, a horseman approached unobserved, from behind and drove his lance into the legate's back. Peter was hurled from his mule and died a few minutes later as dawn broke. His assailant escaped at the gallop to the nearby fortress of Beaucaire, leaving the legate's attendants to carry his body back to St.-Gilles, some ten miles back along the road. In the abbey cloister he was buried by the monks carrying lighted candles and chanting the *Kyrie Eleison*.

The assassin had fled, but not before he was identified as a servant of Raymond VI, count of Toulouse. He had been in Raymond's suite at St.-Gilles on the previous day and may have witnessed the violent quarrel between the count and the papal legate. Some obscure solecism had lost him the count's favour, and he was looking for an opportunity to return to grace. But whether Raymond had inspired his enterprise, or had even known of it, is far from clear. In the course of a tempestuous interview, Raymond was said to have threatened Peter with violence and objected to the bodyguard provided for him by the abbot of St.-Gilles. The count had had both motive and opportunity, and the evidence, which at the time had seemed confused, acquired a misleading clarity by the time it reached Rome. Innocent III declared Peter of Castelnau to be a martyr and unequivocally named the count of Toulouse as his murderer.

15

'Faith and Peace: there are no nobler causes in which to die a martyr's death,' the pope declared in his obituary of the murdered legate. Undoubtedly Faith was better served by Peter's martyrdom than Peace. A persuasive heresy of eastern origin had implanted itself in Raymond's dominions and had succeeded in converting a substantial part of the population. For more than fifty years the church had retreated in the face of a rival organization whose teaching appeared to orthodox theologians to question the foundations of Christian thought. The civil authorities had been unable, unwilling some believed, to prevent the further expansion of the sect. More than that, many of the nobility on whose intervention the church had rested its hopes were themselves infected by the spreading gangrene. Successive papal emissaries were unable to decide whether Raymond himself was among them. What was certain was that he had failed to suppress the heresy by force, and this made him a protector of heretics if not a heretic himself. Persuasion no longer seemed necessary or even useful. An army was recruited in northern France with the promise of indulgences equal to those offered to knights who fought the Infidel in the Holy Land. The death of Peter of Castelnau was avenged by one of the most savage of all mediaeval wars. Faith ultimately prevailed, as Innocent III had predicted, but the consequences of the Albigensian crusade went far beyond its aims. A semi-independent Mediterranean principality was conquered not only by French armies but by the civilization and manners of France. In place of the native dynasty, a member of the French royal family ruled the province from his residence in Paris, leaving the details of administration to bailiffs, officials, and inquisitors. The power of the French monarchy extended for the first time in four centuries to the Mediterranean.

These events marked the triumph of politics over geography. The Massif Central, sparsely populated, with few rivers and no roads, was a formidable barrier to any ambitious centralizing power based in the north. The hills were gentler closer to the Atlantic, but they were divided by great west-flowing rivers—the Somme, the Seine, the Loire, the Dordogne, and the Garonne—which too easily became the frontiers of upstart and independent principalities. The principal route from Paris to the Mediterranean was then, as now, the Rhône-Saône corridor, through which passed one of the richest trade routes of western Europe. But wealth bred power, and the great cities which punctuated the route served no king, for all their outward exhibitions of deference.

# Languedoc

In the seventeenth century, cardinal Richelieu might look on the Rhine, the Alps, and the Pyrenees as marking off the 'natural area' of France. But only the remarkable bureaucratic resources of his own government had made this possible. In the twelfth century when men spoke of 'France' they meant 'northern France' and their terminology, so strange to modern ears, had the sanction of political reality. The authority of the Capetian kings was recognized in less than a tenth of Richelieu's 'natural area'. The territory over which they exercised effective control was smaller still, amounting to no more than Paris, the Ile-de-France, a corner of Burgundy, and isolated enclaves in northern and central France. It is fair to say that their influence extended further than their power. But in the west and south of their kingdom they lacked even influence. The empire of the Angevin kings of England included the entire Atlantic coast of France from the Channel to the Pyrenees, and extended inland as far as Vernon, Tours, Clermont-Ferrand, and Agen. The frontier of the Holy Roman Empire lay not at the Alps but at the Rhône; Provence was an imperial territory; Lyon and Avignon were frontier towns.

Even so, political frontiers mattered less than cultural ones. Poor communications and aristocratic independence left each region to develop its own cultural and political identity. At the margins, distinctions were blurred. But it remained possible for a Poitevin to regard Gascons as foreigners, and for a Burgundian abbot to speak of his native region as having 'no king, no duke, no prince'. The rich province of Languedoc, which lay beyond the Aveyron, between the valleys of the Rhône and the Garonne, probably had less in common with the north of France than many parts of Germany. Its inhabitants, according to a Norman chronicler, were arrogant and hot-tempered and 'as different from the Franks as chickens are from ducks'. The survival of Roman law, the prominent role of women, and the refinement of a society not organized for war, marked it off from the more disciplined north. Its literature was more secular and was written in the *langue d'oc*, a language which Dante's contemporaries, to the poet's great disgust, regarded as finer than either Italian or French. Its prosperity was shaped by the trade routes of the Mediterranean. Its cities developed on Italian, not on northern lines. Historical accident and geographical convenience had contributed to its peculiar development. The break-up of the Roman Empire had had a rather less disturbing effect here than further north, and subsequent invasions by

Frankish armies never penetrated quite as far as Languedoc. Although Charlemagne succeeded where his forebears had failed, his achievement did not long survive his death. The decay of the Carolingian empire was felt first at its extremities. The local counts, originally mere administrative officials, were left in unfettered control of their provinces. They became hereditary and, in time, independent of the Frankish monarchy. In the twelfth century the rulers of the south recognized the suzerainty of the Capetian kings and did homage for their dominions. But they well knew that the Capetians were weak and distant, and their suzerainty little more than nominal.

The greatest of these rulers were the princes of the house of Toulouse, 'the peers of kings, the superiors of dukes and counts', as the Englishman Gervase of Tilbury described them at the beginning of the thirteenth century. The principality of Toulouse was created in 924 when Raymond III Pons, already count of Toulouse, annexed the ancient marquisate of Gothia, comprising the dioceses of Narbonne, Béziers, Agde, Lodève, Maguelonne, Nîmes, and Elne. To these extensive dominions were added the strategic castle of Tarascon on the east bank of the Rhône, acquired by marriage in 990, and a number of scattered footholds in the neighbouring imperial county of Provence. At every death, however, the power of the house of Toulouse was weakened by the practice of partitioning its territories among the sons and daughters of the family. It was left to Raymond IV (d. 1105) to weld his ungainly inheritance into a single, cohesive unit, and make his family the most powerful in the Midi. This he did by a rich marriage, by a series of dynastic alliances, and above all by a shrewd alliance with the church. When Raymond crowned his career by leading the first crusade to Jerusalem in 1096, he was the ruler of thirteen counties, a consolidated domain stretching from Toulouse to Nîmes, from Cahors to Narbonne.

In spite of its formidable size, the power of the principality of Toulouse was more apparent than real. In northern France, the shattering experience of two centuries of Viking invasions had created a strong military society. Land was held in fief, in return for regular military service, court service, and special aids and dues. The great principalities of the north, those of Normandy, Anjou, and Champagne, were centralized, authoritarian states. Languedoc, on the other hand, had scarcely been troubled by the invaders, and constant war had not moulded its institutions. The strenuous efforts of its rulers had signally failed to impose on it the thorough-going feudalism of the north, and consequently it lacked the impressive social cohesion of its neighbours. One symptom of this was the high proportion of allodial land, free land from which no feudal service was due. An allodial landowner was nobody's man and could look to nobody to protect him. For this reason allods had almost entirely disappeared in the north, and become fiefs; in the south, however, the proportion of allods had actually increased during the ninth and tenth centuries. Even where land was held feudally, the bond between lord and man was weak. The feudal lord might be entitled to military service, but more often than not he simply exacted a rent. Herein lay the overpowering weakness of the counts of Toulouse. In a region which was rich enough to excite covetous neighbours, and where private war was endemic, the government could not raise a feudal army. It was dependent on mercenaries whom it could not always afford to pay and whose undisciplined violence only added to its problems.

If social bonds were weaker in Languedoc, this had much to do with the surviving influence of Roman law. 'We have heard', Louis VII of France wrote in 1164, 'that the law of the Empire is applied there and that doctors from Bologna are teaching it.' In fact, southern charters of the twelfth century reveal very little acquaintance with Roman law, but one area where it was undeniably applied was that of testamentary dispositions. The holder of a fief had rights over the land which would have been unthinkable in the north. 'A man may do with his own property whatever he wishes and dispose of it exactly as he pleases,' begins a charter of the period. He could freely sell his land or bequeath it to whomsoever he wished, and the fact that he generally chose to divide it among his children could only exaggerate the fissiparous tendencies of southern society. Several noble houses were reduced to ruin by the constant division of their property, and only extreme good fortune saved the house of Toulouse from the same fate. After Odo, count of Toulouse, divided his immense domains between his two sons at the end of the tenth century, it took more than a century to reunite them. The great county of Carcassonne was partitioned in about 950, and by the middle of the eleventh century there were five counts of Carcassonne. In the course of the twelfth century the greater nobles, including the counts of Toulouse, learned this lesson and adopted the northern practice of primogeniture. But the lesser nobility never learned it. On the eve of the Albigensian crusade, the castle of Montréal was held in undivided shares by thirty-six knights, Mirepoix by another thirty-six, and Lombez by fifty. A fief was thought of as the possession of a family, not of an individual. For this reason women could, and commonly did, inherit in their own right, a notable symptom of the unmilitary quality of southern fiefs. Ermengarde, viscountess of Narbonne, governed her territory, administering justice and fighting off her enemies, for sixty years. Other powerful women were ready to take the field if the occasion demanded. Northern feudalism was more than a convention of land tenure. It was a system of government, and its absence in Languedoc gravely compromised the efforts of the counts of Toulouse to build a southern state on the model of the Angevin empire. Although the extent of their territories was imposing within it they exercised little real power, far less than the Capetians exercised in their own, smaller, demesne. In the Toulousain itself they were in control. Elsewhere they had estates here, legal rights there, a few dependent churches scattered about. Real authority belonged to their vassals.

Who were these vassals? The counts of Foix, although they were nominally numbered among them, ruled a principality which straddled the Pyrenees, and which in practice recognized no suzerainty but their own. The extent of their territory fluctuated with every change in their fortunes, but by the end of the twelfth century they were well entrenched as far north as Pamiers, and were disputing possession of Saverdun with Raymond V of Toulouse. East of the county of Foix stood the small but wealthy territory of Narbonne whose viscounts, supposedly officials of the house of Toulouse, had in fact been independent hereditary princes since the early years of the tenth century. Their uneasy relationship with their neighbours and continuous quarrels with the archbishop of Narbonne were a source of instability in a region of great commercial and strategic importance. More ambitious and more powerful than either of these princes were the Trencavel viscounts of Béziers. Like the viscounts of Narbonne they were ostensibly officials. But their office had become hereditary in the tenth century and by a mixture of dynastic marriages and armed force they gradually added Agde, Nîmes, Albi, Carcassonne, and the Razès to their dominions. From the death of Bernard-Aton IV in 1130, the Trencavels were undoubtedly more powerful than the counts of Toulouse. Their principality extended from the Tarn to the Pyrenees, dividing the territories of Toulouse in two and threatening the Toulousain itself.

The power which these vassals exercised within their own domains, though considerably greater than that of the house of Toulouse, was still far from complete. Even the Trencavels depended on the support of a host of petty lords, such as the counts of Rodez and the viscounts of Montpellier, who supported now one side and now the other in a desperate effort to preserve their independence and pursue the advantages of the moment. Indeed, the vassals of the house of Toulouse faced the same problems, on a smaller scale, as the house of Toulouse itself, problems of military disorganization, fragmented land holdings and enfeebled social bonds. Languedoc in the twelfth century exhibited the classic symptom of social disintegration in the face of constant war: the appearance of a rash of small castles whose garrisons were usually the only authority in the area they dominated. A few of these castles belonged to the counts of Toulouse and rather more to their greater vassals. But by far the greater part belonged to troublesome and semi-independent local landowners. Most of the greater lords forbade their subjects to build castles and exacted oaths from them in which they promised not to do so. However, these prohibitions were not always, or even usually, effective. Roger-Trencavel was unable to prevent the abbot of St.-Pons de Thomières from building a castle on his land, even by sacking the monastery with mercenary troops. As disorder spread through his dominions, demands flowed in for permisssion to fortify, especially from exposed monasteries. If the owner of a castle were rich enough he might entrust it to mercenaries, but more commonly he garrisoned it by dividing it between a number of local knights impoverished by the constant subdivision of their own family properties. In this way even the smallest castles were partitioned between local families. A document of 1126 reveals that the walls of Carcassonne belonged to sixteen different families, each possessing a tower with a small house behind and a field in front.

In this volatile environment, private wars were the rule rather than the exception. The absence of local chronicles makes their course somewhat hard to trace, but constant references in the charters of the period to land acquired 'by conquest' or 'in war' serve as a reminder that the state of Languedoc was very far from peaceful in the two centuries before the armies of the Albigensian crusade arrived to add to its misery. A gift of land to the monastery of St.-Hilaire du Lauquet in 1034 refers to a castle which the donor had captured from an enemy who had killed his son. A quarter of a century later the complaints of

Bérenger, viscount of Narbonne, against the archbishop included the constant wars waged against him by the archbishop's paid mercenaries, sometimes led by the archbishop in person. At Muret the market of St. Germer's day had to be moved inside the walls in 1090 on account of the incessant raids of the counts of Toulouse against their recalcitrant barons.

The strongest card in the hand of successive counts of Toulouse was the fact that their vassals had unruly vassals of their own. When the viscount of Montpellier renounced the suzerainty of the house of Toulouse in 1141, the count, Alphonse-Jourdain, retaliated by supporting a rebellion of its citizens. In the following year the lords of Les Baux found in Alphonse-Jourdain a powerful ally against their immediate superior, the count of Provence. Such methods, if they had been consistently employed, might have been as successful in Languedoc as they were when practised by the Capetians in the Ile-de-France. But they were not consistently employed. Successive counts of Toulouse abandoned the struggle in the Toulousain and succumbed to the lure of the Mediterranean and, beyond the Mediterranean, of the Middle East. They rarely resided in Toulouse, preferring the more hospitable regions of the southern Rhône valley. Raymond IV called himself Raymond of St.-Gilles and died as count of Tripoli. The east retained its fascination for his successors. His son Bertrand embarked for the Holy Land in 1109 leaving his six-year-old brother Alphonse-Jourdain to face a determined attack on his capital by the duke of Aquitaine. Even this harsh lesson did not deter Alphonse-Jourdain in turn from taking the cross in 1146 and dying in the east. Raymond V, who succeeded him, was the first count in more than half a century who devoted the whole of his adult life to the problems of his native land.

For most of his reign, however, Raymond V was occupied in dealing with the most serious crisis which his principality had faced in the two centuries of its existence. The crisis arose out of the alliance of Raymond's unruly vassals with the rising power of Catalonia, beyond the Pyrenees. Catalonia was ruled by the house of Barcelona, whose able and ambitious princes, having already reconquered much of north-eastern Spain from the Moors, now began to interest themselves in southern France. Since the beginning of the twelfth century they had been actively acquiring territories in Provence, a policy which had brought them into sharp conflict with the house of Toulouse. Geography pointed to an alliance with the Trencavels, who had their own quarrels with the counts of Toulouse, and were also in a position to sever western Languedoc from Provence. This formidable alliance came to pass in 1150. Raymond-Trencavel renounced his homage to the count of Toulouse and transferred it to Raymond-Bérenger IV, count of Barcelona. They were joined in the following year by the count of Foix, and in 1158 by Henry II of England, who had recently acquired Aquitaine by marriage and harboured designs on Toulouse. The result was nearly half a century of sporadic but savage warfare, punctuated at times by major international conflicts. The principality of Toulouse survived, but at a terrible price. Any thoughts of internal reform had to be abandoned. Between 1179 and 1185, eastern Languedoc was bitterly fought over by the mercenaries of three nations, and appalling destruction visited on one of the richest areas of western Europe. When the houses of Barcelona and Toulouse were finally reconciled at the treaty of Perpignan in 1198, it became clear how much the counts of Toulouse had lost. Territorially they had ceded most of the northern foothills of the Pyrenees. Not only the original rebels, but Montpellier, Narbonne, Roussillon, Béarn, and Bigorre had accepted the suzerainty of the Catalan dynasty, and Comminges followed them in 1201. Some of these territories remained Spanish until the seventeenth century.

In the lands which remained to the counts much of their power had passed without recall to their vassals. Even in the Toulousain, walled hill-villages and petty castellans had to be forced to submit to the count's authority. The bishop of Toulouse asked for an armed escort before touring his diocese. A northern abbot who passed through the region in 1181 spoke of the 'vast desolate emptiness left behind by mercenary troops, the image of death and the smoke of fire hanging over every town'. How important the anarchy was in assisting the spread of heresy the church itself recognized when, at the Lateran council of 1179, it coupled its imprecations against heretics with a bitter condemnation of the *routiers* who were devastating Languedoc. It was in communities shattered by the war that the heresy took firm root, protected by local lords whom the war had made independent. 'As for I, who am armed with one of the swords of God for the avenging of his anger,' wrote Raymond V to the abbot of Cîteaux, 'I am impotent to put an end to the general desertion of the faith. The task is beyond my feeble resources. The greatest vassals of my dominions are themselves infected with heresy and with them a great number of their subjects. I neither can nor dare impose my will on them.'

In spite of constant war and political disintegration, Languedoc retained an extraordinary vitality. It was, at any rate until the war of 1179, a rich province. Its wealth was the wealth of a developed commercial society straddling the trade routes of the Mediterranean. Its affinities were with Italy rather than with France. There were trade fairs of international importance at Muret, Carcassonne, and St.-Gilles, where business was said to be brisker than at the fairs of Champagne. Their trade was certainly valuable enough for the Pisans and the Genoese to go to war over it in 1166. Surviving tariffs show that silks, spices, and perfumes were traded at St.-Gilles, and an ordinance of 1178 reveals the existence of 109 money-changers in the town. Silver was mined between Béziers and Narbonne and this, combined with the inflow of cash from pilgrims, merchants, and the counts of Barcelona contributed to the creation of a relatively advanced money economy.

A society based on cash rather than services was inevitably rather more fluidly organized than the overwhelmingly agricultural society of the north. It was also naturally an urban society. Raymond VI, remarked the French chronicler William the Breton, had as many towns as there were days of the year. New towns like Montpellier grew up around abbeys and castles and at cross-roads. Old ones expanded beyond recognition. Toulouse, as its consuls informed Raymond VII in 1226, was 'growing daily in size'. Most of these towns developed on Italian, not French lines. They were governed by citizen oligarchies known as *consulates*. In the early years of the thirteenth century the consuls of Toulouse had a town hall and a common seal, and were even attempting, without much success, to subdue the surrounding *patria Tolosana*. The citizens of southern towns were as sensitive in the matter of their privileges as any Italian. Montpellier expelled its count in 1141. The citizens of Béziers lynched Raymond-Trencavel in the cathedral in October 1167. In the 1180s Toulouse was almost continually at war with its counts. But such rebellions were relatively rare because the weakness of the nominal suzerains made them in most cases unnecessary. Far more common were disputes with the bishop who (unlike the count) generally resided in the city and invariably had interests to defend. Lodève rose against its bishop in 1202 and forced him to swear an oath of loyalty to the consuls. The bishop dispensed himself from the oath and excommunicated the citizens, and the revolt appears, at some later stage, to have been crushed. Similar struggles, some of them less violent than this one, occurred at Narbonne, Le Puy, and Mende. Ill-feeling between the bishop and the citizens does much to explain the ease with which heresy penetrated the lesser episcopal cities and the small fortified hill-towns of Languedoc. Here, as in other respects, the experience of the Midi had been anticipated in northern Italy.

There were towns in France as large and prosperous as any in the Midi. Yet France was not an urban society in the same sense as Languedoc, for the separation between town and country in the north, if not absolute, was certainly well defined. The values of the one scarcely penetrated the other. The towns of the Midi, on the other hand, were inhabited not only by bourgeois but by urban knights and local noblemen. At Toulouse, knightly families were enfeofed with parts of the walls and controlled the consulate until 1202. Noble families of the Toulousain, like the Barravi and the Maurand, built towers of their own, much as their counterparts were doing in Italy. The process also occurred in reverse. Rich bourgeois became knights at Narbonne and probably at Toulouse as well. They commonly invested their fortunes in landed estates outside the city, a course which was not unknown in the north but was certainly exceedingly rare. The rise of the Capdenier family of Toulouse illustrates both the fluidity of southern society and the easy intercourse between town and country that gave the civilization of Languedoc its peculiar character. Bernard of Capdenier was born in the village of that name, about ten miles outside Toulouse, and migrated to the city in 1161. He died in 1198 leaving a number of rented houses to his son Pons. Pons became a consul in 1202, made a substantial fortune by speculating in land, and finally retired to his estates outside the city. Thus in two generations the Capdeniers had returned to the countryside from which they had sprung. Pons's will, dated 1229, included 10,000 sols in pious legacies alone, part of which was used to buy the site on which the Dominican church now stands.

The wealth of the Midi was reflected in a taste for luxury and refinement which was by no means confined to the higher nobility. In the streets of every town, a moralist alleged, women could be seen bowed beneath the weight of stoles, capes, and fur trimmings. They washed too often and spent too long arranging their hair. Another believed that they put so much paint on their faces that there was not enough left to paint the statues of the saints. Manuals of courtesy, with injunctions

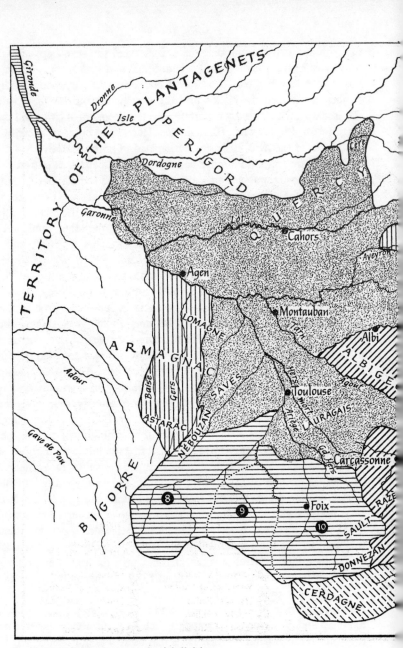

I. Languedoc in 1204: territorial divisions

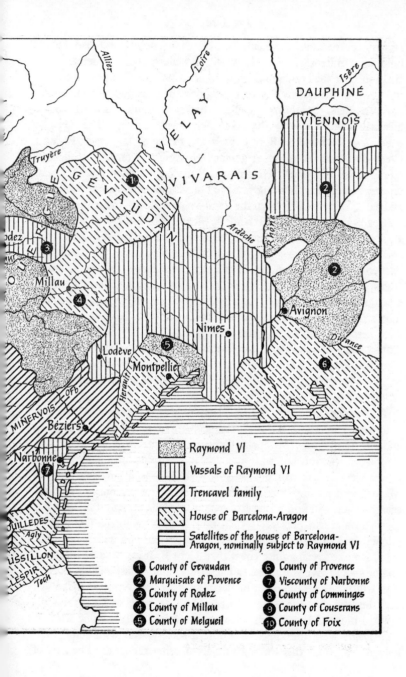

ALLIER
LOIRE
Isère
DAUPHINÉ
VIENNOIS
Truyère
GEVAUDAN
VIVARAIS
Rodez
Ardèche
Rhône
Millau
Avignon
Nimes
Durance
Lodève
Montpellier
Orb
Hérault
MINERVOIS
Béziers
Narbonne
FENOUILLEDES
Agly
ROUSSILLON
VALLESPIR
Tech

Raymond VI
Vassals of Raymond VI
Trencavel family
House of Barcelona-Aragon
Satellites of the house of Barcelona-Aragon, nominally subject to Raymond VI

① County of Gevaudan
② Marquisate of Provence
③ County of Rodez
④ County of Millau
⑤ County of Melgueil
⑥ County of Provence
⑦ Viscounty of Narbonne
⑧ County of Comminges
⑨ County of Couserans
⑩ County of Foix

against coarse table manners, boorish conversation, and bad breath hold up a mirror to a whole world of delicacy and refinement, the creation of a society dominated by women. Such affectations were not unknown in the north, if we can judge by the warnings of contemporary preachers. Southern travellers, however, found northern courts bleak in comparison to those of their own country. The Gascon *troubadour* Bertrand de Born complained of the coarseness of Richard Cœur-de-Lion's court at Argentan. He found women withdrawn, spirits dour, and laughter restrained. Lavish gifts were not showered on every guest, and hunting was the only amusement readily available. Indeed it seems to have been the flamboyant gestures, the cult of pointless extravagance, that Bertrand de Born missed most at Argentan. Both of these were prominent features of the aristocratic life of the south. 'Lordship is largesse', 'donar qu'es la senhoria':[1] the words of a Provencal *troubadour* might have been their motto. It may be that Ebles II de Ventadour did not in fact, as his admirers alleged, destroy a cartload of valuable wax with a hatchet in order to impress his guests. The splendid ceremonies held by Raymond V at Beaucaire in 1174 were certainly less extravagant than is suggested by fanciful reports that valuable horses were slaughtered for ostentation and gold coins ploughed into the ground. But these stories easily gained currency in a society of assertive individuals who valued wealth while affecting to be wholly indifferent to it.

The centre of courtly life in Languedoc was not the court of the counts of Toulouse but the smaller seigneurial courts of the Carcassès and the Laurageais. Mirepois, Cabaret, Lombez, and Minerve were the places remembered with affection in the songs of a generation of *troubadours*. It was to the Carcassès that the *troubadour* Raymond de Miraval sent an impoverished friend in search of patronage. 'At Carcassonne you will find Pierre Roger, lord of Cabaret, and if he does not give you a lavish present, I shall double your retainer. Then on to Olivier, lord of Saissac, who is certain to present you with a fine light robe. No one keeps a finer court than Gent Esquieu, lord of Minerve, and he should give you at least a horse and a suit of fashionable clothes. You will not leave the court of Bertrand de Saissac empty-handed ... and the lord Aimeric is sure to send you on your way with a well-saddled mount.' From such accounts one might well imagine that the *troubadours* were the kings of southern society. But with some well-known exceptions this was very far from being the truth. The best of them were talented amateurs whose fame was ensured by their social eminence as much as by their singing. To this class belonged William IX of Aquitaine and Bertrand de Born; to compose and sing well were accomplishments which became men of their situation. Very few *troubadours* made fortunes by singing and most of them justified the largesse of their patrons in other ways as well. Rainbaut de Vaqueiras, who sang for Boniface de Montferrand, was also his companion in arms and political confidant. Raimon de Miraval performed the same services for Raymond VI of Toulouse. Pistoleta became a successful merchant. Folquet de Marseille became a bishop. On the fringes of these sometime *troubadours* moved a motley collection of itinerant accompanists and cabaret artists who were by no means universally admired; 'base, treacherous, debauched, drunken, lying bar-proppers of taverns' as a contemporary described them. Another listed them with beggars, jugglers and prostitutes among the undesirables of society.

Courtly love and war were the common themes of the *troubadours* and *jongleurs* of twelfth-century Languedoc. Bernard de Ventadour's songs of war and heroism earned him a place in Dante's *Inferno*, together with Mohammed and the fomenters of schism and discord. According to his contemporary biographer, 'he would that there were everlasting war between father and son, brother and brother. . . . And if a peace or truce were made, he would sing of the shame and dishonour which it had brought upon them.' In idealizing their own notions of 'courtly love' the *troubadours* struck another responsive chord in a secular society of small matriarchal courts. The interpretation of the love-songs of the *troubadours* has caused a great deal of scholarly ink to be spilt. To suggest that they invented the literary theme of adultery is unnecessarily slighting to the claims of the *Iliad*. What is certain, however, is that they were among the first to express that theme in an idiom which was readily comprehensible to a mediaeval audience. The intrusion of legal and religious terminology is a noticeable feature of their songs. 'I am your vassal, dedicated to your service, your vassal by oath and homage,' sang Bernard de Ventadour. The lover is the vassal of his lady and she in return owes him her protection. The nature of this protection was outlined in crude terms by some of the early *troubadours*. It is clear that some *troubadours* did nurture carnal desires and sometimes fulfilled them. But the matter is not important, for the essence of courtly love was that it was frustrated love, the 'pleasure of suffering' described by Chrétien de Troyes. 'I love with a love so perfect that I often weep, finding in my grief a kind of ecstasy,' one of them wrote. A recurring theme was the love frustrated by social distance. Another was the idealization of chastity and the worship of frustration, which elevated the man who experienced them above the level of ordinary mortals. This was why Marcabrun denounced marital infidelity with bitterness and why, in many of his contemporaries, there is an undercurrent of reproof against the moral degeneracy which they saw in their patrons.

The *troubadours* supplied the needs of a rich, refined, and educated society, and they articulated some of its values. Their message, however, was neither important nor original. It is far from clear that they had any connection with the spread of the Albigensian heresy. Those *troubadours* (and they were few) who expressed any opinion on the Albigensians were almost invariably hostile, and their hostility must be taken to represent the hostility of most of their patrons. Anti-clerical sentiments, which were extremely widespread in Languedoc, were rare in the works of the *troubadours*. Some of them, indeed, made remarkably pious ends. Bernard de Ventadour and Bertrand de Born both died in the Cistercian abbey of Dalon. Perdigon took the habit at Silvacane. Folquet de Marseille entered the Cistercian abbey of Le Thoronet and finally became bishop of Toulouse, where he made a mark as a fierce opponent of heresy and a formidable antagonist of Raymond VI, the son of his former patron. Judging by what has survived, there does not appear to have been any substance in the bitter claim which the count of Foix made before the Lateran council of 1215, that a whole generation of his peers had been led astray by 'songs whose sound is damnation'.

Nor can it truthfully be said that the *troubadours* were the flower of a civilization which was swept away by the northerners of the crusade. The idiom of the *langue d'oc* was a creation of Gascony, not of Languedoc, and most of the better *troubadours* were Gascons. If any one patron stood pre-eminent it was Eleanor of Aquitaine rather than Raymond V. The itinerant poets who earned their way at the small seigneurial courts of the Carcassès and the Lauragais were generally *jongleurs* whose low reputation is fully justified by those of their works which have survived. Moreover, such as it was, the civilization of Languedoc had already ebbed away before the crusaders finally destroyed the seigneurial courts which had sustained them. The Catalan war had interrupted the prosperity of the Carcassès and the Lauragais. The continuing subdivision of property had ruined many of the patrons. Some of the *troubadours* of Languedoc migrated across the Pyrenees to Spain, where the affectation of the Aragonese court for the civilization of the Midi prolonged their existence for a further century. But it was to Italy that the greater part went, and in Italy that a mosaic of petty rulers with more wealth than taste was arising to replace the one which was declining in Languedoc. What the crusaders encountered in Languedoc was a society in an advanced stage of disintegration which still clung to the husk of a civilization that had all but disappeared.

# The dualist tradition

'The earth is given into the hand of the wicked; He cover-
eth the faces of the judges thereof; if not, where and who is
He?'

JOB IX.24

The heresy which fed on the decomposing body politic of Languedoc
raised questions which were too ancient and too fundamental to be
ignored by the wider world. To one who believes in an omnipotent all-
creating God, it is not easy to explain the existence of evil. God is
infinitely powerful; yet he permits evil to exist and stands aside while
it attacks those same men whom he created in his own image. To this
problem catholic theology offered no satisfactory solution beyond the
historical explanation found in the book of Genesis. But the dualist
had a solution which was both simple and superficially plausible. God,
he said, was not the creator of the world. All matter was the creation of
the Demiurge, a spirit of evil, autonomous, self-creating, who made
man in his own likeness. God had implanted in man the consciousness
of good, thus enabling him to save himself. But He could not control
the material world, and to that extent he was not omnipotent. The
lesson for man was clear. If he would be saved, he must separate himself from all matter and make himself spirit as far as may be. He must
abstain from marriage and procreation which multiplies an evil species;
he must suppress, as far as he can, his every bodily need.

Neither the problem, nor the solution, is peculiar to Christian
dualists. The ancient Zoroastrian religion of Persia presented the world
as the battleground of good and evil, matter and spirit. The rejection
of matter was common to both Stoicism and Neoplatonism, the two
great paganisms of late antiquity. Far away from the world of Rome
and the century of Plotinus, the Buddha had taught his followers to
aspire to *nirvana*, the peace that comes from complete unconsciousness
of the material world.

Christian dualism is almost as old as Christianity itself. The alliance of uncertainty and profound pessimism which was so characteristic of late antiquity gave birth to uneasy speculation about the origin of evil. 'The heretics and pagans constantly return to the same theme,' Tertullian wrote at the beginning of the second century; 'whence came evil, and where is it to be found? Whence came man and how? According to Irenaeus, the dualist answer to these questions was already widely canvassed at the end of the first century. But it was not until the middle of the second century that dualism, or *gnosis*, had any organized existence. The foundation of a gnostic church was the achievement of Marcion, a rich shipowner from Asia Minor who began to organize his sect in Rome in about 144. Marcion was an uncompromising dualist. He did not accept the belief of most gnostics of his day that the Demiurge was a 'fallen angel', himself derived from God. The two were in his mind absolutely distinct. The Demiurge, whom Marcion identified with the Jehovah of the Old Testament, was the creator of the world, the God of retribution. The other, the true God, whose messenger was Jesus Christ, was the God of love. All matter being intrinsically evil, Marcion's followers were taught to avoid it as far as they could. To baptized Marcionites marriage and sexual intercourse were absolutely forbidden, asceticism and self-denial the guiding principles of life. The rigour of Marcion's views encouraged his followers to postpone baptism until late in life, often indeed until the eve of death. Thus arose the distinction between baptized Marcionites, those who submitted themselves to the founder's strict discipline, and mere believers, who accepted his views and intended, perhaps, to be baptized at some future date. For the third class, the non-believers, there was no possibility of salvation.

Not all dualists in the succeeding centuries shared Marcion's beliefs. The niceties of dualist theology differed from one region to the next, and most groups evolved peculiarities of their own. There remained, moreover, a substantial number who held the more moderate but less logical view that the Demiurge was originally derived from God. Nevertheless, after Marcion, all dualists had two fundamental points in common. The first was a belief in the creation of matter by the Devil, or Demiurge, and thus in the desirability of total continence and extreme asceticism. The second, arising out of this, was a church organization which divided its members into practitioners and believers, the two separated by an imposing ceremony of initiation. Hence the distinction between *gnosis*, the knowledge of the initiated practitioner, and *pistis*, the faith of the ordinary believer. The idea of the initiation ceremony, and very often the actual words used, were borrowed from the practice of the early church, which commonly postponed baptism until late in life. St. Augustine was baptized at the age of thirty-three, the emperor Constantine only on his death-bed. The dualist sects merely retained the idea of a spiritual elect long after the orthodox church had abandoned it in favour of infant baptism.

As Pliny makes clear in his celebrated letter to the emperor Trajan, it was precisely their sect-like qualities which had made the Roman authorities suspicious of the early Christians. This suspicion of inward-looking sects was still very much alive under the Christian Empire, and it was naturally directed at those groups, like the Marcionites, which signified the gulf between themselves and the rest of society with an initiation ceremony. The anti-social tendency of gnosticism was even clearer in the case of the most celebrated of all dualist sects, the Manichaeans, who swept across the Christian world in the fourth century, and in western Asia survived as a major church for six hundred years. They derived their name and their doctrines from Mani, a Persian who began his preaching at Ctesiphon in Mesopotamia in 242 and, having aroused the ire of the Zoroastrian priesthood, was martyred in 276 at Gundeshapur in south-western Persia. Though Mani called himself an apostle of Christ, he lived and died in the Zoroastrian kingdom of Persia, and it is not at all clear that he should be regarded as a Christian. Mani considered all the great spiritual leaders to be messengers of the true God. His bizarre theology included elements of Buddhism and Zoroastrianism as well as the classic Christian dualism which commended it to the young Augustine. His stricter disciples went to extreme lengths in avoiding all contact with the material world, refusing to work, fight, or marry. All this does much to explain why the Manichaeans were amongst the first Christian heretics to encounter sustained persecution by the state. Although Mani's contribution to the history of dualism was far smaller than Marcion's, the notoriety which his followers earned by their anarchic attitudes rubbed off on every dualist sect. Throughout the middle ages, the word 'Manichaean' was applied to heretics of whom few had heard of Mani and some were not even dualists.

Heresy, like Christianity itself, tended to move from east to west. But it was not until the eighth century that dualism first gained a firm foothold on the European side of the Bosphorus. The source of the infection was Armenia, where a strong dualist community known as the Paulicians had existed since the fifth century. The Armenians were an aggressive, troublesome race, whose subordination to Byzantium was at times little more than nominal. In the eighth century, colonies of them were transplanted by the emperor Constantine V to Thrace where, it was hoped, their warlike instincts would be put to good use in defending the Balkan frontier. Others followed in about 975 and settled in the region of Philippopolis. These Armenian colonists brought with them not only their military skills but their heretical beliefs. By the end of the ninth century Paulician missionaries had already penetrated the neighbouring kingdom of Bulgaria.

Political circumstances favoured them. Bulgaria had only recently been converted to Christianity by missionaries from Byzantium. But although the Bulgars themselves embraced the new faith readily enough, the Slav peasants who formed the bulk of the population did not. Their hatred of their Greek and Bulgar overlords was extended to the alien church which was now imposed on them. The Paulicians had the considerable advantage that they were not Greeks, and that their austere religious practices contrasted markedly with the elaborate rituals of the orthodox church. During the reign of the Bulgarian Tsar Peter (927–969), the nascent nationalism of the Slavs was skilfully exploited by one Bogomil, an ordinary priest who became the founder of the first great dualist church of Europe. Of Bogomil himself almost nothing is known beyond the fact that he was a thorough-going dualist whose beliefs appear to have been derived from the Paulician settlers of Thrace. These beliefs have an interest of their own, for they are strikingly similar to those which later appeared amongst the Albigensians of southern France. The Bogomils rejected the Old Testament and ascribed the creation of the world to the Devil. They refused the sacraments and did not observe feast-days. They did not venerate the cross for it was the symbol of Christ's death as well as being a material thing. They abstained as far as possible from meat and wine, and from sexual intercourse. Cosmas, the Bulgar priest who describes these aberrations, was shocked by their hostility to their Bulgar rulers, which he mistook for anti-social obstinacy. The Bogomils, it seems, adopted a policy of passive resistance in the face of the authorities. 'They denounce the rich, hate the Tsar, ridicule the elders, and condemn the nobles. They regard all that serve the Tsar as damned, and forbid slaves to do their masters' bidding.'

Such was the creed of the Bulgarian dualists, as described by an intelligent observer who was almost a contemporary of Bogomil. Rather later, Bogomil's followers seem to have come into contact with a Greek sect known as the Messalians, whose dualism was of a rather more limited kind. Thereafter the river of Bogomilism divided into two streams, one group adhering to the strict dualism of the founder while the other, and far larger, group accepted the older gnostic view that the Demiurge was originally created by God. The schism, however, did not interfere with the Bogomils' missionary activity. During the eleventh century they expanded into Macedonia, hitherto the most orthodox Slavonic province, and thence into Serbia and Bosnia, Croatia and Dalmatia. To the south they reached Asia Minor, and briefly established a church in Constantinople itself. And so, when western Christians first came into prolonged contact with the Balkans at the end of the eleventh century, they found a variety of dualist sects firmly entrenched there.

By what channels Balkan dualism first reached the west is very far from clear. Already in the first half of the eleventh century, sporadic outbreaks of heresy were occurring in northern Europe, which contemporaries who had read their Augustine described as 'Manichaean'. But exactly what these heretics believed is not revealed. Neither is the source from which they had learned it. The cloth merchants of the northern towns often had commercial links with the east. So had many Italian merchants, who might have encountered dualism in Constantinople, in the Dalmatian cities of Ragusa and Spalato, or even, rather later, in Serbia and Croatia. Pilgrims too generally followed the great imperial road from Belgrade to Constantinople which took them through the heartland of Paulician dualism. More important than these casual carriers of the eastern heresy were the crusaders, who encountered dualism both in the Balkans and in Asia Minor. The crusaders found a settlement of Armenian Paulicians near Antioch in 1097, and another outside Tripoli in 1099. In the thirteenth century, it was believed that some French crusaders had been converted to dualism by the Bogomil community of Constantinople, and had later returned to disseminate their errors in northern Europe. Such, at least, was the conclusion which the Italian inquisitor Anselm of Alexandria drew from a lifetime's study of western heresy. Anselm may or may not have been correct in this view. What is certain is that those regions in which dualism first made its appearance in the twelfth century, Flanders,

Champagne, the Loire valley, and the Rhineland, were all areas in which the crusaders had, for the most part, been recruited.

Western Europe in the twelfth century was a fertile field for the new heresy. The great reform of the church associated with the name of Gregory VII had brought about a spectacular improvement in the quality of religious life, an improvement which was nowhere more evident than in France. But if the standards of the clergy had risen, so had the expectations of the laity. The new laity, emancipated to some degree from the constrictions of feudal society, richer and more educated than its forebears, was a passionate partisan in the struggle for the reform of the clergy. In parts of France immoral or married clergymen were threatened by mobs. Elsewhere, the growing wealth and institutionalization of the church provoked bitter protest and, on occasion, armed rebellion. The tension was particularly acute in the cities of northern France and the Low Countries, where dualism first appeared and where, as often as not, the feudal overlordship belonged to the bishop. The English satirist Nigel Wireker spoke of baronial gatherings where bishops were indistinguishable from lay magnates.

Long before dualism became a significant force, anti-clerical heresies were causing serious alarm to the ecclesiastical authorities. In the first years of the twelfth century a certain Tanchelm raised a fanatical following in Antwerp by preaching against the lax morals of the local clergy. Tanchelm accepted the need for a virtuous priesthood, but not for a hierarchy of bishops and administrators. The exact nature of his views is hard to disentangle from the mass of hostile polemic directed against him, but there is no doubt that orthodox contemporaries found them deeply shocking. After a brief spell in the episcopal prison at Cologne, Tanchelm escaped to Bruges, where he was murdered by a priest in 1115. Graver still was a succession of violent outbursts of anti-clericalism in Italy. In 1143 the pope's temporal dominion was overthrown by a communal revolution in Rome, which later acquired as its leader a venomous anti-clerical demagogue, Arnold of Brescia. Arnold was an uncompromising opponent of all clerical endowment. He proclaimed that confession should not be made to a priest but to a fellow layman, and denied that the other sacraments had any validity unless they were administered by worthy priests. Unlike Tanchelm, Arnold did not found a church and left few followers. Thrown upon the attention of the world by an accident of Roman politics, he was captured in 1152 and executed by the emperor Frederick Barbarossa. But many of his beliefs were the common property of anti-clerical heretics of his day. The essence of these beliefs was his refusal to accept that the mediation of a monolithic, institutional church was essential for man's salvation. In August 1173, according to tradition, a rich merchant of Lyon called Peter Valdes suddenly resolved upon a life of apostolic poverty, after hearing a minstrel singing of St. Alexis, who had abandoned his wife and property to live as a hermit in Syria. Valdes quickly gathered a following and devoted himself to preaching. In 1882 the church, after some hesitation, finally excommunicated him. The archbishop of Lyon seems to have been less disturbed by the content of Valdes's message than by the fact that it was preached without official permission. Valdes was by no means a theologian, but as far as his views can be ascertained they appear to have been entirely orthodox. His followers, however, who rapidly spread through Lombardy and southern France, adopted within a very few years a position not unlike that of Arnold of Brescia. They condemned the possession of property by the clergy and rejected out of hand the need for a sacramental priesthood.

The speed with which the Waldensians multiplied showed that these ideas struck a sympathetic chord amongst Valdes's contemporaries. The cult of poverty and the veneration of 'holy men' found an orthodox expression as well as a heretical one. Austere hermits in the tradition of Peter Damian, the early Carthusians and Franciscans, these were among the great spiritual heroes of the age. Whether these 'holy men' were revered as saints or excommunicated as heretics seemed to be largely a matter of accident. Valdes was condemned while other itinerant preachers, equally unauthorized, like Robert of Arbrissel, were remembered as great reformers and founders of religious orders. Some of these wanderers, however, were plainly heretics, and a few were equally plainly dualist heretics.

A Champagnard peasant named Clement, who founded a clandestine sect in the Soissonais in about 1114, was one of the earliest western heretics to preach in the dualist tradition. As well as condemning the sacraments, Clement taught that meat should be avoided and that marriage and procreation were evil. Although John, count of Soissons, declared him to be the wisest man he had ever met, this did not save Clement from being imprisoned for life, together with his brother and two other heretics. Stranger still was the career of Odo de l'Etoile, a Breton heretic who was brought before the council of Rheims in 1148. Odo had formed a sect of initiates devoted to austerity and chastity and to attacking hermitages and monasteries. His theology, if indeed he had one, is obscure, but contemporaries described him as a 'Manichaean', and probably with justice.

Early dualist preachers were usually unlettered ex-monks and peasants. It is, on the whole, unlikely that either Clement or Odo had any formal acquaintance with neo-gnostic theology. Not so the sizeable dualist congregations which were discovered in several towns of the Rhineland and the Low Countries in the 1140s. In 1144 highly organized heretical churches came to light in Liège and Cologne, and were suppressed in both places with considerable violence. Those of Cologne exhibited almost all the symptoms of the eastern dualist tradition. They avoided meat and milk, disapproved of procreation, and ridiculed the sacraments. They were strict dualists, ascribing the creation of all matter to the Devil, and holding the Devil to be coeval with God. They divided themselves into believers and initiates, the latter class being called Cathars, a name which was henceforth used to describe all western dualists. The Greek word 'Cathar' ('purified') itself suggests an eastern origin for their creed. And indeed when questioned about the origin of their faith, they asserted that it had come from Greece but at what date they were not certain. By this time dualism was already making rapid advances in the cloth towns of the Low Countries. The archbishop of Rheims admitted in 1157 that the 'Manichaean plague' had affected the greater part of Flanders and was still being actively propagated by itinerant weavers and cloth-merchants. From the discussions of the council held at Rheims in that year, it is clear that the church was by now thoroughly alarmed by the spread of the heresy. The new sects were not only well organized, but included men of education and substance. They were rich enough to attempt, in 1162, to buy the complaisance of the archbishop of Rheims for 600 marks of silver.

Nothing in the long experience of the western church had prepared it for such a crisis. There was no clearly defined crime of heresy, no juridical principles from which to seek guidance, no procedures and no prescribed penalties. Academic controversies had from time to time resulted in denunciations of heresy, but the culprits had been few and usually clerics over whom the church exercised direct authority. Faced with the formidable evidence of organized dissent, churchmen clung for a time to their belief that the most obdurate heretic would ultimately yield to reasoned argument. Most of them would still have subscribed to the advice which Waso bishop of Liège gave to a fellow bishop in 1045. 'We are not entitled,' Waso wrote, 'to deprive heretics of the life which God has given them simply because we believe them to be in the clutches of Satan. . . . Those who are our enemies on earth may, by the grace of God, be our superiors in heaven.' More than a century later Gerhoh of Reichersberg expressed the same opinion when he protested against the execution of Arnold of Brescia. But by then the mood was changing. If the prelates of the eleventh century were inclined to be lenient, it was because they did not seriously envisage the possibility that heresy would displace orthodoxy, even locally. This, however, was the prospect which intelligent churchmen thought that they were facing in the 1160s. St. Bernard, as befitted a man who had undertaken two major missions against heretics, believed in persuasion and reconciliation. 'Errors are refuted by argument, not by force,' he advised the clergy of Cologne. Nevertheless, the saint continued, if after repeated warnings, the heretics persist in their errors they must be excommunicated, 'and if it appears that even then they would prefer to die than to believe, then let them die'. Intellectuals among the clergy continued to refute the opinions of the dualists in reasoned treatises. Peter the Venerable, abbot of Cluny, wrote a tract against the Petrobrusians. Alan of Lille wrote an immense work of refutation which embraced the heresies of the Jews and Waldensians of France. Eckbert of Schonau composed thirteen sermons on the errors of the dualists of the Rhine valley. But in most parts of northern Europe, the church had already embarked upon a policy of violent repression. Eckbert himself presided over the burning of the heretics of Cologne in August 1163.

In an age which cares little for dogma and shares bishop Waso's dislike of persecutors, it is not easy to understand the relentless savagery with which the middle ages attempted to suppress religious dissent. The explanation cannot be found in the theocratic ambitions of the church. Although the thirteenth-century popes assumed the leadership of the persecution and created in the Inquisition its most effective instrument, the initiative had come two centuries earlier from elsewhere —from secular princes and lynch mobs. In a society which regarded religion as the foundation of secular life, their attitude is not surprising. A mediaeval community was defined as much by its religion as by its political allegiance or geographical cohesion. 'Populus et christianitas una est,' declared a treaty concluded by the ninth-century emperor

Charles the Bald. His maxim was applied far beyond the realms of imperial diplomacy. An unbeliever could not belong to a Christian society; he was an alien. And far graver than the unbeliever was the case of the heretic, who accepted the same revelation as his orthodox neighbour but gave it a different interpretation, distorting and corrupting it, leading simpler men away from their salvation. Heresy was a spreading poison and a community which tolerated it invited God to withdraw his protection. An individual's disbelief threatened all about him. Aquinas knew this when he compared heretics to counterfeiters of the coinage; and if the state was justified in killing counterfeiters who undermined the secular foundations of society, was the church not equally justified in killing heretics who undermined its spiritual foundations? These fears were real enough even when the heresies in question arose out of recondite speculation on matters of minimal theological importance. Far greater was the threat of dualism whose adherents were organized and persuasive, and whose teaching raised questions so fundamental as to make it doubtful whether they could be called Christians at all.

In northern France, Germany, and the Low Countries, the suppression of dualism continued at an irregular pace for about eighty years and ended in the almost total victory of the church. There were a number of reasons for this success. The relatively developed judicial organization of the church in the north, a better educated clergy, a generation of exceptionally able and energetic bishops, all contributed to it. Two factors, however, predominated over all the others. The first was the popular rage against heretics, which was at least as virulent as the rage of the heretics themselves against the clergy. The urban mobs genuinely feared the wrath of God upon their homes, and were usually foremost in demanding savage punishments. The heretics burned at Cologne in 1163 had been discovered when neighbours noticed that they did not attend Mass. At Soissons in 1120, at Cologne in 1144, and at Vézelay in 1167, heretics were lynched by the crowd before the ecclesiastical authorities could decide what to do with them. The dualists found at Liège in 1144 only narrowly escaped the same fate.

The second factor in the successful suppression of dualism was the constant support of the civil powers. The church never formally abandoned its objection to clerics imposing a sentence of death. It therefore depended entirely on the willingness of the civil authorities to do it for them. Canon lawyers were beginning to apply the Roman law of *lèse-majesté* to heresy. Theologians invited the intervention of the secular power by pointing out the rebellious undertones of heresy, and the sexual depravity of its adherents. In 1184, pope Lucius III finally agreed with the emperor on a procedure, which was embodied in the decretal *Ad Abolendam*. After solemnly condemning a large number of heretical sects, Lucius declared that those convicted of heresy should be surrendered to the civil power for such punishment as it should think fit. The kings of France, however, had long ago lost patience with the hesitations of the church. As early as 1022, Robert the Pious had summoned an assembly of dignitaries to deal with three heretical priests of Orléans, one of whom was a man of some eminence, a former confessor to the queen. Immediately after the proceedings they were burned to death outside the walls of the city, perhaps the first execution for heresy since antiquity. Louis VII gave constant support to his brother, the archbishop of Rheims, in his campaign against the Cathars, and more than once urged the pope to further action against them.

By the mid-1160s the Cathars of the northern towns had already begun to search for a more hospitable environment. A group of heretics from Flanders were unwise enough to flee to Cologne, where they were promptly detected and burned. Another group of Flemish exiles turned up in the west of England, only to be branded on the forehead and driven naked into the winter snow. But the great majority of the fugitives fled south to Lombardy and Languedoc. In Languedoc they found a society which was, in important respects, quite different from that of the north. It was a society in which the civil power was weak and the nobility had little reason to co-operate with the church. The fierce conformist anger of the northern populace gave way to a mild and cultivated atmosphere in which tolerance, if not actually exalted, was at least a rule of practice. There, alone in France, Catharism took firm root and prospered, until by the end of the twelfth century an entrenched heretical church faced the orthodox hierarchy on something like equal terms. Of this impossible situation, the Albigensian crusade was the outcome.

# ✠ III ✠

## The Cathar church

'Let us go after other Gods which thou hast not known,
and let us serve them.'

DEUTERONOMY XIII.2

The existence of heretical sects in southern France had long been
known to the authorities. If they did not provoke the same panic in the
Midi as they did in the northern towns, this was due as much to the
obscurity of their doings as to the idleness or secular preoccupations of
their persecutors. An inquisitor's task is not easy in a highly mobile,
loosely organized society whose ruler could employ a Jew as his seneschal without protests. Nevertheless, an ecclesiastical council which met
at Toulouse in 1056 perfunctorily excommunicated some heretics of
unspecified views. Another council met there in 1119 under the presidency of pope Calixtus II and drew attention to the activities of those
who denounced the sacraments, opposed infant baptism, and condemned
marriage as sin. These last may even have been dualists, though opposition to a sacramental priesthood was not confined to dualists. The
dissidents in question were anathematized and the secular power
invited to suppress them. But suppression was more than Calixtus
could expect in the fragmented state of Languedoc. Anti-sacramental
teaching never disappeared, even when graver heresies had drawn the
attention of the church. The closeness of mediaeval parish life put a
premium on the unusual. Isolated hermits of no learning but obvious
saintliness became spiritual heroes among simple people who venerated
an impressive appearance and inspiring words.

The beginnings of Catharism in Languedoc are obscure. But it had
evidently made significant inroads into catholic congregations when one
of these violent individualists, a northerner called Henry, abruptly
drew attention to the spiritual condition of the Midi. Henry was in
every way characteristic of his kind. He was tall and lean with close-
cropped hair and a long beard; he ate and dressed austerely; his voice

*43*

was overpowering. Henry had already made a name for himself when he first appeared in the south. In 1116 he had arrived at Le Mans announcing himself as a deacon and requesting permission to preach. When this was granted he and his disciples raised an anti-clerical rebellion and for some weeks virtually governed the city. The bishop, returning from a visit to Rome, was excluded at the gates. Only when a suburb of the city was destroyed by fire did the citizens lose confidence in their prophet, who quietly fled, abandoning possession to the bishop. Henry's subsequent career underlines the range as well as the persistence of these self-appointed prophets. In the next two decades he is heard of at Lausanne, Poitiers and Bordeaux. Finally he joined forces with Peter of Bruys, another heretical demagogue who was active in the Rhône valley in the 1130s. Henry's own ideas do not seem to have been very carefully thought out, but Peter was the founder of a sect to which the abbot of Cluny attached a comprehensive theology and the name 'Petrobrusian'. This theology was still anti-sacramental rather than dualist. Peter disapproved of infant baptism and insisted on the rebaptism of his disciples. He destroyed churches on the ground that God was everywhere and could be worshipped anywhere. He objected to feast-days and to the veneration of the cross. In the course of a few years he left a trail of devastation across Provence, burning crucifixes, destroying altars, attacking priests and monks. Only in about 1140 was his career abruptly ended when he attempted to burn a crucifix at St.-Gilles and was lynched by a catholic mob. In Henry, however, he had found a disciple worthy of his message. Henry had already learned the weakness of his adversaries in 1135 when he was arrested by the archbishop of Arles and taken before the council of Pisa. There he was confronted by St. Bernard, who persuaded him to make a formal retraction of his errors and offered to take him as a monk at Clairvaux. Henry made the retraction but refused the place at Clairvaux. Shortly afterwards he returned to his inflammatory preaching in the Toulousain with a success which was reflected in the mounting alarm of the local clergy. Eugenius III was called upon to deal with the situation almost immediately after his election to the papal throne in February 1145. Writing from Viterbo, whither he had fled from a Roman mob, the pope charged Alberic, cardinal-bishop of Ostia, with the task of restoring order in the troubled province.

Alberic was not the optimum choice for such a mission. He was a Frenchman, born in the Beauvaisis and trained in the somewhat formal piety of the abbey of Cluny. Ten years in the service of the papacy had marked him out as an able diplomat, not a missionary, a fact of which he was perhaps aware for it seems to have been his decision to invite Bernard of Clairvaux and Godfrey bishop of Chartres to accompany him to Toulouse. A year before delivering the sermon which launched the second crusade, St. Bernard was at the summit of his powers. The Cistercian order which he had moulded had become the dominant spiritual influence in western Europe. The force of his personality had succeeded, almost unaided, in bringing an end to the schism of the anti-pope Anacletus. Moreover, Bernard was no stranger to popular heresy, having confronted Henry himself at Pisa and preached against the dualists of the Rhine valley. For such encounters he had obvious qualifications. A taste for theological disputation, combined with a total lack of self-doubt and tremendous rhetorical powers, made him the best possible champion of orthodoxy in a province whose clergy was already beginning to lose confidence in the strength of its cause.

The three emissaries arrived in Toulouse in the summer of 1145 and immediately encountered hostility and silence. The city's heretics refused to meet Bernard in public debate, and even the catholics were not convinced that Henry was a heretic. The count, Alphonse-Jourdain, shared their opinion, and had extended his protection to the arch-heretic. Albi was more welcoming. The citizens cheered his entry and filled the streets and churches to hear his sermons. Emotional crowds raised their hands in front of the cathedral to signify their rejection of falsehood. Bernard was elated; but he had underestimated the resilience of his enemy. Henry's heretical followers had fled from the enthusiastic mobs which Bernard had drawn, leaving only the orthodox to proclaim their support for the true faith. In the small hill-towns of the outlying districts, heresy had firmer roots. At Verfeil, the congregations walked out of the churches as the abbot began to speak, and beat upon their doors to silence his street sermons. Bernard believed that the successes of his mission had outweighed the failures, and he was encouraged in this view by optimistic reports which reached him after his return to Clairvaux. 'The wolves have been tracked down,' wrote the abbot of Grandselve with more enthusiasm than accuracy. Not everyone shared his opinion. Geoffrey of Auxerre, a monk of Clairvaux who had accompanied Bernard on his travels, recognized that the heresies of Langue-doc would not be eradicated in a two-month preaching tour. Even St. Bernard could not fail to notice that these heresies went far beyond

45

the superficial teachings of Peter of Bruys and Henry. In Toulouse, many of the heretics were found to be *textores*, a name which in the north was applied to dualists. The heretics who barracked Bernard at Verfeil had almost certainly accepted the dualism of the Cathars even as early as 1145. Moreover, Geoffrey of Auxerre had noticed something which made even these facts more disturbing than they appeared. The lesser nobility had carried their anti-clericalism to the point of protecting prominent heretics and even, in some cases, of adopting their faith. By comparison the career of the arch-heretic Henry was of small moment. Nor did it have much further to run. Some time before 1148 Henry was captured by the bishop of Toulouse and brought before a council at Rheims where, shortly afterwards, he died in prison.

But Henry was only the precursor. Within twenty years of Bernard's mission, the church of the Midi faced a crisis which seemed all the greater for the failure of its most formidable evangelist. When the council of Tours met in 1163 under the presidency of the exiled pope Alexander III, the heresy was choking the religious life of the Toulousain and spreading outwards into Gascony and the surrounding regions. The serpent had insinuated its way into the Lord's vineyard, the fathers of the council were told. Heretical missionaries had gained many converts. Powerful interests protected them. But the adherents of the rival church were nowhere more than a small minority, and repression was far from the council's mind. Constant vigilance and ostracism of the offenders were still the courses urged upon the faithful. Neither was likely to be effective in loose-knit communities whose leaders were themselves beset by doubts.

The southern bishops had enough faith in the power of persuasion to seek a debate with the heretics on their own ground. The site chosen was Lombers, a hill-town occupying a dramatic position on a spur of land some ten miles south of Albi. Lombers was typical of the small fortified towns, dominated by the sympathetic nobility of the outlying country, where the heretics of the great cathedral cities had found safety in numbers. It became the residence of one of the four Cathar bishops of the Midi. In 1165, forty-four years before it fell to the crusaders, Lombers was the scene of a gentler confrontation. Five southern bishops, seven abbots, and a variety of lesser ecclesiastics were accompanied by most of the more prominent orthodox laymen of the region, including Raymond-Trencavel, viscount of Béziers, and Constance, countess of Toulouse and sister of the king of France. Facing them with a few assistants was one Oliver whom the heretics had appointed as their spokesman. Interrogated by the bishop of Lodève, Oliver admitted that the heretics rejected the authority of the Old Testament and disapproved of infant baptism. Further questioning revealed that they regarded the swearing of oaths as sinful and denied the sacramental power of the priesthood. The heretical delegation did not confine itself to answering the bishop's questions. After violently abusing their interlocutors, they dismissed the catholic clergy as 'false prophets and wolves in the midst of the Lord's flock'. Not surprisingly, the four presiding judges, all of whom were catholic clergymen, declared that the bishop had proved his antagonists to be obdurate heretics. The victory of orthodoxy was perhaps somewhat hollow. But it may have succeeded in persuading some of the audience that, for all their apparent holiness, the heretical preachers were not speaking with the authority of the church; and this was a fact of which many of them were no doubt genuinely ignorant. At the close of the proceeedings the bishop of Lodève formally anathematized the heretics and called upon the castellans of the place to cease protecting them. This, according to the catholic account, they agreed to do. But Lombers, like most of the diocese of Albi, was still in Cathar hands when the crusaders invaded in 1209, and the careful investigations of the Inquisition continued to uncover heretical groups in the town for many years afterwards. Any churchman who still believed that they were dealing with the followers of a charismatic preacher of eccentric views must have been disillusioned by the events at Lombers. Their opponents were seen to have an organization and some degree of intellectual sophistication. Evidently they had been obscurely propagating their views for many years before Henry had drawn off the authorities on what now appeared to have been a wild-goose chase.

The Cathars' views are not easy to reconstruct owing to the efficiency with which their writings were suppressed in the thirteenth century. Robert, count of Montferrand, himself impeccably orthodox, indulged a dilettante interest in heresy by amassing over forty years a great library of Cathar literature; but on his deathbed in 1234 his Dominican confessors persuaded him to burn it, perhaps depriving posterity of a valuable source of insights into the beliefs of those who came near to uprooting the French church in one of its oldest provinces.[2] Nor is it easy to generalize from the works of Italian Cathars which have survived in greater abundance, for there were regional and even individual differences among dualists. Deprived of apologies by the heretics themselves, we are dependent for our knowledge of them on the prolix works of refutation written by catholics such as the Parisian theologian, Alan of Lille. There are also the copious records of the thirteenth-century inquisitors. These have the weakness of all such records, that the inquisitorial mind tends to develop a stereotyped image of the beliefs of its victims, and extracts confessions which accord with it. It is not difficult to make demoralized prisoners mouth the fantasies of their persecutors. Nevertheless on some points all these fragmentary sources of information are agreed, and the outlines of a dualist theology emerge.

At its centre lay that profoundly pessimistic view of the world which characterizes all dualist teaching. 'Everything that exists under the sun and the moon,' an inhabitant of St.-Paul-de-Fenouillet told the bishop of Alet, 'is but corruption and chaos.' All matter is evil and transitory, containing the seeds of its own destruction. What possible connection can it have with a God who is both permanent and perfect? A good God cannot have created a world which the experience of every man shows to be wicked. When the Toulousain heretic Peter Garcia was interrogated by the Inquisition on the origin of the world he replied with this syllogism: 'God is perfect; nothing in the world is perfect; therefore nothing in the world was made by God.' But if God could not have created matter, it was equally clear that the Devil could not have created the soul. Accordingly, Garcia thought, there were two Gods. 'The one, the good God, made the invisible world, while the other, the evil God, made the visible one.' When, therefore, the inquisitor Bernard Gui accused the Cathars of abandoning monotheism, he was in a sense correct. 'The heretics affirm the existence of two Gods, two Lords.'

The dualism of the Cathars necessarily involved the rejection of the Old Testament. Apart from the fact that the book of Genesis proposed a rather different view of the origin of matter, it had seemed to most dualists since Marcion that the capricious, tyrannical, and often unjust behaviour of Jehovah made it inconceivable that he should have been the perfect God. Jehovah was therefore to be identified with Satan, and the Old Testament with the law of Satan. Even the New Testament involved the Cathars in some intellectual difficulties, notably in the matter of the Incarnation. The complete separation between God and matter obliged them to interpret it in a highly symbolic and allegorical fashion. Some heretics who came before the Inquisition had not fully thought out the logic of their views. They continued to talk of God as having taken a human body and been crucified. But the solution of most Cathars was to deny the Incarnation altogether, and to suggest instead that the humanity of Christ was a mere illusion, fostered by Christ to facilitate his mission. It followed that in reality neither the death of Christ, nor his Resurrection or Ascension, had really occurred.

There was another matter on which the Cathars were not agreed. The existence of evil in the world had been explained by postulating the existence of a supernatural spirit of evil. But the origin of this super-natural spirit was the subject of some discord. The thorough-going dualists held that the Devil had always existed. He was as powerful and as old as God himself. The other school of thought, called Monar-chians, clung to a fallen angel theory not unlike that of orthodox catholic theologians. According to this theory the Devil was himself a creation of God and had fallen from heaven after leading a rebellion against God's authority. This division of thought corresponded to a schism which had long ago occurred among the dualists of the Balkans. It was settled in a manner which fully confirms what the details of their doctrines would lead us to expect, namely that the origin of the heresy was eastern and that it retained close links with the dualist churches of the eastern Mediterranean. Until 1167, the French dualists appear to have been Monarchians, in common with most of the Bogomils of Bulgaria. In that year, however, the 'pope' Niquinta, from the strict dualist church of Constantinople, presided over a colloquy in the hill-town of St.-Felix-de-Caraman near Castelnaudary, at which the Cathars of France formally adopted the uncompromising dualism of the Greek.

The meeting at St.-Felix was a formidable display of the influence and organization of a church which had recently debated on equal terms with five catholic bishops. Also present were Robert of Epernon, bishop of the Cathars of northern France, and Mark, Cathar bishop of Lombardy. In addition to settling awkward doctrinal problems the assembly dealt with the organization of the nascent church. The diocese of Albi, where the Cathars were strongest, already had its own heretical bishop. Other bishops were now appointed for the Cathar communities of the regions of Toulouse, Carcassonne, and Agen, and delegates were appointed to draw the boundaries of their dioceses. The functions of these bishops are unclear, but it seems that they were something more than the largely administrative officials which catholic bishops had become. As befitted the leader of a missionary church, the Cathar bishop's principal role was a pastoral one, and he was assisted in fulfilling it by two deputies, the *filius major* and the *filius minor*. Judging by the Italian practice, which may not have been universal, the *filius major* invariably succeeded the bishop in his post. Beneath these two dignitaries came a larger number of deacons who lived with their aristocratic protectors in the fortified towns, and acted as itinerant ministers to a widely dispersed congregation.

Since the Cathars did not recognize the need for the ministry of a sacramental priesthood, the distinction between 'clergy' and 'laity' loomed less large in their eyes than it did among their catholic rivals. The distinction which mattered separated 'Perfects' from others. Perfects were not intermediaries with God like the catholic priesthood; they were merely teachers and exceptionally holy men. The process which transformed a believer into a Perfect had much in common with the spiritual apprenticeship required of catechumens in the early Christian church. Unless he was already dying, the candidate was assigned to an existing Perfect who gave him a foretaste of the austerity which would be expected of him, and satisfied himself that he would not later apostatize. This period of preparation, the *abstinentia*, was a great deal more than a formality. It lasted at least a year, longer in some cases; judging by the experiences of those who came before the Inquisition, it was not always followed by the *consolamentum* which formally admitted the candidate to the ranks of the Perfects. After two years as a candidate, Dulcia of Villeneuve-la-Comtal was found to be too young. The noviciate of Raymonde Jougla was interrupted when the Perfects with whom she had been living were forced to flee to Montségur; and as she was 'insufficiently instructed', they refused to take her with them. After the *abstinentia*, the candidate who had satisfied his Perfect proceeded to the *consolamentum*. The details of this ceremony are known from the accounts of renegades and from a ritual handbook which survives in a manuscript at Lyon. In a brightly lit room filled with believers and sympathizers, the candidate stood before the senior Perfect and two assistants. A long homily outlined the obligations which the candidate was undertaking, and took him phrase by phrase through the *Pater Noster*, the only formal prayer which Christ himself had taught and consequently the only one which the Cathars recognized. The candidate solemnly renounced the cross which had been marked upon his forehead at baptism and accepted instead the baptism of the spirit. He undertook to deny himself all luxuries, to eat no meat, milk, or eggs, to travel always in the company of friends in the faith, and never to allow the fear of death to draw him from his new obligations. The candidate then prostrated himself in veneration before the officiating Perfect. Placing the gospel of St. John on the candidate's head, the Perfect laid his hand upon the book and, in company with the other Perfects present, called upon God to bring down upon the new Perfect the blessings of the Holy Spirit. The impression which the *consolamentum* made on those who received it needs no better testimony than the constancy of the Perfects during the crusade. For although mere believers often returned to the catholic fold, apostasies by Perfects were remarkably rare; and many hundreds of them died at the stake when the hill-towns fell to the crusaders.

At the end of the ceremony of the *consolamentum* the new Perfect was robed with the garb which distinguished his caste until persecution made discretion the better part of valour—a long black robe with a leather belt to which was attached a parchment copy of the New Testament. A Perfect was not often alone. When he was not travelling in the company of another Perfect or of a candidate for the *consolamentum*, he generally lived in a small community of Perfects where the life of the inmates was not unlike that of the more austere catholic orders. These households of Cathar dignitaries were bought and maintained from the gifts or bequests of rich sympathizers. In Cathar strongholds like Laurac and Fanjeaux there were several. The cost of maintaining them was such as to arouse accusations of sharp practice at the death-beds of the well-heeled. But in fact the sympathy and generosity of the local nobility generally made sharp practice unnecessary. The houses of female Perfects were often filled with rich and well-born ladies who, unlike the male members of their families, often carried their conviction to the point of receiving the *consolamentum* in their lifetimes.

Mere believers were certainly not excluded from the internal life of the Cathar churches. The believer also marked his membership of the sect with a ceremony, the *convenientia*, at which he promised to receive the *consolamentum* on his deathbed, if not sooner. The house of Perfects was the centre of his spiritual life, where he prostrated himself before the Perfects, received their blessing, and took the ritual meal which became the basic 'service' of the ordinary believer. Once a month, he attended a general confession known as the *apparelliamentum* at which prayers were recited by a deacon and, commonly, sermons heard. None of the austerities of a Perfect were required of a mere believer. He might marry, eat meat (even in the presence of a Perfect), and indulge in luxuries. His only obligation was to receive the *consolamentum*, an obligation whose performance was, in the case of male believers, almost always delayed until the point of death. Nevertheless, not all Cathars were even believers. Probably the vast majority were sympathizers who offered food to the Perfects, attended the occasional service, and did not object when their wives and daughters celebrated the *convenientia*. Even the soldiers who defended Montségur in 1244 were not properly speaking members of the sect until a mass celebration of the *convenientia* was held shortly before the fall of the castle.

In attempting to deny their humanity and become pure spirit, some Perfects adopted meditative practices similar to those of Buddhists. Many years after she had visited one of these men out of curiosity, a woman of Puylaurens told the inquisitors of the 'extraordinary sight' of the Perfect seated in his chair 'motionless as a tree trunk, insensible to his surroundings'. Taken to its logical conclusion the Perfect's view of life pointed to suicide as the desirable release of a soul enclosed in its bodily prison. This was less common than horrified antagonists alleged. But Perfects did starve themselves to death and on rare occasions imposed a fast to the death on sick men to whom they had administered the *consolamentum*. Occasionally more violent methods were adopted. A certain Guilelma, a Perfect of Toulouse, bled herself, weakened herself in hot baths, and finally drank poison and ate crushed glass. Several are recorded as having slit their wrists. Accounts of these macabre suicides all agree that the dying Perfect was regarded with reverence and admiration by the believers who were present.

Sin, death, redemption, salvation. On all these matters, profound differences of opinion separated Cathars from catholics, and out of them arose radically different codes of social and moral behaviour. The threat of damnation was becoming the central theme of the moral teaching of the catholic church. But the Cathars denied the existence of both Hell and Purgatory. The power of Satan, they asserted, was confined to the material world; even the most sinful soul was beyond his grasp and must inevitably be saved after the appropriate period of purgation. The problem of purgation without Purgatory was one to which not all Cathars addressed themselves. Those that did came to a conclusion not unlike the metempsychosis of Greek and Hindu philosophers. The soul passed from one body to another until it had been cleansed of sin. 'It abandons the body of a dying man to find salvation in the body of a donkey,' one Perfect asserted. Another believed that St. Paul had passed through thirty-three reincarnations before being admitted to Paradise.

More than one Cathar doctrine had anti-social implications which the orthodox were not slow to point out. Some of those who were examined by the Inquisition were anarchists of a kind found on the fringes of every heterodox sect. Those who criticized all criminal justice and held that rulers were damned can have had few supporters even among their co-religionists. Objections to the death penalty were, however, more common, and the condemnation of oaths was universal, a dangerous prejudice in a society which offered no other guarantee of the performance of obligations. Handbooks for inquisitors, which differed on many matters, were all agreed that a Cathar could be identified by his refusal to swear an oath. The sexual behaviour of the Cathars is more controversial. Accusations of sexual depravity are too often levelled at minorities to be accepted without question. There is, however, considerable evidence that the Cathars disapproved of marriage, and this is a view which follows logically from their contempt for the physical world. Human flesh is evil and its procreation unspeakably wicked. 'Carnal marriage has always been mortal sin for them,' wrote Rainier Sacchoni, himself a renegade heretic; 'a legitimate marriage is as severely punished by God as adultery or incest.' Indeed, marriage was worse than these sins for by it sexual relations were given formal sanction. It was more than capricious kindness that led the inquisitors to accept marriage as evidence of a Perfect's reconciliation with the church. Unnatural sexual acts were harder to forgive, and Alan of Lille was not the only catholic who accused the Cathars of favouring sodomy in preference to less sterile sexual activities. Like the allegation that orgies were conducted in the communities of Perfects, these suggestions can probably be dismissed as fantasies of the inquisitorial mind. As propaganda, however, they were effective. The apparent holiness of the Perfects was undeniable. Success had crowned almost every missionary enterprise they had undertaken, and it was far from clear that God was not with them.

The Waldensians were a lesser threat, even though they had formed substantial communities in Languedoc by the end of the twelfth century. They denied that an officiating priesthood was necessary to man's salvation, and they carried this view to its logical conclusion, encouraging laymen to read the Bible in the vernacular, preach, and administer such of the sacraments as they recognized. They also shared the Cathar's disapproval of oaths and capital punishment. But on most essentials the catholics and the Waldensians found themselves in the same camp. One of the first reasoned treatises against Catharism was the work of a Spanish Waldensian, Durand of Huesca, who was later converted to catholicism in the presence of St. Dominic. Indeed St. Dominic paid the Waldensians the tribute of imitation. The sandals of the early Dominicans, and their emphasis on public preaching, were both consciously borrowed from them. There were few Waldensian martyrs of the crusade or even of the Inquisition, a reflection of the sense of proportion which did not desert the church even in its vindictive moments.

Writing to Louis VII in 1173, the archbishop of Narbonne indicated that the clergy of his beleaguered diocese were already thinking in terms of forcible repression. 'The ship of St. Peter is too battered to float for much longer; have you no strength to take up the buckler of faith and the sword of justice in defence of the Lord and our Church?' If the archbishop's appeal was addressed to the king of France and not to the count of Toulouse, it was because he knew how far continuous war had weakened the count's hand. At the time of the Cathar council of St.-Felix, Raymond V was at war with the king of Aragon and most of his greater vassals. Raymond himself was well aware of the progress that the heretics were making in his dominions and of the reasons for it. In a letter addressed to the general chapter of the Cistercian order, he pointed to the disrepair of the churches and the suspension of services. 'Few still believe in the Creation or the Resurrection; the sacraments are despised and the religion of the two principles has everywhere established its hold.' Recognizing his own impotence the count could only hope for the invasion of his principality by the French king. 'I will open my cities to him and deliver up my towns and castles. I will show him where the heretics are to be found and support him to the point of bloodshed if the enemies of Christ can thus be confounded.'

Raymond's summons to a crusade was received with enthusiasm until the difficulties became apparent. In September 1177 Louis VII made peace with Henry II of England, and Henry de Marcy, abbot of Clairvaux, urged both monarchs to turn their swords against the heretics of the south. But the physical and financial exhaustion which had suggested the peace also militated strongly against a crusade. No dramatic event brought catholic armies into existence as it was to do thirty years later. Within a year the abbot was thinking in terms of a preaching mission on the lines of St. Bernard's tour of the province in 1145. The pope gave his approval to this idea and appointed as head of the mission his legate in France, Peter of Pavia, cardinal of St. Chrysogon. He was to be assisted by Henry de Marcy himself and by two Englishmen, Reginald FitzJoscelin, bishop of Bath, and Jean aux Bellesmains, bishop of Poitiers, the latter once a distinguished servant of Henry II.

These four arrived in Toulouse in December 1178. The count's welcome was not reciprocated by his subjects. The heretical community, which had taken umbrage at the arrival of St. Bernard in 1145, met at the gates of the city to jeer at his successor. The missionaries still had a confidence in the efficacy of a public debate which subsequent events show to have been excessively optimistic. After trying in vain to converse with a rabble outside his quarters, Henry de Marcy asked the civic authorities to furnish him with a list of known heretics. There was a delay of some days while a list was prepared, and from it the missionaries endeavoured to select a suitable champion of the Cathar cause. The man chosen was Peter Maurand, a well-known local figure of considerable wealth whose reputation for vanity suggested that he might accept an invitation to a debate. But the outcome was something of a disappointment to those who had hoped to witness a dramatic conflict of principle. Maurand was a frightened old man. Faced with a large and obviously hostile crowd, he lost his nerve, retracted all his heretical views, and was splendidly reconciled to the church in the basilica of St. Sernin on the following morning. His defection brought a number of his fellow Cathars forward to ask for reconciliation, but its principal effect was on the morale of the catholic preachers. They were encouraged to try their skills against other Cathar spokesmen. To this end two prominent heretics from the outlying town of Lavaur, were offered a safe-conduct to and from Toulouse. But the second confrontation was even less satisfactory than the first. The heretics could not speak Latin and the catholic delegation could only with difficulty understand the *langue d'oc*. To the surprise of those catholic spokesmen who understood it, their opponents read out from a parchment a declaration of faith of perfect orthodoxy; when questioned they even agreed that marriage and infant baptism were legitimate and that arch-bishops could be saved. Somewhat nonplussed by all this, the papal legate adjourned the proceedings from the cathedral to the neighbour-ing church of St. James, where a crowd of interested laymen had gathered. Members of the crowd came foward to swear that they had heard the two heretical spokesmen preach that there were two Gods, a good and an evil, that the sacraments were of no value, and that those who lived together as man and wife could not be saved. Although the spokesmen denied it, when asked to confirm their declarations of faith on oath, they proved to be evasive and finally refused outright. The papal legate excommunicated them for contumacy and Raymond declared them to be outlaws. But if the catholics had proved their adversaries to be heretics, neither side could be said to have gained any points. The safe-conduct was respected and the two outlaws escaped to the protection of the count of Béziers. Shortly after the new year the catholic delegation dispersed, Henry de Marcy returning to Bur-gundy and the papal legate embarking for Rome.

On his arrival the legate delivered what must have been a sombre report to Alexander III, and the matter of Languedoc was duly raised at the third Lateran council which opened two months later on 5th March 1179. The council was unable to do more than utter another excommunication against the heretics and their allies. The pope, however, thought it worth attempting another mission. Henry de Marcy, who had by now arrived in Rome, was created cardinal-bishop of Albano and despatched to France with general powers to act in the pope's name. It is not clear whether the action which Henry took was what Alexander had in mind. What is certain is that Henry had gained enough experience of the southern Cathars to realize that little could be done by unarmed missionaries. In July 1181, after disposing of other business, he gathered a small army and marched on the town of Lavaur, the home of the two heretical spokesmen whose safe-conduct he had respected two years earlier. A hill-town between Toulouse and Albi belonging to Roger II Trencavel, in 1181 it was the strongest Cathar town of the Toulousain, 'the very seat of Satan and capital of heresy' as the southern bishops described it many years later when it had fallen to the crusaders. It was the residence of the Cathar bishop of Toulouse and contained a number of houses of Perfects. The castellan was openly sympathetic to the heresy and his wife, a Perfect and a notable virago, was later to meet a brutal death at the hands of the crusaders. Taken by surprise, the citizens did not have time to make use of the town's formidable defensive strength. The wife of Roger II, who was in the town when the legate arrived, had the gates opened for him. The two heretics were quickly found and brought before the legate who harangued them at length and induced them to retract a long list of dualist errors. Probably, there was more to this encounter than the sources tell us, for they appear to have been quite sincere in renouncing in an afternoon the beliefs of a lifetime. Some years later they are both found in Toulouse, one of them among the canons of St.-Sernin and the other assisting the bishop as a canon of the cathedral.

Henry de Marcy cannot have hoped to achieve more than this with the small force at his disposal. Spectacular as it was, his intervention at Lavaur remained his only significant action against the heretics in a legation of nearly ten years. The eight years of life which were left to him were passed in attending to the great affairs of the church at the French court and in preaching the third crusade. In Languedoc dualism, though never the religion of the majority, reached the fullest extent of its power by the closing years of the twelfth century. Had the strength of the Cathars been concentrated in the great urban centres, as it was in the north, an alliance between the count of Toulouse and the local bishop would probably have checked their progress at an early stage. But although the Cathar bishops took their titles from large cities they did not live in them. Toulouse, Albi, and Narbonne were by now relatively minor centres of the heresy. Béziers was more important, but the only large city which the heretics ever succeeded in controlling was Carcassonne. Catharism put down its deepest roots in the small country towns subject to the Trencavel viscounts of Béziers. In the southern half of the diocese of Albi dualists were sufficiently numerous for the crusaders to apply the name 'Albigensians' indiscriminately to all the heretics of the south. In Lombers and Lautrec they probably had the sympathy if not the formal adhesion of a majority of the population. The same may have been true of Verfeil in the diocese of Toulouse, where St. Bernard was humiliated in 1145, and Lavaur, where his successor enjoyed such a notable triumph in 1181. Further south, Laurac, Fanjeaux, and Montréal were typical of innumerable walled towns where the benevolence of the seigneurial family provided a safe haven for the Cathars and their leaders. Such statistical evidence as can be found (and there is not much) suggests that between a quarter and a third of the population of western Languedoc may have sympathized with the Cathars. In the outlying regions, Gascony, Quercy, the Rouergue, and the Rhône valley, the proportion was certainly smaller. The church was slow to appreciate the gravity of the situation. But in the last resort it was the unusual experience of an alliance between popular religion and aristocratic force which convinced it that only a crusade would carry the day. Nothing comparable occurred in France until the sixteenth-century wars of religion threw precisely the same regions into the hands of a militant and puritanical creed.

The chronicler Peter of Vaux-de-Cernay, who came south with the crusaders, found that the supporters of the Cathars included 'almost all the baronial families of the province who gave them hospitality, friendship, and protection against God and His Church'. This conclusion is substantially borne out by the records of the Inquisition which, although not compiled until after the 1230s, include depositions to events as far back as the 1180s. On the eve of the crusade, more than a third of all known Perfects were of noble birth. At St.-Paul-Cadajoux, as at many similar towns, the communities of Perfects were filled with the womenfolk of the dominant seigneurial family; the Cathar cemeteries with the unmarked graves of their husbands and sons who had received the *consolamentum* on their deathbeds. Tradition, pride, often some unrevealed grievance against the catholic clergy, combined to create ties between Cathar communities and local families, many of which survived for several generations. The seigneur of Laurac, who was hanged for his resistance to the crusaders, may have been no more than a sympathizer, but he numbered his mother, three sisters, and two nephews among the sect's initiated believers.

To describe the persistence of heresy in such families as the fruit of envy and anti-clericalism is only half of the truth. Those noblemen who supported the Cathars in their lifetimes but died with the absolution of the church, may well have been guided by such considerations. But the lesser nobility had little to gain by embracing heresy. And if their hatred of the catholic clergy was nonetheless venomous for that, it requires rather more to explain why an important class of southern society behaved in a manner so radically different from that of their equally anti-clerical brethren in the north. These men had all the intensified consciousness of guilt of the twelfth-century nobility, but few of the means of appeasing it. They needed a religion that set a premium on personal piety and individuality. An increasingly institutional church did little to satisfy them by conventional formulae which had long lost the edge that once made them inspiring. The greater nobility found satisfaction in the endowment of new orders—the Cistercians of Grandselve and Fontfroide, the order of the Holy Spirit at Montpellier. Such endowments formed part of the continuous exchange of land and rights over land which bound together the ecclesiastical masters of a province with the political masters. But what was there to impress the master of a hundred acres and a quarter of a dilapidated castle? The abbot of Grandselve offered him no greater consolation than a price for his land, a price which reflected the buyer's market in a region where death and subdivision had made seigneurial estates uneconomic. The monasteries did not die; their estates were divided by force or not at all. Elsewhere, in Normandy and Burgundy, strong spiritual currents had made knighthood an honorary order of the church and reconciled it to its losses. But since the second crusade, these currents had passed Languedoc by. The small seigneurial landowner was left with the guilt of sins unexpiated, with a parish priest whose ministrations bored even the illiterate members of his flock, and with an estate reduced by the pious bequests of his grandfather. The Cathars offered him an alternative, and he took it.

The greater nobility found it harder to detach spiritual issues from their political consequences. While the rural nobility had themselves carried when dying to the houses of Perfects to receive the *consolamentum*, the greater feudatories almost invariably died with the sacraments of the church and still filled their wills with pious legacies. Roger II, viscount of Béziers, though not himself a heretic, was certainly a friend of heretics, and the heretics of Lavaur, Laurac, Fanjeaux, and Minerve lived under his protection. On his death in 1194 Roger named a notorious heretic, Bertrand de Saissac, as his son's guardian, an act which does not necessarily imply Cathar leanings, for Bertrand was also the strongest of his vassals and any other appointment would have been an act of political folly. Though the appointment did not make the young count into a heretic, it did put Bertrand in control of the viscounty during his minority. In 1197, the regent forced the monks of Alet to elect one of his creatures as their abbot at a chapter presided over by the exhumed corpse of their previous abbot.

The count of Foix was no more restrained in his use of power. Although he stopped short of membership of the Cathar sect, he declined to take his hat off as processions passed him with holy relics

59

in the streets, and did nothing to prevent his relatives and friends from receiving the *consolamentum*. In 1204 he attended the ceremony in the castle of Fanjeaux by which his sister Esclarmonde became a Perfect; his wife, an aunt, and another sister also became heretics. The count's persistent quarrels with the abbot of St. Antonin at Pamiers had become a *cause célèbre* even in a region famed for its anti-clerical excesses. He installed a house of Perfects, presided over by his mother, on one of the abbey's estates. When the canons of St. Antonin attempted to expel them by force, one of their number was hacked to death at the altar by a knight in the count's service; another had his eyes put out. The lordship of Pamiers, held jointly by the count and the abbot, was for many years a bone of contention. In defending their rights the monks were repeatedly assaulted and robbed, and on one occasion blockaded in their monastery for three days without food. The nature of the count's own religious beliefs is now impenetrably obscure. But there is little doubt that he agreed with his illegitimate brother, who was once heard to declare that the Perfects were holy men and that salvation would not be had from the catholic clergy.

The catholic clergy of Languedoc certainly lacked the personal charisma and obvious holiness of many Cathar missionaries. But their vices may have been exaggerated both by the heretics and by catholic missionaries who could find no other excuse for the failure of their church. Cistercian missionaries in the province were regularly reminded by hostile audiences of the deplorable conduct of the catholic clergy by comparison with the austere lives of the Perfects. But even the Cathars rarely condemned them as harshly as Innocent III, who called them ignorant, illiterate, and irredeemably corrupt, 'watchdogs who have lost their bark', 'hirelings who abandon their flock to the wolves'. Between his accession in 1198 and the beginning of the crusade in 1209, Innocent III deposed no less than seven southern bishops including those of Toulouse and Béziers. Most were replaced by Cistercian monks, or at any rate by outsiders who could be expected to be free of the retentive web of corruption and aristocratic influence. Yet Innocent was perhaps unrealistic in expecting triumphs where even St Bernard had failed, and it may well be doubted whether he ever truly understood the situation in Languedoc. His letters, which presumably reflect the prejudices of his informants, reveal an excessively simple view of a delicate problem. Certainly it is hard to take seriously his suggestion in 1200 that the sole cause of the spread of heresy in the province of Narbonne was the venality of its archbishop. The archbishop of Narbonne was no more venal than many of his northern colleagues. If his wealth was considerable the use to which he put it was not always bad; and there was noticeably less heresy among his own flock than among those of the penniless bishops of Toulouse and Carcassonne. Bishops like those of Narbonne and Montpellier who ruled minor principalities and employed small mercenary armies, may not have been an edifying spectacle; but there is no doubt that they were by far the most effective opponents of a heresy which could rely on the armed support of the rural nobility. Less powerful ecclesiastics faced the problems of revenues eroded by aristocratic appropriations, and an anarchy which made the performance of their pastoral duties impossible. Fulcrand, bishop of Toulouse, had to negotiate with local castellans each time that he toured his diocese; he lived 'like a bourgeois' and after his death in 1200 only ninety-six sous were found in the episcopal chest.

Laymen, observed William of Puylaurens, were in the habit of exclaiming that they 'would rather be a priest than do such and such'. Not surprisingly, it had proved hard to find acceptable clerics to take on such thankless duties. In the north, the practice of primogeniture had made priests of ambitious and literate younger sons; in Languedoc there was not even this leaven to improve a clerical class which shared all the limited horizons of its parishioners. Unlettered candidates were accepted for ordination before they had reached the canonical age, and even they could only cover the entire province by holding benefices in plurality. Most were more demoralized than corrupt. They would have liked to follow Otto, bishop of Carcassonne, who begged to be relieved of his functions in 1198. Others relapsed into despair, brushed their hair forward so as to conceal their tonsures, or strove to make what agreements they could with the Cathars. Some became heretics themselves, like the monks of Alet and St.-Hilaire, who were dispersed by a papal legate after the crusade.

At a distance of eight centuries it is possible to be more sympathetic to these churchmen than their contemporaries were. If the establishment failed to rally to the church in Languedoc as it had in the Rhineland or the Ile-de-France, it was because its members were deeply divided among themselves. When Raymond V told the abbot of Cîteaux that the schism had divided husbands and wives, fathers and sons, he was uttering more than the cliché that such expressions normally imply in the words of mediaeval letter-writers. The abbots of St.-Papoul and of St.-Volusien de Foix belonged to heretical families. There is no evidence that they were even clandestinely sympathetic to the Cathars, but their effectiveness as leaders of a catholic resurgence can only have been weakened. Probably they felt much as William Peire, bishop of Albi, did when his own cousin told him that he would be buried in the Cathar cemetery if he had to crawl there on his hands and knees. Several years later the bishop of Toulouse asked a catholic knight why he did not expel the heretics from his lands. 'How can we?' he replied. 'We have been brought up side by side with them. Our closest kinsmen are numbered among them. Every day we see them living worthy and honourable lives in our midst.' The answer showed how far the heretics could now rely on the forces of social conservatism for their survival.

# ✠ IV ✠

## 1194–1208: Raymond VI

'He that being often reproved hardeneth his neck, shall
suddenly be destroyed.'

PROVERBS XXIX.I

Raymond V died at Nîmes in December 1194. His long reign had
witnessed the defeat of the catholic Church by an upstart heresy and
the dismemberment of his inheritance by rebellious vassals and aggressive neighbours. Raymond had fought bitterly against both these misfortunes, but although he was the most energetic and resourceful of
his dynasty, his enemies were too many and too strong. He lacked the
military skills and the political brilliance by which Henry II of England
had survived still greater assaults on his power. That he was charming
and generous where Henry II was rude and mean is of small moment
beside the impoverished and disordered condition in which he left his
principality. He had had the virtues of his vices, and the eulogies which
accompanied his burial in the cloister of Nîmes cathedral were sincere,
if conventional, tributes to the last count of Toulouse who could
plausibly claim to be the 'peer of kings'.

As to the qualities of his successor, there was less agreement. Raymond VI was already thirty-eight years old when he entered into his
inheritance. He had not had the brutal training of his predecessors, all
of whom had come to power very young and learned from the experience. He had his father's charm, but unlike his father he was tactless
and vacillating, and lost his nerve in crises. Equally serious were his
failings as a soldier in a principality where vassals respected few other
arts. In 1194, Raymond's experience of war was limited to a few pilla-
ging expeditions against his father's enemies. On both occasions that
he faced the crusaders in battle, he left the field without drawing his
sword. His mother, Constance of France, was a daughter of Louis VI
but she had left him none of the toughness and certainty of purpose of
the Capetians.

Raymond VI's personal attractiveness was not in doubt. He kept a splendid and expensive court, which made him popular with the nobility and the *troubadours*. He was fond of luxury. He was also a notable womanizer, and an admirer of the songs of Raimon de Miraval, one of the last *troubadours* of the first rank, whose command of the art of seduction is said to have endeared him to the count. If Raymond's detractors are to be believed, he had little need of such advice, having seduced his father's mistresses at an early age, committed incest with his sister, and repudiated two of his five wives. He cut a romantic figure in contemporary eyes, but his incompetence as a ruler brought disaster on his dominions and would have done so even if he had not faced in Innocent III one of the ablest statesmen of mediaeval Europe.

No aspect of Raymond's personality was as obscure or as controversial as his religion. If history has condemned him as a cynic and a hypocrite, this is very largely due to the venomous testimony of one man, the chronicler Peter of Vaux-de-Cernay, a Cistercian and a northerner whose first encounter with the south came, perhaps revealingly, three years after the beginning of the crusade. The prime count in Peter's indictment was that Raymond was a believing heretic 'from the very cradle'. He surrounded himself with heretical courtiers and always kept a Perfect with him to administer the *consolamentum* should he suddenly be taken ill; he protected Perfects, giving them money and food, and even prostrating himself before them; he was heard to dismiss the Old Testament as worthless, and to ascribe to the Devil the creation of the world 'because nothing that happens in it ever goes my way'; he invited the bishop of Toulouse to hear Cathar sermons in his palace in the middle of the night; he refused to punish a heretic who urinated on an altar; he disposed of his second wife by forcing her into a Cathar community. Many of these allegations were entirely baseless, but there was enough truth in Peter's earnest litany of hatred to carry conviction among those who did not know the true weakness of the house of Toulouse. Raymond VI undoubtedly kept heretics about him, including his second wife Beatrice of Béziers who probably needed no prompting to enter a Cathar convent in 1193. He was also hot-tempered and capable of being extremely rude to clergymen. In 1209 it was possible to draw up a list of twenty-six towns of the count's private demesne where heretics practised their faith with impunity. But such lists could have been drawn up for many private demesnes. They reflected the political condition of Languedoc, not the religious sympathies of its rulers. Raymond may well have lacked the will to destroy heresy; that he lacked the means to do so is beyond question. He belonged to a generation which had grown up with heresy and become reconciled to its existence. He recognized, as ultimately the church recognized, that only a bloody war would eradicate Catharism, but unlike the church he did not think the price worth paying. None of this proves that his own sympathies lay with the heretics, and what little is known of his personal life suggests that he was a man of unexceptional, entirely conventional piety. After Raymond's death, evidence of his orthodoxy was presented to a papal commission appointed to decide whether he should be allowed a Christian burial. His son compiled a memorandum of the dead count's pious benefactions and charitable deeds, and 110 witnesses, most of them priests and monks, came forward to give evidence of his orthodoxy. The commissioners were not impressed by this testimony, but much of it is borne out by charters in which Raymond showed himself to be a generous benefactor of the church, including those orders such as the Cistercians which were particularly associated with the crusade. His will, drawn up while he was besieged in Toulouse, was a model of catholic piety, expressing the hope that he might die in the habit of the Hospitallers of St. John, and leaving them a large legacy.

Raymond's first embroilment with the church came within a few weeks of his accession. He had built a stone castle called Mirapetra on land belonging to the abbot of St.-Gilles. The abbot's protests were met by violence, and an appeal to the pope produced an angry remonstrance from Rome threatening the count with excommunication. The dispute showed how difficult it was to disentangle the secular from the spiritual in the government of a mediaeval state. The abbey of St.-Gilles had long enjoyed the special protection of the papacy; but it owed its survival and most of its land to Raymond's ancestors. Their motives had been only partly spiritual. The abbey stood in the most sensitive parts of the count's dominions, close to the great arteries of the Rhône and the Domitian Way, and close to the rebellious petty lords of western Provence who had repeatedly disturbed the count's grip on his richest possessions. An owner did not part with land when he gave it to a monastery in such circumstances. He placed it in the safe-keeping of a community whom he expected to watch over his interests and maintain his presence. No count of Toulouse could accept spiritual theories scarcely a century old by which the church sought to emancipate itself from these ill-defined obligations. From such seeds grew most of Raymond's disputes with the clergy: his seizure of the fortified cathedral of Rodez; his appropriation of two castles belonging to the bishop of Carpentras; his expulsion of the bishop of Agen from the city; his imprisonment of the bishop of Vaison and the abbot of Montauban; recurring quarrels with almost every ecclesiastical landowner as to fields, villages, and vineyards whose ownership was disputed or whose boundaries were uncertain. Raymond's dispute with the abbot of St.-Gilles was not to be cut short by threats from Rome, and in 1196 he suffered the first of many excommunications. Although it was lifted in 1198, Raymond's submission was not the end of that matter. Repeated complaints from the pope and the abbot of St.-Gilles demonstrated that Raymond followed his ancestors in rating the preservation of his power above his spiritual well-being.

Celestine III did not live to see his commands flouted. The ninety-two-year-old pope died in Rome on 8th January 1198, and on the same day the cardinals met in the ruinous remains of the palace of Septimus Severus to elect a thirty-seven-year-old canon lawyer as his successor. Lothaire de Segni, who took the name Innocent III, was probably the most powerful, certainly the most impressive of all mediaeval popes. He was descended from the petty nobility of the Roman Campagna, a background which gave him something in common with the Cathar nobility of Languedoc. But such sympathy as he might otherwise have had for them did not survive his legal training at Bologna, the birth-place of the juridical theories of the reformed papacy. The modesty of the conventional formulae with which he announced his election to the world only briefly concealed his authoritarian nature. Innocent had an exalted view of the powers of his office. He was called 'to reign over kings from the throne of glory'. He was the first pope to use the title 'vicar of Christ'. In his youth, Innocent had written some treatises on the spiritual life, and his sensitivity to spiritual matters survived his election to the papacy; he befriended the early Franciscans in spite of the hostility of the bishops; even his treatment of heretics shows some awareness of the church's failure to satisfy spiritual aspirations with orthodox alternatives. By temperament, however, he was a politician and a lawyer, and if he had a politician's autocratic ways, he had a lawyer's stickling for procedural formalities and constitutional niceties.

Innocent believed that princes were charged with the sword of God for the avenging of his anger. If they would not use it or, worse, turned it against God's church, they might be reproved and ultimately destroyed. With his strong views on the unity of the church, he could not be indifferent to the spread of heresy in Languedoc. References in his letters to the 'hateful plague', 'spreading canker', or 'vile wolves among the Lord's flock', suggest a fanatical, even hysterical hatred of heresy. But Innocent's letters were manifestos; his use of resounding biblical expressions was a symptom of their public nature as well as a natural instinct in one whose education had taught him to think in scriptural phrases. Innocent's actions were more restrained than his words. He had a sense of what was possible, a sound political wisdom which his legates on the spot, carried away by the rapid succession of events, frequently lacked. His legal training constantly reminded him of the judicial procedures and cogent evidence that were required before an incompetent bishop could be deprived or a heretical prince deposed. The enthusiasm with which the crusaders dispossessed their enemies without trial or investigation caused Innocent a distress which was by no means hypocritical. More than once he pointed out to his legates that Raymond VI had never been proved a heretic, and for this reason he strongly objected to their attempts to put another in his place. But the fanaticism of a crusader was as little understood by Innocent as the fanaticism of a heretic. He had fired his mine, and could not control the destruction which followed.

Innocent had first to learn the frustration of dealing with a fast-changing situation at a distance of a month's journey. Being one of those men who would have liked to handle every detail of a complex administration himself, he chafed at the necessity of relying on legates, and his first appointments were bad ones. In April 1198 he nominated Rainier da Ponza, a mild Italian Cistercian, once the disciple and friend of that strange Calabrian mystic Joachim of Fiore. Rainier had neither time nor taste for his task, which he was expected to combine with an important diplomatic mission to the Spanish and Portuguese courts. More than once he indicated his desire to have done with ecclesiastical politics and return to the peace of his cloister. His sole achievement in two years was to accept the resignation of the infirm and incapable bishop of Carcassonne. It was doubtless he who was responsible for the official wisdom in Rome that the solution to the Cathar problem lay in removing the archbishop of Narbonne from his post, for a rigorous investigation of the archbishop's deficiencies was the principal task with which Innocent charged his next legate, John cardinal of St.

Priscus. John arrived in Montpellier in the autumn of 1200, but his activities in Languedoc have left no trace, and he lost little time in returning to Rome in the following year.

Three years of inactivity followed, in which the southern nobility predictably failed to respond to the promise of the indulgences of Rome and Santiago for expelling heretics from their lands. Not until the summer of 1203 did Innocent find in Peter of Castelnau a legate equal to the problem. Peter was a monk of the abbey of Fontfroide, near Narbonne. He was a theologian and a canon lawyer, able and energetic, but with all the narrowness of view which his background implied. He was a Cistercian like all his predecessors, but unlike them he had the advantage of being a man of the Midi, born in the flat, vine-growing country north of Montpellier which remained throughout his life the stronghold of catholicism in the south. Another monk of Fontfroide, one Ralph, was joined with Peter as co-legate, but he rarely emerged from the shadow of his autocratic colleague. More powerful reinforcement came in the following year with the appointment of a third legate, Arnald-Amaury abbot of Cîteaux. Arnald-Amaury was also a southerner, having been abbot of Grandselve and of Fontfroide's Catalonian daughter-house at Poblet, before being elected to the highest office of his order. Of all the ecclesiastics concerned with the Albigensian crusade, Arnald-Amaury came nearest to fanaticism. He was more comfortable leading 40,000 men to the battlefield of Las Navas de Tolosa than attempting the arduous, often unrewarding work of converting the Cathars. The restraint which was forced upon him by his status as a legate and a priest cramped him. Innocent had given him a mission and he did his best to fulfil it. But his heart was not in it until the crusade gave him an opportunity for resolute action of a kind which was more to his taste. 'Kill them all; God will recognize his own,' may not have been Arnald-Amaury's phrase; but it summed up the instinct of a man who, better than St. Dominic, deserves to be called the father of the Inquisition.

Innocent's legates enjoyed absolute powers. The jurisdiction of the bishops over heresy was transferred to them; they were empowered to enforce their wishes by excommunication and interdict; any ecclesiastic who seemed to them to be obstructive or unworthy of his office, they might remove without notice or right of appeal. These powers were not calculated to ingratiate the legates with the local clergy and may well have proved more of a hindrance than a help. The archbishop of Narbonne complained that the legates had been high-handed and rude, failing to notify him of their presence in his diocese in accordance with accepted courtesies, and issuing peremptory instructions to him as if he were a mere acolyte. He refused to accompany them to the presence of Raymond VI or even allow them an armed escort. With some difficulty he was persuaded to assign a single knight to protect them on the road. The bishop of Béziers and the bishop-elect of Maguelonne were equally adamant in refusing to attend on the pope's legates. At Toulouse, however, which the party reached with its small escort in December 1204, a warm welcome belied the city's reputation as a 'poisonous nest of heresy'. The bishop, the abbot of St. Sernin, and the consuls were persuaded to swear that they would tolerate no heretics in their midst. In return for this, their civic privileges were confirmed, a high-handed assumption of power which must have irritated the count as much as the bishop. The citizens of Béziers, less orthodox perhaps, or less amenable to bribes, refused to swear a similar oath; nor would the bishop agree to make them do so until he had been menaced with excommunication in the presence of his own clergy.

Three months of his legation were enough to convince Peter of Castelnau that his first quarrel was with Languedoc's bishops. His reaction was characteristically extreme. The bishop of Béziers was deprived forthwith and replaced by an administrator. The bishop of Viviers was suspended after his canons had accused him of a variety of malpractices, and would have been deposed had he not belonged to a powerful family. Even aristocratic connections did not save the bishop of Toulouse, Raymond de Rabastens, who was forced to resign after the revelation that he had bribed his electors and sold off the assets of the bishopric to finance a private war. The case of Bérenger, archbishop of Narbonne, required greater circumspection. The deposition of an archbishop was a grave matter, particularly when he was the uncle of the king of Aragon in whom Innocent already saw the leader of a possible crusade. Bérenger was a master of the elaborate procedure by which the papal curia failed to make decisions, and he remained archbishop of Narbonne until 1212. By this time, however, scarcely any of his colleagues survived in the posts they had held on Peter's arrival, nine years earlier.

Peter II of Aragon was particularly important to the legates in 1204. The possession of extensive, if somewhat nominal feudal rights in

Languedoc, made Peter an acceptable substitute for the count of Toulouse, who would not co-operate with them. In February 1204 he presided over a formal debate at Carcassonne at which both Waldensians and Cathars were represented. It was a dramatic occasion and for the legates a revelation of the extent of their problems. But the inevitable excommunication of the heretics served little purpose. The time was long past when conversions could be made simply by pointing out that the Cathars spoke without the authority of the church. Taking stock of his achievements at the end of his first year as legate, Peter of Castelnau recognized that they amounted to very little. He began to experience that weary nostalgia for the life of the cloister to which earlier legates had succumbed, and he needed to be reminded by his distant master that 'faith shines out in adversity . . . and effort is as pleasing to Our Lord as achievement'. *Sursum corda.*

Innocent himself was already thinking in other terms. Learning that the Cathars had taken control of Lescure, a property of the Holy See, he offered the town as a fief to Peter II of Aragon if he could take it. Peter, always anxious to add effective power to the somewhat shadowy rights which he already held in western Languedoc, seized the town at the beginning of the following year. The pope was less fortunate in his other champions. He had already written once to the king of France, Philip Augustus, about the spread of heresy in the southern part of his kingdom. In February 1205, within a fortnight of his reassuring letter to the legates, Innocent appealed once more to Raymond's nominal suzerain, begging him to intervene in the Midi, or at least to send his son to do so. The pope's letter found Philip preoccupied with plans for an invasion of England, and his army fully stretched before the walls of Loches and Chinon. His reply has not survived, but it is unlikely to have been encouraging. The mounting evidence of papal indignation was, however, beginning to alarm Raymond VI. In the summer of 1205, he decided to placate the legates by swearing an oath to expel the heretics from his dominions. It was a promise which he knew it was beyond his power to keep, and one which the legates did not forget.

Towards the end of a June day in 1206 an accidental encounter inside the eastern gate of Montpellier altered the direction of Peter's mission. Two Castilians, Diego, bishop of Osma, and the subprior of his cathedral, Dominic de Guzman, were returning homeward after three years of fruitless travel on the business of Alfonso VIII of Castile.

With them were some Cistercian monks and the bedraggled remnant of what had once been an imposing diplomatic retinue. The Roman road was carried through the town by a winding street which took them past the church of Notre-Dame des Tables. Here almost certainly, where public ceremonies were held and money-changers kept their tables, Diego and Dominic found the papal legates conducting official business. The legates were demoralized and exhausted. They complained that the continuing battle with the southern clergy had spared them little time for preaching; what preaching they had done was coldly heard by hardened, obstinate audiences; all three were on the point of renouncing their mission. The two Castilians had encountered Catharism once before, three years earlier in a Toulouse hostelry where Dominic had discovered that the innkeeper was a believer and had confronted him for most of the night with the earnest orthodoxy of a graduate of Palencia university. The memory of that occasion may have given him an optimism which three years of failure had drained from the papal legates. Diego suggested that they should try again, travelling from town to town without shoes or money preaching by example as well as by word. 'It is the pretence of poverty which has won the heretics their victories; turn their arms against them, and preach by example, opposing true faith to illusion.' The legates had to be persuaded. They thought the idea unusual, and therefore wrong, and they doubted whether they had authority to accept the bishop's proposal. But it had the merit of adopting for the catholics an evangelical method which had proved strikingly successful when practised by their heretical adversaries. Diego sent his baggage train and attendants on to Spain. Arnald-Amaury left for Cîteaux to hold the general chapter of his order. The others, Diego, Dominic, and two legates left Montpellier unescorted and on foot along the Domitian Way towards Béziers.

Diego's mission to the Cathars was a failure, but for the future development of the church it was an instructive failure marking the end of many centuries of official optimism about the church's capacity to persuade. Out of it arose not only the foundation of the Dominican order but the attitude of mind which made inquisitors of so many of a later generation of Dominicans. At Servian the missionaries found a well-entrenched heretical minority living under the protection of the largest local landowner, Etienne de Servian. Four years later this man was to confess to sheltering in his castle a number of distinguished heretics, including the Cathar bishop of Carcassonne and a former canon of Nevers who had changed his name and fled south to escape persecution at home. In July 1206 the latter, and a companion of his, engaged the legates in debate for eight days without admitting their error. But the catholics of the town were cheered by the display and escorted the party for a league outside the walls when they left. At Béziers Diego's party 'confirmed the faith of the catholics and confounded the heretics', an encouraging but still negative work which by now was as much as the more experienced legates hoped to achieve. From Béziers they trudged to Carcassonne and thence, in the wake of the equally penniless but more splendidly dressed *jongleurs*, from one seigneurial city to the next, moving steadily in the direction of Toulouse.

Dominic had scarcely emerged from the shadow of his bishop. He had not yet developed the rhetorical methods by which the mendicant orders were to transform the art of preaching to popular audiences. His discourses were still severe, uncompromising theological disputations without the histrionic tricks and naive 'examples' which delighted late mediaeval congregations. The Cathars were more skilful. At Montréal in April 1207, Dominic and his companions faced a formidable team of Cathar champions including a celebrated preacher Guilabert de Castres, the heretic bishop of Toulouse. Written lists of arguments and authorities were exchanged, and then verbally denied, distinguished or refined. The four arbiters, two townsmen and two knights of Montréal, all sympathetic to the heretics, refused to give a verdict, sensitive, perhaps, to divisions among the population. But others had been convinced and were converted, perhaps even as many as the 150 suggested by contemporaries, notoriously loose in the matter of statistics. The missionaries were still in Montréal at the end of April when Arnald-Amaury returned from Cîteaux bringing with him some thirty Cistercian preachers. The missionaries, now forty strong, separated into small groups and went different ways. Dominic and the bishop of Osma went south to Pamiers where they confronted a deputation of Waldensians in a formal deputation held under the auspices of the count of Foix. The bishop's claim to have had the better of this argument is borne out by several well-documented conversions and also, perhaps, by the heckling from the count's sister who had to be silenced by a monk. 'Go away, woman, and spin at your distaff; these are not matters for you.' The debate at Pamiers was a powerful boost to the catholics' morale, since the converts included prominent and educated men. One of them, the Spaniard Durand of Huesca, later formed an obscure association of poor preachers which was the first of the mendicant orders.

Not everyone found catholic preaching convincing. The heretics of Carcassonne expelled the bishop in the summer of 1207, and the citizens were warned by the town crier not to associate with him or supply food to his household. At about the same time, the Cathars were able to hold an assembly of some six hundred believers at Mirepoix in the dominions of the count of Foix. Evidently the missionaries themselves had few illusions about the permanence of their achievement, after the initial enthusiasm had waned. Some of the Cistercians brought by Arnald-Amaury drifted back within a few weeks of their arrival, and all had left by the end of the year. Ralph of Fontfroide, Peter's co-legate, withdrew to the abbey of Franquevaux to die in July 1207. In September, Diego of Osma returned to settle the affairs of his diocese where, a few weeks after his arrival, he too died. Dominic devoted himself increasingly to the foundation of a community of converted Cathar women at Prouille, an alternative to the houses of Perfects where penniless knights tended to leave daughters whom they could not afford to endow. He did not abandon his preaching mission. But in 1208 political events had overtaken it and the religious future of Languedoc was being decided elsewhere.

Peter of Castelnau left the other legates during the debate at Montréal and crossed the Rhône at the end of April 1207. It was almost exactly two years since Raymond VI had promised to destroy heresy by force and his failure to take action was manifest. Peter had already decided that no further progress could be expected in the Toulousain without the co-operation of the count. In Provence he negotiated a truce among the count's warring vassals and formed a league devoted to the preservation of peace and the destruction of heresy in the province of Narbonne. This league Raymond was invited to join. But the legate's unforeseen boldness had taken him too much by surprise. The delicate balance of power which the count had established in the Rhône valley was now disturbed, and it irritated him to be asked to join a league so obviously directed against himself. He refused and was immediately excommunicated. Raymond's alleged protection of heretics was only one of the charges against him. He had employed foreign mercenaries to fight his private war; he had violated the truce declared for the great feast-days of the church; he had appointed Jews to public offices; he had pillaged monasteries, and turned churches into fortresses. In Rome, Innocent confirmed his legate's sentence and addressed to the count a letter of unparalleled violence:

'Do not forget that life and death themselves are in God's hands. God may suddenly strike you down, and his anger deliver you to everlasting torment. Even if you are permitted to live, do not suppose that misfortune cannot reach you. You are not made of iron. You are weak and vulnerable, like other men. Fever, leprosy, paralysis, insanity, incurable disease may all attack you like any other of your kind. ... Are you not ashamed of breaking the oath by which you swore to eradicate heresy from your dominions? ... Are you already so mad that you think yourself wiser than all the faithful of the universal Church? ... The hand of the Lord will no longer be stayed. It will stretch forth to crush you, for the anger which you have provoked will not lightly be evaded.'

The three archbishops of the Midi were ordered to publish the sentence in their churches each Sunday until Raymond submitted. No religious service was to be held in any place where the count was staying. No prince, knight, castellan or official was to associate with him on pain of excommunication. No judge, notary, or doctor was to serve him, 'not even the farrier who shoes his horse'. His vassals were released from their oaths of homage, his subjects absolved from their duty of obedience. Worse was threatened if the count did not submit. Innocent reserved the right to depose him and invite neighbouring rulers to invade his principality.

Having launched his thunderbolt, Peter of Castelnau arrived at Raymond's court to inform him personally of its consequences. He was received with a characteristic display of ill-temper. The count boasted, if the legate is to be believed, that he could find plenty of heretical bishops to prove their church superior to his. Many years later Raymond's arrogant demeanour in the face of the legate was denied by his friends; Raymond's son asserted that he had sincerely regretted the denial of the church's services to his household, even saying his prayers outside the closed doors of churches on Sundays and holy days. Probably, neither version was very close to the truth. The excommunication was an irritant, but Raymond certainly knew that his cousin Philip of France had suffered a papal interdict of two years unscathed. He did not yet have the example of John of England to warn him of the effect of excommunication on a monarch who did not fully control his own subjects. Innocent's strength was the strength of his allies and in Languedoc his allies were few and feeble.

Knowing the weakness of his position, Innocent III revived a project which had twice before passed through his mind, an invasion of Languedoc by the king of France. On 12th November 1207, he addressed a further appeal to Philip Augustus. The heretics of the Toulousain, he said, had shown themselves impervious to arguments or threats. The verdict of the church had been declared, but had carried no weight, and the time had now arrived for the sword of the civil power to come to its assistance. 'Let the strength of the crown and the misery of war bring them back to the truth,' the pope declared. Innocent offered the indulgences of the crusades to all who would follow the French king against infidels who had embedded themselves in the heart of the Christian west. Copies of the pope's appeal were sent to some of the prospective crusaders: the count of Flanders, the counts of Bar, Dreux, and Nevers, and the duke of Burgundy; instructions were given that its contents should be made public in the Cathar towns of the south.

News of the pope's pronouncement quickly reached Raymond VI. The proclamation of a crusade was entirely unexpected, and the count immediately moved to forestall any threat from the north. The papal letter arrived at the French court at Paris in mid-December, and Philip instructed the bishop of Paris to draft a reply. In the south, Raymond hastily attempted a negotiated surrender. At the end of December he sent word to Peter of Castelnau that he was ready to satisfy all his demands if the excommunication were lifted, and invited the legates to a meeting at St.-Gilles in January. Two legates, Peter himself and the bishop of Couserans, arrived at St.-Gilles in the second week in January. On the 13th they were received by a moody, resentful count. Raymond knew nothing of the deliberations in Paris, and he was determined to satisfy the legates while retaining as much freedom of manœuvre as his vulnerable situation allowed. He alternated between moods of humble submissiveness and angry defiance. By the end of the afternoon the legates had still not extracted any concessions of substance and Peter announced that they proposed to leave. The count insisted that they stay, angrily threatening that 'there was no place on land or water where he would not be watching for them.' An ill-timed intervention by the abbot of St.-Gilles and leading citizens of the town failed to calm Raymond's temper, and as darkness fell the legates left the town with a body-guard of the abbey's retainers, riding eastward along the marshy bank of the Petit Rhône.

In Rome, papal officials were studying the French king's reply. This was far from encouraging. Philip did not refuse to invade the county of Toulouse, but he imposed severe conditions. King John had succeeded in raising a rebellion against him in Poitou, and his allies had shut themselves in the stronghold of Thouars. Philip could not conduct two wars at the same time. But if the pope would arrange a truce with John and his allies, and ensure that the French clergy and baronage would contribute to the cost, the king would consider a campaign in the south. Should John break the truce, Philip reserved the right to recall his army immediately. Philip knew that Innocent was in no position to meet these conditions. The English king was under threat of interdict, a threat which was actually fulfilled only two months later. The pope's influence over John was negligible. Nor were the French nobility likely to be more accommodating than their sovereign. The resolution of Innocent's quandary was still far from clear when a wholly unforeseen event transformed the situation. On 14th January Peter of Castelnau was assassinated by an officer of the count of Toulouse.

# ✠ V ✠

## 1208–1209: The launching of the crusade

'Lo, I will bring forth a nation upon you from far . . . ; it is
a mighty nation; it is an ancient nation; it is a nation whose
language thou knowest not.'

JEREMIAH V.15

In February 1208 the news of the murder reached Rome. The pope,
according to the Navarrese ambassador, sunk his head into his hands and
retired to pray at the shrine of St. Peter below the high altar of the
Vatican basilica. The abbot of Cîteaux and the bishops of Toulouse
and Couserans arrived a few days afterwards with a full report of the
circumstances of the legate's death. They left Innocent in no doubt
that Raymond was responsible. The pope was probably told of malicious
rumours that Raymond had publicly honoured the assassin as 'the only
man loyal enough to rid me of my enemy'. These stories were certainly
untrue, but it is by no means certain that the count was innocent; the
identity of the murderer was well known, and to many of his contemporaries Raymond had lost the benefit of the doubt by his failure to
punish him. Memories of the death of Thomas Becket must have
sprung to many minds. Later, Innocent admitted that the evidence
amounted to no more than a 'strong suspicion', but at the time the
dignity of his office required an immediate reaction. With the abbot of
Cîteaux and twelve cardinals forming a circle round him, Innocent
renewed the excommunication of the count of Toulouse, extinguishing
a lighted taper as the tradition of the occasion required. On 10th March
he addressed a new letter to the knights and barons of France inviting
them to lay hands on the count and appropriate his property. 'Forward,
soldiers of Christ! Forward, volunteers of the army of God! Go forth
with the church's cry of anguish ringing in your ears. Fill your souls
with godly rage to avenge the insult done to the Lord.' For executing
God's vengence they would have a plenary indulgence equal to the
indulgence of the crusaders in the Holy Land.[3]

With the news of Peter of Castelnau's death still fresh, Arnald-

Amaury had no difficulty in recruiting Odo III duke of Burgundy, and Hervé de Donzy count of Nevers, both of them among the most prominent noblemen in France. The former was a recruit of considerable importance. His duchy was one of the richest fiefs of the crown and his retinue of knights was the largest in the royal army after the king's. The crusading tradition was strong in his family, for his ancestors had been among the leaders of the Spanish crusades of the eleventh and twelfth centuries. The motives of Hervé de Donzy are less clear, but a fondness for fighting was certainly among them. Ten years earlier he had been an unimportant baron of the Nivernais. In August 1199 he had defeated and captured the count of Nevers in battle, and had forced his prisoner to cede to him both his county and his daughter. Hervé accounted for only eleven knights in the books of the royal army, but he could probably produce three or four times that number for his own purposes. Between them, they told Arnald-Amaury, they could muster five hundred knights, already the nucleus of a substantial army. But since those knights were owed first and foremost to the French king they made their support conditional on his approval.

Philip Augustus' co-operation was important for another reason since, as Raymond's feudal suzerain, it was for him to retake possession of the county of Toulouse. Innocent had written an ingratiating letter to him in March congratulating him on the achievements of his reign and indicating that there was no better use to be made of his God-given strength than to fight the church's battle in the Midi. When this epistle reached France, Philip Augustus was still engrossed in the affairs of Poitou. He was with his army, marching against king John's allies at Thouars, and he was feeling ill. Instead of the hoped-for promise of help, Innocent received a gratuitous law lecture. The count of Toulouse, Philip replied, was no friend of his, but it was not for the pope to invite Frenchmen to help themselves to the count's dominions. If Innocent notified him in proper form that the count had been convicted of heresy, which he had not done yet, then he would confiscate the fief in due course. Philip was not impressed by the pope's instructions to various French prelates to negotiate a truce between him and his enemies. Nor was he pleased to see his military strength reduced, even temporarily, by the recruitment of a crusading army among his vassals.

In May, as he was recovering from campaign sickness, Philip was visited at Chinon by the sub-cellarer of Cîteaux who asked him, on behalf of the duke of Burgundy and the count of Nevers, for permission to take the cross. This the king reluctantly granted, with the proviso that no other barons would be permitted to follow their example. Had this proviso been enforced the crusade would have been still-born. But later in the month Philip's armies were victorious in Poitou, and his attitude softened. Moreover, it was becoming apparent that the indignation aroused by the death of Peter of Castelnau was too strong to be contained by Philip's passionless political calculations. The proviso was cancelled and forgotten.

Having won over the few leading noblemen whose support was essential, Arnald-Amaury waited until 14th September before formally proclaiming the crusade at the general chapter of the Cistercian order. The Albigensian crusade did not have the powerful emotional appeal of the Middle Eastern crusades, nor was Arnald-Amaury a St. Bernard or an Urban II. But it was preached with vigour by the Cistercians throughout the winter of 1208-9, and the response among the French nobility was most encouraging. Contemporaries were not as shocked by the idea of a crusade in a Christian land as were anti-clerical historians of the nineteenth century. In a society founded on community of religion, were heretics not foreigners? Were they not, as Innocent insisted in his letter to the French king, even worse than Saracens because closer to the heart of Christianity? The promise of a plenary indulgence for destroying such vermin was too good an offer to be spurned. 'I promise categorically,' a preacher of the fourth crusade had declared at Basle only four years earlier, 'that every one of you who takes the cross and makes his confession will be entirely cleansed of all his sins.' This promise was now repeated throughout Burgundy and northern France. Those who heard it knew nothing of the theological scruples which distinguished between the remission of guilt and the remission of penance. They wished to be numbered among the 'shrewd businessmen' to whom St. Bernard had appealed at the time of the second crusade in 1146. The cross, he had said, was a bargain not to be missed: 'It will cost you little, but if you wear it with humility, it will be worth the kingdom of heaven.' Many accepted, from the thief of Lille, whom the countess of Champagne would have preferred to see in prison, to the count of Auvergne who was made to join the crusading army as a penance for laying hands on a bishop.

To the nobility there were temporal as well as spiritual reasons for joining the crusade. Their possessions, at least in theory, were protected in their absence by a vigilant church. The interest on their debts was remitted by the pope's orders and there was a moratorium on repayments of capital. This concession alone must have been irresistibly appealing to the knightly families of Burgundy eking out a living on their reduced and fragmented estates, in conditions very similar to those of the Cathar nobles themselves. There was also the prospect of the rich fiefs to be distributed when the crusade had been brought to a successful conclusion. Innocent III's decretal *Vergentiis in senium* of 1199 had permitted the confiscation of the lands of heretics, and the pope's crusading bulls unequivocally offered these lands to those who could take them. Philip Augustus, it is true, had strong reservations on this point. But these were not generally known. Nor would it have made a great deal of difference if they had been, for if Hervé de Donzy, without a shadow of right, could conquer the county of Nevers in battle as recently as 1199, then a shrewd fortune-hunter with the full support of the church could conquer the county of Toulouse from its unworthy holder.

Innocent would have liked Philip Augustus to pay the considerable expenses of the crusade. But the French king was as unhelpful on this point as on every other, and Innocent was therefore obliged to act as his own treasurer. The French clergy were invited to mortgage their incomes for two years. Bishops and nobles were asked to contribute one-tenth of their revenues towards the cost of the enterprise. In addition, noblemen who had taken the cross were expected to arm and supply themselves and their contingents, a considerable expense which even the duke of Burgundy could only meet by mortgaging his revenues to monastic houses.

Raymond VI found himself weak and friendless in the face of the gathering storm. In the autumn of 1208 he travelled north to see Philip Augustus. But although the king had shown no enthusiasm for the crusade, he had not forgotten that Raymond had married the sister of the English king at a time when England and France were at war, nor that Toulousain soldiers had been found among the garrison of Falaise when it surrendered to the royal army in 1204. Whatever affection the French king had shown for his troubled cousin certainly disappeared when the count proceeded next to the court of his enemy, Otto IV of Germany. Otto was Raymond's suzerain for his Provençal dominions. But the purpose of this visit is unclear, and it is difficult to see what benefit from the weak and distant emperor could have been worth the implacable hostility of Philip Augustus. Otto was in the process of negotiating an alliance with king John. Raymond almost certainly knew this, and he may have hoped that a military diversion in the north would draw off the crusaders who were already preparing to invade Languedoc. But Otto, who was at the nadir of his fortunes in Germany, was in no position to offer the count more than sympathy and advice. It was no doubt on his way back from this fruitless journey that Raymond visited Arnald-Amaury at Aubenas in the final hope of averting the threatened invasion. It was the first time that they had met since the murder of Peter of Castelnau. Raymond knelt at the abbot's feet with every sign of humility and contrition, and begged for forgiveness. But Arnald-Amaury refused to forgive him now that preparations for the crusade were so far advanced; the pope had excommunicated him and the pope alone could lift the excommunication.[4]

Raymond returned home shortly after Christmas to an atmosphere soured by the papal interdict. The Cistercians had been preaching the crusade in Provence and in the northern part of his own dominions. At St.-Gilles the monks exhumed the body of Peter of Castelnau on the anniversary of his death to find it still incorrupt. The sarcophagus, now moved to the crypt of the abbey church, gave off the 'odour of sanctity' which indicated a life pleasing to God, although in fact it was frequently the result of the anointment of bodies with Arabian myrrh and other gum resins.[5] The initiation of a martyr's cult was the unpropitious background to Raymond's frenzied attempt to find allies in his own principality. The citizens of Nîmes were publicly forgiven for having supported his enemies and sacked his palace in the previous year. He confirmed the privileges of the tiny county of Melgueil where, since it was held as a papal fief, he was particularly vulnerable. In mid-January he visited his nephew, Raymond-Roger Trencavel viscount of Béziers, and suggested an alliance or at least a truce in the face of the common peril. But old hatreds were too strong for the viscount, who did not appreciate that he was as much threatened by the crusade as his overlord. He refused to co-operate and Raymond withdrew in a high temper to the Rhône valley.

In Rome, Innocent had issued yet another summons to the baronage of France and had begun to make detailed plans for the conduct of the crusade. 'Use cunning and deception as weapons, for in the circumstances deceit is no more than prudence,' Innocent advised his legates. They should not start by attacking the count of Toulouse, but should first attack the heretics themselves. The count would not wish to risk his principality by helping them, and when his allies had been picked off then the legates would be able to deal with him at leisure. 'Such is my advice,' the pope concluded; 'but since you will be on the spot, use your own judgement as the circumstances of the moment and the inspiration of the Lord seem to suggest.'

Raymond cannot have known of this letter, but he had already realized that his only hope lay in complete surrender. This was itself no easy matter. It involved circumventing the intransigent abbot of Cîteaux by appealing over his head to Innocent III. An embassy was therefore despatched to Rome at the end of January with instructions to agree to any terms, however humiliating, if the pope would only send him a legate less unbending than Arnald-Amaury. Raymond promised to do all that the pope asked of him, even undertaking to make over to the church seven castles and the county of Melgueil as an earnest of his good behaviour. If further evidence were needed of Raymond's ineptness as a diplomat, it was provided by his choice of ambassadors. They included Raymond de Rabastens, the former bishop of Toulouse, and Bernard de Montaut, archbishop of Auch; both had a reputation for eloquence, but the former had been deposed by the legates in 1205 for bribing his electors, and the latter was to be invited to resign in 1211 on account of his lack of evangelical zeal. Nevertheless, these unpromising emissaries did succeed in securing the appointment of two special legates to receive the count's unconditional surrender. The new legates, the apostolic notary Milo and a Genoese canon called Thedisius, were both Italians entirely without experience of Languedoc's affairs. For a while Raymond's delight knew no bounds. He would have been less pleased had he read Milo's secret instructions. For Innocent was no more inclined than Arnald-Amaury to abandon his crusade now that the preparations were almost completed. Without the constant threat of war there was no guarantee that Raymond would be either able or willing to keep his promises. Accordingly Milo was to be no more than a voice-pipe for Arnald-Amaury. 'The abbot will make the decisions,' Innocent told him; 'you will be his instrument, for the count suspects him, but not you.' Arnald-Amaury met the new legates at Auxerre, and gave them their instructions. There was to be no question of abandoning the crusade against Raymond's subjects, even if the count himself chose to submit. Moreover, Arnald-Amaury strongly suspected Raymond's sincerity and enjoined the two Italians to treat the count with the greatest possible circumspection.

Preparations for the holy war proceeded throughout the spring and early summer of 1209. Innocent's problem was still the lack of an effective commander. In the forefront of his mind was the dreadful experience of the fourth crusade which in spite of his efforts had degenerated into a war against the Christians of Dalmatia and Constantinople. It had had too many leaders. Many of them had supplied their own contingent and their vanities and conflicting ambitions could not be ignored. Innocent had the experience of the twelfth century to teach him that the most effective crusading armies were national armies under national leaders. In February he had written to the French king suggesting the appointment of the dauphin Louis, but had received no reply. The ambassadors of the emperor Otto were at the English court when the letter arrived. If Philip knew, as he almost certainly did, of the warmth with which John had received their suggestion of an anti-French alliance, he cannot have listened very sympathetically to the pope's request. On 1st May 1209 Arnald-Amaury and Milo attended a royal council at Villeneuve-sur-Yonne to receive the king's reply. Philip told them that he had 'two fierce lions at his flanks', the emperor Otto and the king of England. He could neither leave northern France himself nor spare the services of his son. But he did agree to send a contingent of knights which, if it was not fifteen thousand strong as his biographer asserted, was at least large enough to make an impression among the army of God. The crusaders' muster was fixed for 24th June at Lyon. Later in the month, when the dauphin was knighted by his father at Compiègne, crusaders' crosses were seen on many tunics in the crowd of attendants.

While Philip was arming his son at Compiègne, Milo was consulting the southern bishops gathered at Montélimar. Their advice, submitted in writing under seal, was unanimous. The bishops thought that the church should take possession of the seven castles and the county of Melgueil, which Raymond had already offered to surrender as security, and that the consuls of Avignon, Nîmes, and St.-Gilles should be made to swear that in the event of the count breaking his promises they would renounce their allegiance to him. On those conditions, Raymond might be re-admitted to the church. The terms were put to Raymond at Valence and he reluctantly accepted them. The final act of the tragedy of Peter of Castelnau was played a month later at St.-Gilles. On 18th June a consecrated host and a small collection of relics were laid out on a table in front of the central door of the great west front of the abbey,

perhaps already adorned with its fine sculptures of the life and resurrection of Christ. The count, stripped to the waist, was led up the
steps, where three archbishops and nineteen bishops were assembled.
He swore to obey the instructions of the church and its legates in all
matters and in particular to redress a long list of accumulated grievances: his favour to Jews and heretics, his use of mercenaries, his
violation of the Peace of God, his fortification of churches, his setting
up of toll-gates, his assaults on the bishops of Vaison and Carpentras,
and above all his protection of the murderer of Peter of Castelnau. A
significant reserve spared him the humiliation of admitting that he had
actually ordered the murder. He merely avowed that he was 'suspected'
of having done so. Milo then passed his stole round the count's neck
and pulled him into the church flogging him all the way with a switch.
Absolution was finally pronounced from the altar. When the ceremony
was over Raymond was unable to leave by the west door which was
blocked by a crowd of pilgrims, dignatories, and idle spectators. Instead he was hurriedly taken out through the crypt and made to run
half-naked past the sarcophagus of the murdered legate.

Raymond remained for the next four days at St.-Gilles to complete
the humiliating process of surrendering the control of his dominions to
the papal legates. His officials were instructed to implement the
promises of the 18th. The garrisons of the seven castles were told to
hold them at the legates' command. Promises of co-operation were extracted from the principal towns and barons of the Rhône valley.
Then, on 22nd June, Raymond took the cross himself, promising on
the Gospels to help and advise the army of God and to do all that its
commanders asked of him. This last act was possibly Raymond's
shrewdest political stroke, certainly the only one which bears out Peter
of Vaux-de-Cernay's description of him as the 'cunning subtle serpent'.
Raymond knew that it was too late to halt the crusade. The muster was
due to be held in less than a week. But by taking the cross he would
earn the immunity of a crusader; his titles and dominions would be
protected except perhaps for those that were in the hands of the Cathars.
He would become a leader of the crusade which would thereby be
transformed into a war against Raymond's greatest enemy, Raymond-
Roger Trencavel, viscount of Béziers. When the crusaders had destroyed the Trencavels, their resources and perhaps their enthusiasm
would be exhausted and Raymond would be left in effective control of
his principality for the first time since his accession. So things might

well have come to pass had Raymond been as skilful in the execution
as in the conception of his plan.

In the western part of the county of Toulouse, the crusade had
already begun. A smaller army, drawn from Quercy, Auvergne, and the
Atlantic provinces had met at Agen in May under the command of the
count of Auvergne and the archbishop of Bordeaux. The expedition
began with the advantage of surprise but came to very little. It captured
the bastide of Puylaroque without difficulty and sacked the surrounding
villages, sending many heretics to the stake. Panic gripped the Cathars
of the province. More than sixty miles away, the inhabitants of Villemur
burned their town and fled. But the invading army seems to have consisted principally of feudal levies, who were not obliged to give their
lords more than forty days of free service. It could not undertake
protracted sieges. At Casseneuil, a strong fortified place on the Lot, the
crusaders encountered determined resistance from a force of Gascon
crossbowmen brought into the town by Seguin de Balenx. The crossbow, though short-ranged and cumbersome to reload, was so effective
when fired from higher ground that the church in 1139 had forbidden
its use between Christians. As the crusaders encamped out of range
of the walls they were harassed by sorties of *dardasiers*, unmounted
soldiers who threw a thin, shortened spear that penetrated chain mail
at considerable distances. The Gascons, whose skill in the use of these
unorthodox weapons was celebrated in the epic of *Girart de Roussillon*, had made a national sport of the *dard*.[6] The count of Auvergne,
who had never been a particularly enthusiastic crusader, insisted on
making terms with the garrison and moving elsewhere. The archbishop
accused him of betraying the expedition, and the first crusading venture
petered out in a welter of recriminations. A similar fate overtook another small expedition, mounted by the bishop of Le Puy, which, after
extracting protection money from a number of towns of the Rouergue
appears to have abandoned the effort altogether.

The main body of crusaders mustered at Lyon on 24th June. It was
the feast of the patron of Lyon, John the Baptist, and the city was filled
with crowds of hawkers, pilgrims and pickpockets, as well as with the
knights of Burgundy and northern France. The latter, conspicuous by
the silk crosses worn on their chests, were the mounted élite of what the
legates proudly called 'the greatest Christian army ever mustered'. 'The
army of Milan' was the only comparison which leapt to William of
Tudela's mind—a significant tribute to the Italian city, whose size and

wealth, magnified no doubt by distance, had captured the imagination of the twelfth century. Arnald-Amaury's exaggeration can perhaps be forgiven, and the statistics offered by his contemporaries have to be accepted for the misleading round figures that they are. Estimates of the army's size ranged from 40,000 to 220,000, but a figure of 20,000 would probably be closer to the mark. Of these many, perhaps half, were clerics, craftsmen, wives, camp-followers, and other non-combatant hangers-on.

Mediaeval armies were small. At the crisis of his reign, Philip Augustus could muster no more than 800 mounted knights in an army whose total fighting strength was perhaps 9,000. Since the role assigned to infantry by the tacticians of the thirteenth century was largely defensive, major battles were in effect decided by absurdly small forces of heavily armed men. Major battles, however, had become the exception rather than the rule. They continued to dominate the heroic literature of the knightly class, but the continual refinement of the art of fortification had transformed twelfth-century warfare into a succession of unglamorous sieges. The anarchy in which Catharism had prospered in Languedoc owed a great deal to the advantage which the castle had given to defensive over aggressive warfare. If nine men in 1138 could hold at bay the entire army of David of Scotland, then a Trencavel could defy the house of Toulouse indefinitely. No part of the army of the crusade was more important than the siege train which was sent ahead by river to await the main force at Avignon. Its sappers, carpenters and military engineers were ridiculed in the satires and *chansons de geste*, but they kept mediaeval kingdoms in being and their value was reflected in the very high salaries which they were paid.

Arnald-Amaury's army had many weaknesses. Its obvious leader, Philip Augustus, had refused to join it or even appoint a representative. This left Arnald-Amaury himself as its only effective leader, for among the military chiefs there were too many rivalries and personal animosities, the seeds of future discord as Arnald-Amaury was sensitive enough to realize. Hervé de Donzy was a quarrelsome, ambitious man with many enemies. There were ambitious fortune-hunters like Peter d'Anduze and Simon de Montfort. Several were friend sand relatives of Raymond VI, who suffered from conflicting loyalties when Raymond himself became the victim of the crusade. Peter and Robert de Courtenay were his cousins; Adhémar de Poitiers was his vassal. There were also problems of recruitment and finance to which the legates had not perhaps paid as much attention as they might have done. Volunteers could not be made to fight indefinitely. Forty days was the length of service suggested by feudal practice, but it is far from clear that this was the period that Innocent had in mind. Officially, no term had been set to the crusade and no city presented itself as the great target whose capture would mark its triumphant conclusion. The crusaders, says William of Tudela, had originally thought of Toulouse as their destination, but the submission of the count of Toulouse had left them with the vaguer objective of capturing 'the Albigeois'. A man more experienced in military affairs than Arnald-Amaury would have foreseen that the enthusiasm of the holy war would be dissipated in a long war of sieges, and the army would be left with only the pious, the ambitious, and the well paid. But these doubts were far from his mind as he led his host down the Agrippan Way which followed the left bank of the Rhône from Lyon south to Tarascon.

# ✠ VI ✠

## 1209: Béziers and Carcassonne

'I will bring evil from the north and a great destruction; the lion is come up from his thicket and the destroyer of the Gentiles is on his way.'

JEREMIAH IV.6–7

The army left Lyon at the beginning of July with the abbot of Cîteaux, the archbishop of Sens, the bishops of Autun, Clermont, and Nevers, and the duke of Burgundy marching, pennants flying, at its head. As it approached, the nobility of the south hastened to make its peace with the church. William Porcelet, the bitterly anti-clerical Provençal nobleman who had sheltered Peter of Castelnau's murderer in his household, submitted at the end of June. The legate Milo personally supervised the demolition of two churches at Arles which William had converted into fortresses to dominate the passage of the Rhône. Twelve castles standing in the crusaders' path were surrendered to the legate by their owners, including the great stone fortresses of Rochemaure and Roussillon.

Raymond VI himself met the crusaders at Valence. He was well aware of his vulnerable situation. He had promised to dismiss his Spanish and Brabancon mercenaries, which left him without an army; and his strongest castles had been surrendered to the church. Unless his unaccustomed role as a crusader could be made to seem convincing, his lands would shortly be defenceless against a powerful and enthusiastic northern army. Plainly his survival depended on turning the crusade against his nephew, Raymond-Roger Trencavel, viscount of Béziers, a fate which the viscount had no doubt brought upon himself by his refusal to consider an alliance earlier in the year. Raymond had come ready to make further concessions. He promised to abide by the decisions of the commanders of the crusade, and to find them supplies and suitable encampments in his dominions. He was willing to surrender more strongholds, and even offered them his twelve-year-old son as a hostage. Guided by the count, the army crossed the great eighteen-arch bridge which St. Bénézet had recently built over the Rhône at Avignon, and reached Montpellier about 15th July. There they were met by Raymond-Roger Trencavel.

Raymond-Roger was a young man of considerable charm, but of greater pride than ability. He had inherited his powerful fief at the age of nine, and was still only twenty-four when he saw it invaded by his uncle with a large northern host. Raymond-Roger was not himself a Cathar. But his vassals had joined the sect in large numbers, and had taken advantage of the long period of his minority to emancipate themselves from his control, transforming their castles and hill-towns into the capitals of petty Pyrenean kingdoms. In Béziers and Carcassonne, the viscount held two of the strongest cities of the south; but elsewhere his authority was of no account. Raymond-Roger's inaction in the face of the preparations for the crusade can only be explained by his conviction that his uncle alone was threatened. At first, when he heard of Raymond's submission at St.-Gilles, he refused to believe it. But as his weakness and isolation became apparent, and as his allies deserted him for their mountain castles, Raymond-Roger swallowed his pride and went to meet Arnald-Amaury at Montpellier. He pleaded that he had done nothing to favour the heretics; that he could not control his heretical vassals. He begged forgiveness for his anti-clerical excesses and professed himself willing to submit to the church on the same terms as Raymond VI. The legate dismissed him from his presence.[7] Raymond-Roger turned back and summoned his vassals to meet him at Carcassonne. He had left himself very little time. To assemble an army and prepare his strongholds would take at least a week, and Béziers was only two days' march from Montpellier. Since Béziers dominated the bridge which carried the Roman road over the river Orb, his best hope was that the citizens would delay the crusaders for long enough to enable him to gather his strength at Carcassonne. With only a few hours' start on the crusading army, Raymond-Roger rode through the night to arrive at Béziers before dawn on the following morning. A meeting of the citizens was summoned at which the viscount asked them to defend the city as best they could until he was able to send them help. He then rode west, taking with him the entire Jewish community of Béziers.

The Jewish communities of the southern cities were too valuable a source of taxes and administrators to be left to the mercy of the crusaders. Raymond-Roger, in common with most seigneurs of the province, protected them jealously. His representative in Béziers had at one point been a Jew called Samuel. Other Jews owned houses, toll-gates, salt-pans, extensive estates. Celebrated schools of Talmudic law existed at Narbonne, Lunel, and Beaucaire, where the itinerant rabbi Benjamin of Tudela had found Jewish students from 'distant lands' in 1160. Rich, secure, living in constant contact with a larger world than their Christian protectors, these communities had contributed much to a flourishing renaissance of Jewish letters. The growing power of mysticism, as marked in the Jewish world then as it was in the Christian and the Islamic, was born in Languedoc with the *Bahir* and the Kabbalistic writings of Abraham ben Isaac 'the Blind'. These men were respected by many southern rulers, even some clerical ones, in a manner unthinkable in the north. Isaac's father, a celebrated Talmudic scholar, had been rescued by Roger II Trencavel from a seigneurial prison at Posquières and installed at his court at Carcassonne. Side by side with the conquering asceticism of the Cathars, another mysticism had taken root among the Jews which had much in common with it. Benjamin of Tudela had met a Jew at Lunel who 'discarded all worldly business, studied day and night, kept fasts, and never ate meat'. This world, the Albigensian crusade was to banish to that diminishing part of Spain where fluid religious loyalties enabled three faiths to thrive together. The word crusade had sombre associations for Jews. The massacres perpetrated in the Rhineland by the soldiers of the first crusade were still fresh memories, and the crusade against the Spanish Moors which passed through southern France in 1065 had slaughtered all the Jews in its path. The Jews of Béziers were glad to leave the city with the viscount. They fared better than their Christian neighbours.[8]

On 21st July the crusaders crossed the river Hérault which marked the eastern boundary of Raymond-Roger's lands. The summer of 1209 was unusually hot, and eastern Languedoc was in any case more humid then than it is now. The canals which had drained it in Roman times had not been maintained after the sixth century. Stagnant land-locked pools had formed in the basins of the Orb and the Aude, and in the long ribbon of land on the seaward side of Béziers and Narbonne. The salt-pans which covered the entire coast of the Golfe du Lion were too profitable for the owners to consider reclamation. Inland, the flat southern plain, through which the Roman road ran, offered the cru-saders a landscape in some ways strikingly different from that which they had known in the north. The constricting mantle of forest was less

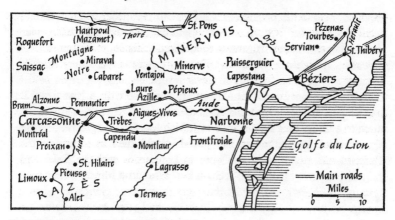

II.   Carcassonne–Minervois–Narbonnais

noticeable. An agriculture which allowed half the fields to lie fallow instead of a third left extensive tracts of yellowing scrub to join the acres of land which were too poor for any cultivation at all, moorland, hard stony ground impenetrable to wooden ploughs. Only fruit trees— olives and almonds—lent themselves well to such land. In the cultivated fields which, in spite of the fragmentation of holdings, still bore the imprint of immense Roman *villae*, the staple cereal was barley, not the ubiquitous rye which brought the terrors of ergotism to northern peasants. At the edges of the plain was the evidence of another war. The struggle of vines against cereals, still scarcely a century old, had left vines in possession of the roadsides and of the belt of smallholders' plots round tiny hill-towns of crumbling re-used stone and pink Roman tiles on flat roofs. With the vines came the chequerboard pattern of stone walls which kept out free-running goats and sheep, and very slowly altered the ancient landscape. In the time of Pliny, Béziers had produced the finest wine in France. Only recently had the rich commerce of Italy and the Levant allowed such towns once more the luxury of keeping vines and buying their cereals elsewhere. Montpellier, so its citizens told Gregory X, was self-sufficient in nothing but wine; but thanks to its excellent communications and the 'profit-lust of its merchants', the citizens never went without and the fathers of the council which Gregory was thinking of holding there would be well fed.[9]

Servian, where St. Dominic and his companions had spent a fruitless week arguing with prominent Cathars in 1206, surrendered without resistance on 21st July. At Béziers, eight miles away, the citizens were digging trenches beneath the city walls and taking in supplies. The crusaders anticipated a prolonged siege. On 22nd July they sent the bishop, an old man who had accompanied them from Montpellier, to ride ahead on a mule and negotiate with the citizens. At a public meeting in the cathedral the bishop emphasized the strength of the crusading army and the imminence of its approach, and advised them to surrender. He had brought with him a list of more than two hundred known heretics. If the catholics were prepared to deliver these people into the legates' hands, or alternatively to walk through the gates leaving the heretics alone in the city, their lives and their property would be respected. Otherwise they would be at the mercy of the crusaders. These terms were not acceptable to the majority of the citizens. Their city, built on a strongly fortified escarpment overlooking the river Orb, was well stocked with food. They believed that it could hold out for at least a month. By that time, they reasoned, the unwieldy mass of crusaders and camp-followers would have exhausted all the supplies that could be had in the area. Moreover, reinforcement was expected imminently from Carcassonne. While these deliberations continued, Arnald-Amaury's army was already taking up positions on the south-eastern side of the city, beneath the rock terrace on which the cathedral itself stood. The bishop, seeing that his pleas carried no weight, left hurriedly, taking with him the handful of citizens whose nerves were not equal to the ordeal.

He had scarcely passed through the gates when hostilities began. A sortie of citizens rode out with white pennants, uttering blood-curdling yells, and releasing a shower of arrows on the crusaders. A crusader who had ventured onto the bridge below the walls was cut down. The sight of this greatly enraged the camp-followers, who were setting up their masters' tents a few hundred yards away. Seizing clubs and tent-poles they furiously rushed the city, and attempted to dig into the base of the powerful walls. Others threw themselves against the gates and began to smash the wooden beams. The citizens had not expected an assault so soon. The walls were not properly manned. While the bells of the city began to ring out the alarm, panic-stricken defenders were already abandoning their posts and fleeing to the sanctuary of the churches. The crusaders had watched with astonishment as their ragged orderlies stormed the city. They armed and mounted themselves and arrived on the scene as the gates were giving way before the pressure of the uncontrolled horde outside. Within two or three hours the crusaders were masters of Béziers.

The camp-followers were intoxicated with success, inflamed by fanaticism and greed. They had learned from the preachers of the crusade that the southerners were instruments of Satan, protectors of Jews, immeasurably rich. Once they had penetrated into the streets, they rushed howling through the streets, killing all who had not had time to hide. Appalling scenes of destruction and violence followed. The heavily armed knights, not to be outdone in the pursuit of plunder, charged through the gates and invaded the houses, barging aside the camp-followers with cudgels and seizing valuables from their grasp. The camp-followers, frustrated in their hopes of a rich booty, spread through the city filled with a lust for the destruction of what they could not take for themselves. They invaded the churches and slaughtered the terrified citizens who had gathered there for safety. Priests, women, and children were cut down indiscriminately, as they clung to reliquaries and crucifixes. Of the crowds which had packed the cathedral and the church of the Madeleine, there was not one survivor. As they passed through the city, the camp-followers lit brands and set fire to all the finer houses which they came upon. The flames spread rapidly through the wooden buildings. In the south-eastern corner of the walls, the timbers of the cathedral caught fire and the high vault collapsed to entomb the bodies of the massacred citizens inside. The work of pillage ended only towards the evening when the heat of the blazing city became intolerable and the crusaders were forced to withdraw to the meadows by the river.

Although it had been unplanned, the sack of Béziers was not unwelcomed by the clerical leaders of the crusade. Providence had dealt those 'disgusting dogs' their just punishment, reflected Peter of Vaux-de-Cernay. A German monk repeated a story that Arnald-Amaury, when asked in the middle of the slaughter how the catholics could be distinguished from the heretics, replied 'Kill them all; God will recognize his own'; and this motto has passed into history as the epitome of the spirit which had brought the crusaders to the south. Whether Arnald-Amaury was consulted, or ever uttered any such sentiment, remains unclear. But it is not important. The legate reported the massacre without comment to Innocent III, remarking only that 'neither age, nor sex, nor status had been spared'. Neither he nor his clerical colleagues had any sympathy even for the catholic victims. They had, after all, been offered peace if they would surrender their heretical neighbours, and they had rejected it. The military leaders, it is true, regretted the fire, for much of their booty was destroyed in it. But they reflected that the news of the massacre would discourage resistance in the other cities of Languedoc. After the city had fallen, they met in council and resolved that in every city that resisted them the entire population would be put to the sword.

The first fruits of this decision almost immediately manifested themselves. A few days later, as the crusaders were resting from their exertions, a deputation arrived from Narbonne with an offer of complete submission. The citizens were conscious that only a day's march separated them from the smoking ruins of Béziers. They undertook to deliver all known heretics to the legate immediately, together with all the property owned by heretics or Jews. In addition they promised to supply food to the army and to pay a tax of a sixtieth on their possessions towards the expenses of the crusade. On these terms, the leaders of the army offered them their protection. Further evidence of the chastening effect of the sack of Béziers confronted the crusaders on their march up the valley of the Aude to Carcassonne. They passed through a succession of ghost towns. They found villages and towns empty and silent, but with bursting granaries and fruit-stores from which they were able to help themselves freely. Some were strong-walled villages, like Nissan south of Béziers, which might have delayed the crusaders for several weeks. Their garrisons and inhabitants had fled to the forests. Others, further west, had taken their chickens and donkeys and joined the growing crowd of hungry, penniless refugees at Carcassonne.

The advance guard of the army arrived outside Carcassonne on the evening of 28th July, as the bells of the city were ringing for vespers. Carcassonne was incomparably the strongest city in Raymond-Roger's possession. It was built on a steep escarpment some six hundred yards from the marshes of the river Aude. Its walls, originally the work of the Vizigothic kings of the fifth century, corresponded roughly to the inner circuit of the present fortifications. The ambitious and aggressive viscounts had kept them in good repair. Twenty-six towers pierced them in 1209, and the fortified palace of the Trencavels powerfully reinforced them on the western side. Carcassonne had expanded with prosperity and had acquired suburbs. Two of these, the *bourg* to the north and the *castellare* to the south were surrounded by walls and ditches of their own. A third, the suburb of St.-Vincent, which included the Jewish quarter, lay unprotected between the city and the

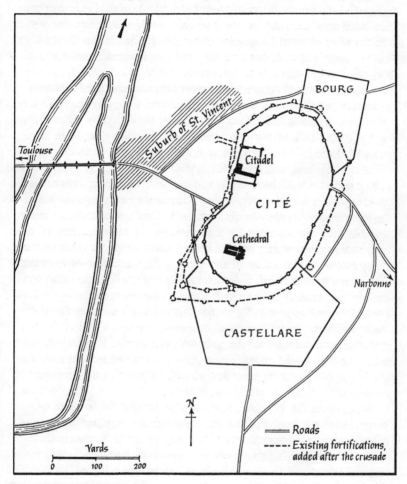

III.  Carcassonne in 1209

river. Carcassonne had one serious weakness. It was too far from the river, so that the garrison were unable to command the narrow wooden bridge and, once invested by a besieging army, were dependent for their water supply on deep wells, sunk within the walls.

Raymond-Roger cannot have anticipated that the crusaders would be upon him so quickly. But he had made good use of his ten days' respite. The wooden galleries which surmounted the battlements in wartime, and enabled the garrison to protect the bases of the walls from sappers, had been assembled by carpenters at astonishing speed. The refectory of the cathedral canons had been demolished for its stone, and even the canons' stalls had been sawn up for use in repairing the fortifications. Raymond-Roger hoped, like the citizens of Béziers before him, that the crusading army would prove too large for the resources of the surrounding countryside, and would run out of food before the garrison. Outside the city everything edible was collected or burned. The water-mills of the Aude, still of the old-fashioned kind which floated in mid-stream held to both banks by hawsers,[10] had been efficiently destroyed to prevent the besiegers from milling their grain.

The main body of the army arrived on 1st August, four days behind its advance guard, and at once began to invest the city. An inspection of the ground soon revealed its weak points. The walls of the suburbs were low and sparsely defended by towers; once the besiegers had penetrated them, they would be able to approach within bowshot of the city walls, under the cover of the houses. On the following morning they began to occupy the unfortified suburb of St.-Vincent. This had the effect of cutting off the city's access to the river, and was bitterly resisted by the garrison. Raymond-Roger led a sortie out from the castle gate and a sanguinary battle followed beneath the walls, culminating in the withdrawal of the garrison. The fortified suburb to the north, known as the *bourg*, was taken by storm on 3rd August, its defenders fleeing as the northern clergy, gathered in the crusaders' camp, intoned the *Veni Sancte Spiritus*. This hymn, the 'golden sequence' ascribed to Innocent III, had been adopted by those great patrons of fine hymns, the Cistercians, and had won immediate popularity in northern France. It was to become the anthem of the crusade.[11]

After the capture of the bourg, its walls were razed to the ground, and the stone used to fill in the ditch around the northern sector of the city walls. Emboldened by their success, the besiegers resolved to assault the far stronger *castellare* suburb on the southern side of the city. On 4th August they rushed it with scaling ladders. The garrison, however, defended the walls with a courage which even the ungracious Peter of Vaux-de-Cernay was forced to recognize. The crusaders succeeded briefly in occupying the ditch below the walls, but were repelled by a shower of arrows and stones, and retired with heavy casualties. Three days later a further attempt was made with siege engines, which bombarded the walls of the *castellare* throughout the morning of 7th August. A party of sappers approached beneath a specially constructed wheeled shelter and succeeded, before the shelter was finally destroyed by the deluge of blazing missiles, in mining the base of the wall. At dawn on the following morning the mine was fired and the wall subsided. The crusaders entered noisily through the breach, and advanced, street by street, until they were masters of the suburb. But in the exuberance of victory they failed to leave a large enough guard when they withdrew to their camp. In a bold sortie, the garrison succeeded in regaining possession of the *castellare* for long enough to burn it, thus denying the besiegers the shelter of the houses clustered beneath the walls of the city itself.

At this indecisive stage of the siege, Peter II of Aragon arrived in the crusaders' camp with an escort of a hundred knights. Peter's interest in the progress of the crusade is at first sight surprising. In 1204, the king had concluded a defensive alliance with Raymond VI whereby each undertook to assist the other against 'any man in the world', a class which clearly included Arnald-Amaury's crusade. But Raymond was not yet threatened by the crusade, and Peter was more interested in the fate of the Trencavels than in the adaptable count of Toulouse. Peter was descended from the Trencavels' traditional allies the counts of Barcelona, who had become kings of Aragon in the time of Peter's father. His dynastic ambitions were closely bound up with the fate of Carcassonne. A combination of accident and diplomatic skill had made it the pivot of the Mediterranean empire which his ancestors had been assembling for more than a century.

This empire had arisen on the ruins to which the southern laws of succession had reduced the county of Provence. In the course of the eleventh century all the male branches of the ancient comital family of Provence had died out. This had left the county to be held in undivided shares by the representatives of the three surviving female lines, and these representatives were the heads of the southern dynasties which at various stages had married into the comital family: the counts of Forcalquier, the counts of Toulouse, and the house of Barcelona-Aragon. All of them, in 1112, were jointly counts of Provence. Evidently some territorial partition was essential. But the exact form of that partition was the cause of sporadic wars between the three families throughout the twelfth century. In 1198 the treaty of Perpignan had restored the peace between the houses of Toulouse and Barcelona-Aragon. Shortly afterwards Raymond VI had married Peter II's sister. But these arrangements did no more than confirm the dominant position which the Catalan dynasty had acquired in the southern Rhône valley. Peter II's younger brother was a count of Provence, and he himself had become count of Montpellier by marriage in 1204. These complicated transactions made the Trencavel viscounties of Béziers and Carcassonne more important than they had ever been. They were the link between Catalonia and Provence. Whoever ruled them could sever the land and sea routes which were the lifeline of Peter's youthful empire. As a vassal of the church and a man of strong, if conventional piety, Peter had little sympathy for the Cathars or their allies. On the other hand he claimed, as his ancestors had claimed for a century and a half, to be the immediate feudal superior of the Trencavels. Twice, in 1067 and 1150, the Trencavels had renounced their homage to the house of Toulouse and transferred it to that of Barcelona-Aragon. The rights which these acts of homage conferred on the Catalan dynasty were somewhat shadowy, and their legality was open to question. But Raymond-Roger Trencavel certainly recognized them as valid; and Peter II nursed ambitions of transforming them into the foundation of an extensive southern principality straddling the Pyrenees. These ambitions depended on Peter's continuing relationship with his Trencavel clients. He was not pleased by the prospect of their removal and replacement by some northern baron or, worse, by the count of Toulouse. Such considerations made it highly desirable that Raymond-Roger should be reconciled with the church, and Peter had come to offer his services as mediator.

The crusaders were at dinner when he arrived. Raymond VI received him courteously in his opulent tent by the river, and he was allowed to enter the city on condition that he went unarmed and with only three companions. The garrison were overjoyed by his arrival, having assumed that he had come to reinforce them. But they were quickly disillusioned. Peter testily pointed out that if Raymond-Roger had listened to his advice to expel the heretics he would not be in his predicament. His escort of Spanish knights was not strong enough to break through the besiegers' lines, and even if it were no purpose would be served by it. There were too many hungry non-combatants in the city. Its population had been swollen by frightened refugees, many of them hysterical women and children. The wells had dried up in the intense heat of the summer, and disease had already begun to spread among the crowded inhabitants. The humidity, the mosquitoes, and the smell of rotting animal carcasses were oppressive. The crusaders, on the other hand, lacked nothing. They had found shady trees under which to pitch their tents and were enjoying the first fruits of an early harvest. They had taken over the salt-pans in a nearby marsh, and in spite of the destruction of the water-mills they were able to exchange salt for bread with local peasants. The garrison, whose morale was at its nadir, agreed to let Peter II negotiate a surrender on their behalf. Arnald-Amaury, however, was aware of his strength and in no mood to compromise. Carcassonne was a nest of heretics. It had resisted the army of God, and had exposed itself to the fate of Béziers. Only as a special favour to the Aragonese king would he allow Raymond-Roger himself to leave the city with eleven companions of his choice and as many of their possessions as they could carry. 'When donkeys fly we shall see that happen,' Peter muttered audibly. Raymond-Roger rejected the terms out of hand, and the siege continued as Peter returned to Barcelona.

By 14th August Arnald-Amaury's intransigence had softened. A number of assaults had been repelled by crossbowmen, and the northerners' siege train had failed to make any impression on the walls. The crusaders had already decided to replace Raymond-Roger as count of Béziers and Carcassonne by one of themselves; and at a meeting of the leaders it was pointed out that if Carcassonne were to suffer the fate of Béziers whoever was chosen would be left with nothing to rule. New terms were therefore offered to the garrison. Their lives would be spared if they surrendered, but they and all the inhabitants were to walk in single file out of one gate, wearing only their shirts and breeches and leaving all their possessions behind them. A parley was held under the city walls. Raymond-Roger, with nine leading members of the garrison, accepted a safe-conduct to negotiate with the crusaders in the count of Nevers's tent. No sooner had the terms been agreed than Raymond-Roger was seized and taken away in chains in flagrant breach of his safe-conduct. On the following day, 15th August, the remaining inhabitants left Carcassonne in accordance with the agreement, carrying nothing but their sins, as Peter of Vaux-de-Cernay crowed.

As the crusaders poured in and began to help themselves to fine war-horses and select suitable accommodation in the city's mansions, heralds passed through the streets summoning them to hear the abbot of Cîteaux preach. The abbot, standing on a lump of marble, urged them to restrain themselves. He reminded them that they owed their victory to God. Let them put aside all thought of personal gain and instead carry all the booty to a central place, where it would be placed at the disposal of the new viscount, shortly to be elected. This proposal, though it cannot have been welcome to all the crusaders, was accepted. The common hoard of valuables was placed under the guard of some trustworthy knights (who later embezzled 5,000 livres of it), and the leaders of the army proceeded to the election of Raymond-Roger's successor.

The viscounty was offered first to the principal barons of the army. But the duke of Burgundy, the count of Nevers, and the count of St.-Pol all refused to take on the thankless burden. An electoral committee consisting of four knights, two bishops, and the abbot of Cîteaux, was appointed to consider the matter. The crusaders were becoming restless and anxious to return home. Few of them were interested in a principality which had been conquered by the sword and might well be reconquered by the sword when the army of God had departed. Some thought the Trencavel dominions cursed. Eventually the committee lighted upon Simon de Montfort, a minor baron of the Ile-de-France who, after raising some formal objections, agreed to accept the honour. Peter of Vaux-de-Cernay says that he had to be begged, bullied, and ultimately ordered to accept it by the abbot of Cîteaux. But Simon was precisely the kind of knight whose ambition, cramped by a small northern fief, found an outlet in the crusades. His show of reluctance may have won him better terms from the legate, but it is unlikely that he intended it to be taken seriously.

Simon de Montfort was the father of the turbulent politician whose career was to be such a formative episode in English history. Father and son had much in common. Both were rootless, moody, introspective men of strong piety and strong ambitions, who did not let opportunities pass them by. In the course of a century, the expansion of France into England, Spain, southern Italy, and the Middle East had offered such families unmatched opportunities for self-advancement. Certainly the elder Simon had been destined for greater things than the lordship of Montfort-l'Amaury and Epernon. Through his mother, he was the heir to the important English earldom of Leicester. But the death of his uncle, Robert earl of Leicester, coincided with the climax of the war between England and France. French barons like Simon saw their

English lands confiscated by king John, and themselves left with greater status than wealth to support it. In 1202, Simon had joined the fourth crusade. He had been genuinely shocked by the cynical manner in which the Venetians had used the holy war to serve their own ambitions. When the crusaders had besieged the Christian city of Zara in Dalmatia, Simon had refused to take part in the assault. Instead of following the expedition to Constantinople and assisting it in the destruction of the Byzantine empire, he had returned to Italy and embarked for Syria to fulfil his vows by fighting against Moslems. Less than three years after his return to Montfort-l'Amaury, he had taken the cross against the Albigensians at the special request of the duke of Burgundy, one of the first barons of the Ile-de-France to do so. Simon had distinguished himself on the crusade. He had led the assault on the *castellare* of Carcassonne on 4th August, and had rescued a wounded knight from the ditch beneath a rain of arrows while the rest of the army was retreating.

In 1209 Simon de Montfort was in his late forties, an old man by mediaeval standards. He was a tall, ox-like man with a striking shock of hair, capable of extraordinary feats of physical endurance in spite of his advanced age. His contemporaries were almost unanimous in their admiration, and theirs is an opinion which must be respected. He was certainly brave and persevering, a model Christian of austere personal morals, and a military leader of genius. He inspired extravagant loyalty in his soldiers. Others have judged him more harshly, accusing him of abusing the crusade to serve his own ambitions in a way that sometimes seems as cynical as Dandolo's attack on Zara in 1202. Simon was undoubtedly ambitious, and he was entirely ruthless in pursuing his ambitions. But he was not cynical. He hated heresy with a fierce hatred, and genuinely regarded his own advancement as part of the design of Providence to encompass its destruction. 'Do you think I am afraid?' he was to ask a Cistercian who came to reassure him at a crisis of his adventure; 'My work is the work of Christ and the entire Church is praying for me. We cannot be defeated.' Simon was an 'athlete of Christ', an instrument of God's anger. Among politicians he was an ascetic, a fanatic after Arnald-Amaury's own heart.

Not everyone welcomed Simon's election. There were some, as Arnald-Amaury darkly hinted to the pope, who were 'with us in body but not in spirit'. Others were aware that they had served for more than forty days and that the harvest was approaching at home. The count of

Nevers in particular regarded Simon as a protégé of the duke of Burgundy with whom he had violently fallen out in the course of the campaign. Now that Carcassonne had fallen, he announced his intention of returning to the north with his men, and left forthwith. More than half the army accompanied him.

The Duke of Burgundy agreed to stay behind until the new viscount had been properly installed in his dominions. This was more time-consuming than difficult, for the crusaders were welcomed by the catholics, and the Cathars had fled. Fanjeaux was occupied without difficulty. Castres, the centre of an important network of roads, sent a deputation to submit to Simon, who went north to take possession of the town personally, and to watch the first public burning of heretics. This was followed by a triumphal tour of the northern part of the county of Foix. Mirepoix had been abandoned by its garrison and surrendered immediately. The abbot of Pamiers and the citizens of Saverdun were delighted to throw off the harsh government of the count of Foix, and welcomed Simon as a liberator. Finally the count of Foix himself, unable to put an army in the field and unwilling to be dispossessed like Raymond-Roger, came before Simon as he was besieging the castle of Preixan, south of Carcassonne. He accepted onerous terms, obliging him to submit himself entirely to the wishes of the papal legates and to leave his youngest son with Simon as a hostage. Preixan, which was a dependancy of Foix, was ordered to surrender to its besiegers. The bulk of the army did not follow Simon on these expeditions. It remained in the duke of Burgundy's encampment at Alzonne near Carcassonne; but its presence was felt throughout the region, and the lesson of Béziers was not forgotten. The duke, however, could not remain in Languedoc indefinitely. At the end of September, he left for home, taking with him all but a handful of the army which had met at Lyon three months earlier.

On 10th November, Raymond-Roger Trencavel died of dysentery in his prison near Carcassonne. His death was undeniably convenient for the crusaders, and more than one voice was raised to accuse Simon of his murder; but dysentery was too common in the insanitary conditions of a mediaeval castle for such allegations to carry any weight. Simon himself was the first to pay his respects to the dead man. He had the body laid out in state in the cathedral and allowed the train of mourners from the outlying countryside to file past it. An allowance of 3,000 sols was promised to Raymond-Roger's widow. It was the first irony of the

Albigensian crusade that an army raised to fight an excommunicate accused of the murder of a papal legate had instead destroyed a young man of twenty-four who had not been convicted, or even accused, of any crime. Raymond-Roger's political incompetence was only partly to blame for his fate. He was the victim of his uncle's predicament, from which Raymond had been unable to escape except by diverting the crusade against Béziers and Carcassonne. The true author of Raymond-Roger's destruction was Arnald-Amaury who had refused, in defiance of the principles of canon law, to accept the viscount's submission at Montpellier. But the codes of canon law were framed on the assumption that rulers were able as well as willing to suppress heresy. This political truth was never grasped by Innocent III, but Arnald-Amaury knew it. Innocent was a legist; Arnald-Amaury was a conqueror. If the canon law was to be respected in Languedoc, its existing rulers had to be replaced, and its institutions remoulded.

## ✛ VII ✛

## 1209–1211: The breach with Raymond VI

'Can two walk together except they be agreed? Will a lion
roar in the forest when he hath no prey?'

AMOS III.3–4

A month after his election, Simon de Montfort wrote to the pope. He
informed Innocent of the victory of the crusading army and of his own
unanimous election to the viscounties of Béziers and Carcassonne, both
of which were due, as he believed, to the intervention of God and his
church. In recognition of that fact he proposed to pay the yield of a
threepenny hearth tax annually to Rome. In return Simon hoped that
the pope would confirm him and his heirs in the possession of a principality which, to minds trained in the conventions of feudal politics, had
been so irregularly acquired.

Simon's letter was not a song of triumph, and he made it abundantly
clear that he expected more than moral support from Rome. He controlled two substantial cities, one of which was a heap of charred ruins,
and the other full of booty but entirely without inhabitants. In addition,
some two hundred villages and towns had been occupied by the army on
its march from Béziers, or had surrendered to him after the fall of Carcassonne. But his hold on these places depended more on bluff than
force. The army which had conquered them had departed leaving him
with no more than thirty knights to defend them, adventurers, landless
fortune-hunters and younger sons, friends from the neighbourhood of
Montfort-l'Amaury. There was a force of foot-soldiers in addition to the
knights whom alone contemporaries troubled to count, but it was not
large. Simon's entire strength cannot have amounted to more than 500
men, and even they had demanded twice the normal wage for their
services. With this force he had to garrison at least a dozen important
castles, and keep an army in the field strong enough to face the enemies
of Christ 'who prowl freely among the crags and mountains of the land'.
Raymond-Roger was dead, but his army had been allowed to leave Car-

cassonne alive, and the greater part of it had reassembled in the three impregnable rock-fortresses of Termes, Minerve, and Cabaret. Their presence was felt everywhere.

Innocent replied fervently congratulating the new viscount and confirming his election. Reinforcements were promised as soon as they could be found. During November, the papal chancery despatched requests and commands to the princes of Europe, and instructed the French bishops to recruit crusaders in their dioceses with promises of indulgences and privileges as generous as those of the original crusaders. To the emperor Otto, Innocent boasted with pardonable exaggeration of 500 towns conquered from the heretics. Simon's companions at Carcassonne were commended for their faith and urged to be patient; the following year would bring reinforcements from the north and money to settle their arrears of pay. He would have done more, Innocent explained to Simon, but the pressing needs of the Holy Land could not be ignored; the Latins were struggling to maintain their precarious grip on Constantinople and the pope had already received complaints that the indulgences of the Albigensian crusade were choking off recruitment to the Christian armies of the east.

He had done enough to ensure that Simon's army was constantly reinforced by fresh crusaders from the north. Each winter for the next ten years the Cistercians preached the crusade in northern France, the Low Countries and Germany; each spring the steady trickle of recruits began to percolate to the south. Small bands of crusaders came and went throughout the summer, serving for a short while and departing to be replaced by others. As winter approached, the entire army disappeared, leaving Simon with a small band of devoted followers to preserve his conquests by energy, ruthlessness and bluff until the arrival of the next band of knights in March. Perhaps, as Innocent himself had observed, the slow progress of the crusade was part of the wonderful design of God to allow ever more northern knights to save their souls by taking the cross. But from a military point of view it was far from satisfactory. Few of the new recruits had much enthusiasm for the enterprise. Having saved their souls, they were anxious to return home as soon as possible. The legates were obliged to decree that no one could gain the indulgence without serving for at least forty days; and even forty days was a short time in which to master the peculiar problems of fighting an enemy who was everywhere around them, and was conquered only to reappear again when the army had moved on. Simon never knew more than a few weeks in advance how strong his army would be. He never began an enterprise in the knowledge that he would be able to finish it.

The persecution of heresy had already begun in the spirit in which it was to continue. Substantial fines were decreed for those who were named by the legates as protectors of heresy and failed to submit within forty days. In castles taken by storm they were summarily hanged. The heretics themselves were burned in scores on huge pyres of wood and straw, the penalty prescribed by the tradition which the crusaders had brought with them from the north. The crusaders knew nothing of the calculated judicial safeguards which the Inquisition was to introduce to the persecution of heresy. At Castres they could not decide whether penitent heretics should be burned along with impenitent, a subject on which the inquisitors of another generation were to write that 'mercy, in such circumstances, is preferable to the rigour of justice'; and more acceptable, they added, to a feeble and cowardly public. But the church, in 1209, did not yet have the police system to pursue those whose penitence was insincere, and Simon ordered that both alike should die. These holocausts were an essential part of his purpose in Languedoc. But there is little doubt that they stiffened the resistance of the nobility, and made enemies of many moderate catholics.

Arnald-Amaury was not a man to respect the liberties of free townsmen or the petty privileges of self-important city fathers. In September 1209 he named a number of citizens of Toulouse as heretics, and peremptorily demanded the surrender of their persons and property. The consuls of the city indignantly denied that there were any heretics in the city; those named by Arnald-Amaury, they asserted, had professed sentiments of the most fervent orthodoxy. They refused his demand and appealed to Innocent III. Arnald-Amaury laid an interdict upon the city. The anomalous position of Raymond VI was a more intractable problem. Until he was removed from the government of his dominions, there was little that could be done about the powerful heretical communities among his vassals. But Raymond had submitted to the church. Arnald-Amaury distrusted and disbelieved him. He thought his submission hypocritical, a mere device to ward off the punishment which he deserved. But Innocent's judicial scruples would not allow the legates to invade the county of Toulouse until the count had given them just cause, and Raymond went to extreme lengths to avoid doing so. He brought his son, whom he had offered as a hostage, into the crusaders' camp at Alzonne and promised him in marriage to the daughter of

Simon de Montfort. He destroyed a number of castles on the frontiers between his land and Simon's, lest they should give rise to disputes. Repeatedly he protested his orthodoxy and his willingness to submit to the legates' every demand.

Arnald-Amaury had not forgotten the promises which Raymond had already made at St.-Gilles, promises which would be hard to keep. The persecution of heresy, the abolition of toll-gates, the immediate dismissal of mercenaries and Jewish administrators from his service, none of these could be achieved quickly without inviting the disintegration of his government. Nevertheless, complaints of Raymond's tardiness were heard within a few days of the capture of Carcassonne. In September 1209 the three legates, Milo, Thedisius, and Arnald-Amaury, presided over a council at Avignon, at which they excommunicated Raymond and laid an interdict on all his dominions. Raymond protested in vain that only three months had elapsed since his promises at St.-Gilles, during two of which he had been actively assisting the crusade. The council merely consented to delay the execution of the sentence for six weeks. He had until 1st November to satisfy the legates on all the points raised at St.-Gilles or see his county confiscated by the church. Raymond immediately appealed to the pope. He announced his intention of going to Rome to prosecute his appeal in person and made preparations which bore all the marks of earnest intention. The legates were visibly disturbed. They had exceeded the letter of their instructions, and they knew Innocent's attachment to formalities. They determined to forestall Raymond's appeal by sending to Rome an ambassador of their own. 'If it should happen,' the legates wrote to the pope, 'that the count of Toulouse, that enemy of peace and justice, should come before your holiness, take care that you be not deceived by his lying tongue.' They listed the complaints against Raymond, who had deceitfully evaded his promise at St.-Gilles. The inhabitants of Avignon, Nîmes, and St.-Gilles were ready to renounce their allegiance to him in accordance with their oaths in June. The count's castles were in their hands. He would be powerless to resist them. 'He is so well trussed up by the power of God and the efforts of your holiness that the struggle would be beyond his strength.' The agents who carried these letters to Rome received exact instructions. Every possible argument in the count's favour was anticipated and the correct reply set out for them to put to the pope.

Arnald-Amaury's agents were followed at a short distance by two ambassadors of Raymond himself, sent to prepare the ground and acquaint Innocent with his appeal. The count had decided to go first to Paris in order to put his case to Philip Augustus, and to find allies among the northern barons. He did not arrive in Rome until after Christmas, and when he eventually reached the papal curia he was embarrassed to discover that he had been preceded not only by Arnald-Amaury's agents but by the bishop of Agen, who had come to complain of the ill-treatment which he had suffered at the count's hands. How Innocent received him cannot now be known. According to one account the pope delivered a bitter harangue to the startled count, who was accused of being a murderer, a protector of heretics, and a persecutor of the cross. But another contemporary believed that he had been received warmly, showered with presents, and offered a private viewing of one of the Vatican's most precious relics, the napkin of St. Veronica. The conflict of testimony remains insoluble, a lesson to those who look for certainty in history. What is certain is that the outcome was a humiliating defeat for the legates in France. Innocent was irritated by their unjudicial behaviour. He was impressed by the references that Raymond was able to produce, showing that he had made good many of his depredations against individual churches. The count had plainly kept some of his promises, and had professed his willingness to keep the others. Was it right that the church should enrich itself at his expense, confiscating his castles and invading his dominions?

In January 1210, the pope set aside Raymond's excommunication. He appointed Thedisius as co-legate in place of Milo, who had died in December, and instructed him to summon a new council in three months, at which anyone might come forward to accuse the count of heresy or complicity in the murder of Peter of Castelnau. But if no such evidence was forthcoming, the count was to be reconciled with the church and left in peace. Even if some credible accuser came forward, Thedisius was on no account to pass judgement himself, but was to send the dossier to Rome to await Innocent's own decision. Worse was to follow. The legates were ordered to proceed personally to Toulouse, where they were to absolve the consuls, lift the interdict, and come to an agreement with the citizens. If the citizens refused to accede to reasonable requests, they might be excommunicated. But in any case no action was to be taken against them by a single legate. Innocent did not trust Arnald-Amaury to act alone. The pope followed these humiliating injunctions with a personal letter to Arnald-Amaury. After flattering and congratulating him at interminable length, Innocent admitted that he had blunted Arnald-Amaury's weapon. He had charged Thedisius with the delicate matter of the count of Toulouse, but this was not to be taken as a public rebuke. Thedisius was quite capable of dealing with the count and would be expected to take his instructions from Arnald-Amaury. Raymond, the pope pointed out, might accept terms from him which he would throw back at Arnald-Amaury.

Innocent's words can have done little to sugar the bitter pill which Arnald-Amaury had to swallow. And they came at a particularly unfortunate time, for Simon de Montfort had suffered serious reverses in the autumn of 1209. Reinforcements were expected imminently from the north, but it was far from clear that he would be able to survive the winter. The principal author of his troubles was Peter II of Aragon. Peter, as nominal suzerain of the viscounties of Béziers and Carcassonne, was exceedingly displeased to have acquired a new vassal without his consent. In November 1209 he spent a fortnight with Simon at Montpellier but could not be persuaded to accept his homage. This refusal cast serious doubt on the legality of Simon's rule, for even the canon law allowed a suzerain some discretion in these matters. Moreover, Peter indicated to the nobility of Simon's dominions that they would have his support in resisting their unwanted overlord. They did not need to be told twice. Not long afterwards the bodies of two Cistercian monks in the service of the legate Milo were discovered on a lonely path near Carcassone. One of them had been stabbed thirty-six times.

The leader of the resistance was Pierre-Roger, lord of Cabaret. He was an old man in 1209; but age had not diminished his independence of mind or even his formidable physical powers. He had a reputation for extravagance and large gestures, for his court was one of those which the *troubadour* Raimon de Miraval urged his accompanist to visit in pursuit of a patron. Pierre-Roger had played a prominent part in the defence of Carcassonne. After its fall, many of the garrison had escaped with him to Cabaret where they were shortly reinforced by petty seigneurs of the region, refugees from castles abandoned or lost. Of all the remote hill-fortresses of the Carcassès, Cabaret came nearest to being impregnable. Properly speaking it was not one fortress but a line of four independently fortified keeps occupying an irregular ridge some three hundred yards long, above the village of Lastours. It was surrounded on three sides by sheer cliffs. There was no access road wide enough to take a carriage until 1847. Early in September the crusading army had penetrated up the valley of the Orbiel and attempted to take the place by storm. But they were repelled without difficulty and the approach of winter prevented them from contemplating a long siege. As the last crusaders withdrew to the north, the defenders of Cabaret began to launch raids deep into Simon's territory. At the beginning of November, some fifty northerners, commanded by Simon's kinsman Bouchard de Marly, were ambushed near Cabaret and put to flight with considerable losses. Bouchard himself was captured and kept chained in a cell for sixteen months.

Simon could ill afford such losses. But the winter weather was on the side of his enemies. A wet and bitterly cold November had succeeded the glorious summer of 1209. The river Aude was swollen by the flood-waters of the Pyrenees and there was no usable bridge downstream of Carcassonne. Since the river divided his thin ribbon of territory in two, Simon was unable to bring rapid reinforcements to his small, widely scattered garrisons. He was leaving Montpellier when the news of Bouchard de Marly's capture was brought to him. Immediately afterwards he learned that two of his knights were besieged with a handful of troops in a castle south of the Aude, but before he had completed the long detour by Carcassonne the castle had been captured and its defenders killed. The news of a more serious revolt in the Minervois forced him to return to the bridge at Carcassonne and back east along the Roman road. The cause was one of those obscure quarrels which repeatedly hindered Simon's efforts to find allies among the southern nobility. One of his companions had murdered the uncle of Giraud de Pépieux, a southern knight in the service of the crusaders. Simon had sentenced the murderer to be buried alive. This barbarous mode of execution was well known in the south, a custom of Béarn and Bigorre whose infliction on a northerner and a nobleman should have satisfied Giraud.[12] Nevertheless at the end of November he introduced himself with a few friends into the castle of Puisserguier, west of Béziers, over-powered the garrison, and shut them in the keep. Simon took more than a week to reach the castle, and then the local levies who were with him refused to storm the walls. Without a siege train he was impotent. Giraud set fire to the castle the following night and escaped, throwing the fifty soldiers of the garrison into the moat. The two knights whom Giraud had found in command of the place were taken to the Cathar stronghold of Minerve. There they were savagely mutilated and driven naked from the gates to rejoin their master.

Further south the count of Foix had torn up his treaty with the crusaders and recaptured Preixan. An attempt to storm Fanjeaux by night was only narrowly beaten off. Simon's principality appeared to be disintegrating. Castres and Lombers threw off their allegiance and imprisoned their northern garrisons. Montréal was surrendered to its former seigneur by the priest whom Simon had appointed to command it. In Carcassonne the newly appointed bishop arrived to find Simon's soldiers making hasty preparations for flight. Before the snow had begun to melt in the narrow valleys, yielding their passes to Simon's siege train, the crusaders had lost more than forty castles and were clinging to eight isolated strongholds separated by large tracts of hostile country.

Help began to arrive in March. A contingent of knights led by Simon's wife Alice de Montmorency reached Languedoc on about 3rd March. Simon went to meet them at Pézénas. A warm spring and a constant trickle of fresh troops enabled him to return to the offensive. With the Aude now fordable in several places Simon demonstrated his remarkable capacity for being everywhere at once. A rising at Montlaur was brutally suppressed before the citizens had succeeded in overcoming the garrison. Most of the townsmen fled in the confusion, but those who could be found were hanged. Simon had learned the value of these hideous examples. At Bram, which he captured later in the month, the entire garrison had their eyes put out except for one, who was spared to lead the wretched column to Cabaret. The priest who had betrayed Montréal in December was found among the defenders. He was stripped of his clerical status by the bishop of Carcassonne, and dragged through the streets from a horse's tail to be hanged from a gibbet on the walls. In April, a rapid march through the Minervois brought new surrenders from frightened townsmen. Where isolated garrisons still held out, the land was wasted and the vines uprooted as they were coming into leaf. Alaric, the last enemy stronghold in the Aude valley, was recaptured in the teeth of a screaming gale at the end of April 1210.

Simon's sudden abasement and recovery had provoked a bitter struggle in Toulouse, as the friends and the enemies of the crusade fought for control of the city. Toulouse was nearly fifty miles from the boundary of Simon's principality. But its population and wealth, and its situation at the junction of several major roads, made its alliance too valuable a prize to be ignored. Toulouse was an important ecclesiastical capital, one of the holy cities of France. Its position on the pilgrims' route to Santiago had made it a city of chapels and hospitals, and of inns numerous enough in 1205 to be worth regulating with a prolix ordinance. The basilica of St.-Sernin, completed some fifty years earlier, had been built to hold the great processions of clerics and pilgrims which honoured the saints on their feast days. But of the other treasures which brought pilgrims to Toulouse, many have gone. The church of the Daurade, with its famous mosaics of Christ with Abraham and the Virgin, is now an empty square by the Garonne. The sculptured cloisters of St.-Sernin and St.-Etienne have given way to roads, victims of the passion of nineteenth-century engineers for straight lines. Toulouse had expanded more than any southern city except Montpellier. North of the parchment-makers' shops of what is now the rue Pargaminières, a new suburb known as the *bourg* had sprung up in the course of the eleventh century around the vast monastic outbuildings of St.-Sernin. The suburbs of mediaeval cities often drained the vitality of the centres, leaving them as silent ghost-towns populated by ecclesiastics and officials. But this had not happened in Toulouse. The *cité* retained its Jewish quarter, its busy tenements, its streets of small craftsmen's workshops, its licensed salt shops behind the count's palace in the south. The *bourg* became the residential quarter of the rich. Ancient patrician families like the Maurands built rambling mansions and towers there, reminiscent of the aristocratic towers of Italian cities. There was far less heresy in Toulouse than the legates imagined. But what there was, was concentrated in the *bourg*, in the fashionable houses beneath the spire of St.-Sernin and, closer to the Garonne, in the workshops of the bleachers, cobblers and tanners, who had been squeezed out of the *cité* to establish themselves round the church of St.-Pierre-de-Cuisines. The new men of Toulouse, successful immigrants like Bernard Capdenier, fiercely catholic, slightly vulgar, dominated the politics of the *cité*. The old wealth moved to the *bourg*, and with it the tradition of protecting heresy, born of a bitter anti-clericalism and of an outlook which the urban nobility shared with the older aristocracy of the outlying country.

Simon's principal ally in the city was the bishop, Folquet de Marseille. He was a politician of remarkable talents who had had an unusual career. His father had been a Genoese merchant in Marseille, and had left him a substantial fortune at an early age. He had become an itinerant *troubadour*, popular with the southern aristocracy, and talented enough to find a place in Dante's *Paradiso*, in the Heaven of

Venus among those who had been lovers on earth. He was a man of extremes. In 1195 he had abruptly abandoned his wife and two sons, to enter the austere Robertist abbey of Le Thoronet. He remained there for ten years, until the deposition of Raymond VI's friend Raymond de Rabastens from the bishopric of Toulouse gave the papal legates an opportunity to appoint a man closer to their own heart. Folquet was promoted to fill the vacant see, and as the ruler of the largest diocese of the Midi, he amply justified the legates' confidence in him.

Toulouse offered a promising prospect to a shrewd politician. The war had aggravated the tensions of the expanding city, and swollen its heretical population with the refugees of Carcassonne and the tributary valleys of the Aude. But Simon's enemies in Toulouse included many who were not heretics. There were those who were tied to Raymond VI by bonds of sentiment or self-interest, and others who saw in the high-handed behaviour of Arnald-Amaury a threat to hard-won civic privileges. But Folquet, unlike Arnald-Amaury, knew how to divide his enemies. To create a party for Simon de Montfort in Toulouse, he raised the one issue which cut across the divisions of class and party: usury. The victims of Christian usurers included men who had nothing else in common, small artisans, allodial landowners of the outlying district, aristocratic families who had seen better days. The church had the strongest possible objections to usury. It had repeatedly and vainly asked Raymond VI to suppress it. Now Folquet saw the political advantages of taking action himself. He organized the catholics of the *cité* into a popular society which called itself the White Brotherhood. They wore robes and crosses and were entitled to the indulgences of the crusade. They held processions, hunted out heretics, and broke up the premises of the usurers. It was probably the latter activity as much as their savage orthodoxy which offended the inhabitants of the *bourg*. For the patrician families who lived there had close business connections with the usurers, and offered them the protection of their fortified towers. The *bourg* responded to Folquet's demagogic activities by forming a Black Brotherhood of its own, and the two mobs, armed with swords and banners, sometimes even mounted, clashed frequently in the narrow streets of Toulouse.

At the end of March, in the midst of this violent civil war, Arnald-Amaury arrived in the city to negotiate with the consuls, in accordance with Innocent's instructions. He had come without any of the other legates, a plain breach of those instructions as the consuls did not fail to point out. The consuls, however, were anxious to be absolved from the stain of heresy and did not wish to stand on formality. They were persuaded to waive this irregularity, and peace was concluded on terms which the citizens could reconcile with their privileges. The legate was promised assistance in the pursuit of heretics, and a subsidy of 1,000 livres 'for the cause of the holy church'. But if this agreement satisfied the *cité*, it smacked of discreditable surrender in the eyes of the *bourg*. The consuls were unable to collect the money, and were obliged to return to the legate with a smaller offer of 500 livres. With a characteristic lack of political finesse, Arnald-Amaury chose to regard this as an act of open defiance. Once again the consuls were excommunicated and an interdict laid on the city. The bishop, who perceived that Arnald-Amaury's affront to civic liberties was likely to unite the city against him, intervened with the legate and persuaded him to lift the excommunication on lighter terms. Instead of finding the remaining 500 livres, the consuls surrendered a number of distinguished citizens as hostages for their good behaviour. In return the legates 'permitted' them to remain in the allegiance of the count of Toulouse. It was an unsatisfactory compromise on both sides, and it did not heal the deep divisions within the city.

Folquet was undoubtedly assisted by Simon's victories, for there were many, both inside Toulouse and elsewhere, whose sole desire was to be on the winning side. In a war that was as much psychological as military, the appearance of permanence was as valuable to the new viscount as several castles. Much depended on the attitude of Peter II of Aragon, who was in a position to deny Simon's government the clothing of legality which he desperately craved. But at this moment, Peter hesitated. He knew that if he did not support his clients north of the Pyrenees, his influence there would rapidly evaporate. Yet he could not bring himself to defy the church openly, nor was it clear that his finances would be equal to the strain of a long war in Languedoc. In April, Peter crossed the Pyrenees to attend a conference at Pamiers, at which all the leading actors of the drama were present, including the count of Toulouse, who had now returned in triumph from Italy. The negotiations were inconclusive, and as soon as the conference broke up, Simon rode to Foix with a small force to try the defences of the castle and uproot the vines on the surrounding hillsides. Peter was less resolute. At the end of May he went to Montréal to meet the leaders of the resistance. He toyed briefly with the idea of accepting them as his

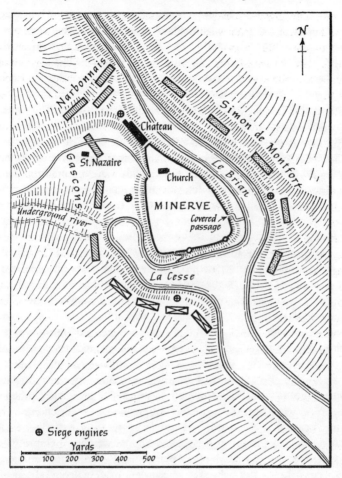

IV.   Minerve in 1210

vassals, an act which would certainly have committed him to the enemies of the crusade. But this came to nothing, and after persuading Simon to grant a truce to the count of Foix until Easter 1211, he returned empty-handed to Aragon.[13]

With the count of Foix reconciled for the next ten months to his losses, Raymond VI anxious at all costs to avoid a new quarrel with the church, and Toulouse neutralized by its bishop, Simon de Montfort had a free hand to deal with the garrisons which still held out against him. On about 3rd June he laid siege to Minerve, the base from which his enemies had launched repeated raids against the Narbonnais in the course of the winter. Minerve was a remarkable natural fortress. It was a large fortified village some six miles north of the Aude, sited at the confluence of two steep river gorges and protected on three sides by sheer ravines up to three hundred feet deep. On the fourth side, it was approached by a narrow isthmus of land defended by a powerful citadel and by steep fissures in the rocky ground. Simon's army was the strongest he had assembled since the previous year. In addition to a motley force of French and German volunteers, there was a substantial Gascon contingent recruited by the archbishop of Auch, and some levies from the city of Narbonne, who were repaying the injury which the inhabitants of Minerve had done to their trade. These last invested the village on its landward side, but it was immediately apparent that it could not be taken by storm. Its one weakness was the weakness of all fortresses built on rock, the shortage of water. A natural cleft in the rock had provided Minerve with its only well, but it was situated at the very edge of the ravine, some 250 feet above the river Briant and only sixty yards from the weapons of the besiegers on the opposite side. The well was protected by a thick wall, and was approached by a covered passage from the village. Without rain to fill its storage tanks, the garrison could survive for no longer than the covered passage. It was opposite this point that Simon sited his siege engines and his own headquarters. The most powerful of these machines were trebuchets, immense mechanical slings mounted on wooden frames, and clothed in hides to protect them from the lighted arrows of the defenders. The military science of the north had only very recently perfected them, replacing with a system of pivots and counterweights the springs of twisted rope that powered older machines. Experiments conducted with reconstructed trebuchets on the orders of Napoleon III suggest that they could hurl a twenty-five pound ball nearly 200 yards to destroy the upperworks of the walls and towers. These bulky machines were generally assembled on site by specialist carpenters, and their operation required considerable skill. Simon's largest machine, a monster called Malevoisine, was attended by engineers who cost him 21 livres a day in wages. These were the men whose skills were derided in the name of a fading chivalrous ideal by that ingratiating gossip of baronial halls, Guiot de Provins; did Alexander have sappers, or king Arthur use siege engineers?[14] Guiot's protest fell on deaf ears. Simon de Montfort employed both, and their wages were well earned. From the opposite side of the Briant ravine, the largest trebuchets were able to destroy the upper storeys of the citadel. Three hundred yards away, smaller machines were finding the range of the covered passage, and on the other side of the village the Gascons had erected trebuchets of their own with which they kept up a continual bombardment throughout the day and night.

Once the engineers had found their range and height, there was little that the garrison could do to protect themselves. Thick walls could reduce the damage, but even Château Gaillard, Richard Cœur-de-Lion's great fortress on the Seine which had been deliberately constructed with siege engines in mind, had succumbed six years earlier to sappers and trebuchets. On the night of 18th July, after six weeks of bombardment, the garrison attempted a daring sortie to destroy Malevoisine. This involved evading the sentries posted on the landward side of the village and making a long detour by the north to reach the other side of the ravine. They succeeded in reaching the giant trebuchet, which was unattended, and set fire to it with animal fat and bales of straw and flax which they had brought with them in baskets. But as the flames began to rise, the alarm was given by an engineer who had left his tent to relieve himself. This man was quickly silenced with a lance, but the crusaders, awakened by the noise, succeeded in repelling the raiding party and extinguishing the fire.

The position of the garrison now seemed untenable. The well and the covered passageway had been destroyed. The citadel had been so badly damaged that it was doubtful whether the defenders would be capable of repelling an assault. On 22nd July, William of Minerve came into Simon's camp to ask for terms. Within the camp, the negotiations provoked acrimonious disputes. The conventions of war, founded on Christian principles as well as military wisdom, required the besiegers to spare the lives of a garrison which surrendered. But this convention seemed hard to reconcile with the crusaders' mission to destroy heresy, for the defenders of Minerve included many Cathars, and an even greater number of sympathizers. While the crusaders attempted to resolve their differences on this point, Arnald-Amaury arrived in the camp with his co-legate Thedisius. Simon announced that the decision would be left to the abbot, who as the director of the crusade would be able to give an authoritative ruling. These words, says the monk of Vaux-de-Cernay, caused the abbot of Cîteaux deep discomfort. 'He passionately desired to see God's enemies die, but as a monk and a priest he did not dare to strike the blow himself.' Instead he suggested that each side should reduce its terms to writing, hoping that their demands would prove to be incompatible and that the village would be taken by assault. William of Minerve set out his terms. They were read to Simon de Montfort and found unacceptable. But instead of returning to continue the siege, William announced that he would accept any terms which the crusaders chose to impose. The decision was again delegated to Arnald-Amaury. With evident reluctance the legate ordered that the inhabitants' lives be spared, including those of Cathars who were prepared to renounce their errors. This news was greeted with indignation when it was announced to the other crusaders. Robert Mauvoisin, one of Simon's principal officers, exclaimed that he had come to kill heretics, not to watch them escape freely by feigning conversion. Arnald-Amaury reassured him. Very few, he thought, would be converted.

Arnald-Amaury's judgement was sound. On the same day, the clergy led the crusading army into Minerve past the shattered citadel, singing the *Te Deum* and bearing a large crucifix to be placed on the tower of the church. The leaders of the heretical community did not trouble to conceal themselves. Both Arnald-Amaury and Simon passed from one house of Perfects to the next in an unavailing attempt to persuade them to recant. 'Why preach at us?' the male Perfects replied to the legate; 'we care nothing for your faith, we deny the church of Rome.' The female Perfects were even more dismissive. Three of them were persuaded to return to the church by Matilda de Garlande, the mother of the crusader Bouchard de Marly, who was even then lying in a cell at Cabaret. The others, some 140 in number, were taken to a clearing outside the village and thrown onto a huge blazing pyre. Few of them offered any resistance. Many were seen to throw themselves joyfully into the flames, embracing martyrdom and the end of the tyranny of the flesh with the same enthusiasm as the heroes of the early Christian church. None of the ordinary believers was willing to share the fate of the Perfects. They accepted the mercy of the church with gratitude.

The holocaust of the Perfects of Minerve brought to a fitting end a long siege which had embittered both sides, hardening religious sympathies. From the other hill-towns, more Cathars fled to the comparative safety of Toulouse. For the army, the campaign took on more of the savagery of a holy war. Reports of God's miraculous intervention became more common. Vultures never flew above the army. The land gave forth its produce when the army was hungry, and dried-up rivers became torrents when it was thirsty. The Lord guided the missiles of their siege engines, and warded off the bolts of their enemies. Silver crosses were seen on the whitewashed walls of Toulouse churches.

The subjection of most of the Trencavel dominions had brought the county of Toulouse once more into the forefront of men's minds, for Arnald-Amaury had by no means accepted his six-month-old defeat. Raymond VI was anxious that his reconciliation with the church should be formally recognized. He felt that Innocent III's bulls entitled him to this, and he knew that without it his territory would always be at risk. In May, he received Arnald-Amaury in Toulouse and delivered up to him his fortified palace at the southern gate, the Château Narbonnais, an act which even his catholic allies felt to be an unnecessary humilia-tion. Nevertheless, Arnald-Amaury refused to allow him the formal reconciliation which he sought, on the grounds that his co-legate, Thedisius, was away in Rome. When Thedisius returned to Languedoc in the middle of June, there seemed to be no alternative to recognizing Raymond's orthodoxy. But Thedisius was a 'man of intelligence and vision, who devoted himself heart and mind to the matter, in the hope that some juridically acceptable excuse might be found for rejecting the count's submission.' At a secret conference of the legates it was agreed that to reconcile Raymond would be to tie their own hands and to allow him the benefit of his own duplicity. Perusing the bull, Thedisius lighted on a sentence in which Innocent had said that until the count's reconciliation, he would be 'expected to obey the instructions of the legates'. The count had received many instructions, he reasoned. Not all of them had been obeyed. There were, for example, still heretics in his dominions, and toll-gates on his roads. Could the count's submission properly be accepted while these matters were outstanding? It was clear that excessive haste should be avoided, as Innocent would un-doubtedly consider it unjudicial. So they would summon a council at St.-Gilles, and would invite Raymond himself to appear before it.

The council met at the beginning of July 1210, and Raymond appeared with his legal advisers, expecting to be reconciled. A cynical charade then followed. The abbot of Cîteaux rose and announced that he had no objection to the count's reconciliation. But Thedisius came forward with the papal bulls and read out the passage requiring Raymond to ac-cept the legates' instructions. No evidence could be heard, he declared, on the matters of the count's heresy or his complicity in the murder of Peter of Castelnau, until these instructions had been complied with. A list of them was read out to him, including the immediate dismissal of the foreign troops who garrisoned his few remaining strongholds. Raymond protested vigorously that the legates' demands would cost him his county. Finally he broke down in tears, tears of guilt and rage, Thedisius sanctimoniously suggested. But not discreditable tears, three centuries before the Renaissance cult of manliness made sentiment contemptible.

The church's insistence on the dismissal of Raymond's mercenaries was motivated by something more than a desire to see his castles ungarrisoned. In a province where feudal bands were weak and feudal armies rare, it undoubtedly had this effect. But the church's reasoning was more like that of those eighteenth-century Englishmen who distrusted a standing army because it 'tended much to tyranny'. The church had sanctified the feudal bond, and in so doing had subtly weakened it. A vassal's obligation to fight for his lord was tempered by other obligations of a more spiritual kind, by rules which prescribed the proper treatment of non-combatants, respect for ecclesiastical property, and the observance of truces on holy days. It was these rules that St. Bernard's biographer had in mind when he described the saint's father as a man of 'ancient and legitimate chivalry, waging war according to the holy law'.[15] It was as near as the twelfth century came to a Geneva Convention; and if, like its modern counterparts, it was frequently honoured in the breach, it could never be entirely ignored, as Philip Augustus had discovered when some of his vassals refused to invade the lands of Richard Cœur-de-Lion during the third crusade. Wisely, the church refused to say what it meant by a 'just war'. But it suspected that a prince who dispensed with the services of vassals, employing mercenaries instead, knew his war to be unjust. These suspicions were often justified in the event. Mercenaries were men of low birth who did as they were told. They fought in just and unjust causes alike, provided that they were paid. Their avarice and brutality were notorious. Nevertheless, Henry II of England had employed an army composed entirely of professionals and in doing so had conclusively demonstrated that the ancient verities no longer made military sense. Military sense, however, did not govern the views of the church which persisted in regarding the feudal army as a guarantee of virtue in war. Even that stern realist Joinville, writing nearly a century later of the crusade of St. Louis, thought that Guy de Mauvoisin's force had distinguished itself at the battle of Mansourah because it consisted entirely of his kinsmen and vassals.

After his humiliation at St.-Gilles, the count returned to Toulouse by the valley of the Aude, passing the evident signs of Simon's tightening grip on the province. Two major fortresses, Ventajou and Montréal, had surrendered on the news of the fall of Minerve. Simon's base camp at Pennautier, north-west of Carcassonne, was filled with fresh crusaders from the Ile-de-France, and there were reports of a large contingent of Bretons on its way south. In the castle, the viscount was holding court in rooms decorated with silken carpets, supported by his wife and kinsmen, and by the barons of his new principality.

At the end of July, it was decided to attack Termes, the one remaining hostile fortress south of the Aude. This involved leaving Cabaret to be dealt with last, a decision which may well have made sense on logistical grounds, but one which they almost had cause to regret. Simon left immediately for Termes leaving instructions for his unwieldy siege train to follow him. The siege engines were packed into ox-carts by the garrison of Carcassonne and left outside the walls on the gravel by the Aude. A small detachment of troops had been ordered to escort them to Termes. This intelligence was quickly carried to Pierre-Roger of Cabaret by the spies whom he had set to observe the movements of the crusaders. In the middle of the night the siege train was attacked by a force of knights commanded by Pierre-Roger in person. Their approach had been observed from the walls, and they were chased off by the garrison. But shortly before dawn they returned, and had already begun to break the machines with axes and burn them with bales of straw, when the alarm was raised. As dawn broke a minor battle was fought on the gravel banks of the river. William of Contres, the commander of the garrison, fought his assailants hand to hand in the water. In the fighting around the ox-carts, the crusaders gradually gained the upper hand, inflicting heavy casualties on the raiders. Pierre-Roger himself was trapped by the river while his men were making good their escape. He saved his life only by passing himself off as a crusader, and riding through the garrison crying 'Montfort! Montfort!'

Simon, unaware of how close he had come to disaster, arrived outside Termes with the body of his army towards the middle of August 1210. The castle of Termes was of little strategic importance. But it was among the largest as well as the strongest of Languedoc and

Simon could not afford to leave his enemies a safe haven from which to raid his dominions. The castle dominated a narrow river valley in the northern part of the Corbières, a region of few roads, of sharp, thickly wooded peaks and of valleys which remained snowbound until well into April. The village stood, crushed by the mass of its castle, on a sheer rock, from which two narrow fingers of land extended north towards the valley of the Orbiel. One of these fingers was protected from assault by vertical cliffs, the other by a small isolated turret known as the Termenet. To the south, there was a fortified suburb, and a thin neck of rocky land which offered the only means of access to the fortress. Raymond de Termes, who was its lord, was an aged, hardened man cast in the mould of Pierre-Roger de Cabaret, and in his time he had fought both the counts of Toulouse and the Trencavels. He had no intention of making his peace with Simon de Montfort. In spite of the speed of Simon's approach, he had been able to take in supplies and to reinforce the garrison with mercenaries hired in Aragon, Catalonia, and Roussillon.

Having committed his reputation to the capture of Termes, Simon found that he had under-estimated the difficulties involved. His siege train had been delayed by the activities of Pierre-Roger and by the rough roads of the Corbières. The immense circuit of the walls defied Simon's attempts to surround them, and for some time the defenders were able to come and go freely within sight of the crusaders' camp. Reinforcements trickled through slowly, and left promptly when their forty days were done. Raiding parties from Cabaret swept the roads north of Termes, picking off small groups of crusaders and sending them on to Simon's camp with pierced eyes and severed lips and noses. The garrison shouted abuse from the walls, and amused themselves by capturing the crusaders' banners and carrying them off within the gates. Simon's situation began to improve at the end of August. The promised contingent of Bretons arrived with his siege engines, followed, shortly afterwards, by a large army from the Ile-de-France led by the bishops of Chartres and Beauvais and the counts of Dreux and Ponthieu. For the first time the crusaders were able to cut off access to the castle. Simon's trebuchets were set up on the south-western side of the castle and the archdeacon of Paris, who had accompanied the northern host, organized a religious confraternity among the numerous idlers and non-combatants in the camp to keep the machines supplied with wood and stones. The outworks of the castle succumbed quickly. The suburb, weakened by the continual bombardment, was destroyed and abandoned by the garrison at an early stage. The defenders of the isolated Termenet turret, frightened by the accuracy of the trebuchets, and cut off from the castle by the soldiers of the bishop of Chartres, slipped away in the night, abandoning possession to the crusaders.

In spite of their early successes, the crusaders were unable to make any impression on the castle itself. The trebuchets were only just within range of the walls and their operators had difficulty in finding the correct height. Some damage was done to the walls on the eastern side but the garrison repaired them as fast as the besiegers shattered them. Each time an assault party penetrated a breach, it found its path blocked by a makeshift barricade of wood and stone, and was forced into retreat. Moreover, the defenders had machines of their own, which they began to use to great effect. Their mangonels fired huge boulders into the crusaders' camp with results that were no doubt more psychological than practical, but nonetheless effective for that. More dangerous, because more accurate, were the ballistas, giant crossbows mounted on wooden frames which were wound back with winches to fire long bolts. The barons who required king John at Runnymede to dismiss his foreign *ballistarii* evidently had a high opinion of this weapon which recent wars had done much to justify. Professionally handled, they could be aimed with great accuracy and used to pick off individual besiegers at considerable distances, as some of the crusaders in Simon's army had discovered before the walls of Constantinople in 1204. On one occasion a bolt from a ballista penetrated Simon de Montfort's tent while he was hearing Mass and killed the soldier standing immediately behind him. On another, a boulder fired from a mangonel within the castle crushed a sapper with whom Simon was talking. Simon's attendants did not fail to point out the miraculous implications of these narrow escapes, but to the viscount himself they were a source of worry and gloom. The vigour of the garrison's resistance had not been foreseen. Each day that passed brought nearer the departure of the northern crusaders, with the prospect of a damaging psychological defeat and a second winter in Languedoc as terrible as his first. On some days Simon refused to take food and instead anxiously examined his positions, encouraging his men and pleading with northern crusaders whose thoughts were turning to their homes.

Periodically the garrison conducted carefully timed sorties to cut down straying groups of crusaders who had penetrated the abandoned suburb, or to attack vulnerable parts of the besiegers' positions. The only trebuchet which had inflicted serious damage on the castle was attacked and set alight one day by some ninety horsemen. The machine, sited on a cliff opposite the walls, was separated from the crusaders' camp by a deep cleft in the rock. The guard of more than three hundred men, which Simon had assigned to its defence, melted away on the approach of the attackers, and the trebuchet was saved from destruction only by the bravery of a single knight, William de l'Ecureuil. He held off the raiding party for several minutes while the army mounted a diversion at an exposed part of the walls. The raiders rode off and the fire was put out.

Inside the castle, though Simon did not know it, things were far from well. The defenders were well supplied with food, but water had run seriously short. Raymond de Termes's Spanish mercenaries knew that they could expect no quarter from a crusading army, and were anxious for a negotiated settlement. Towards the middle of October, Raymond offered Simon terms which fully reflected the continuing strength of the castle. He was prepared to surrender it, he said, for the duration of the winter, but Simon was to leave him in possession of the surrounding lands, and was to restore the castle itself the following Easter. The terms offered Simon scant reward for an exhausting and expensive siege which had already lasted two months. But he accepted them, and with reason. The bishop of Beauvais and the counts of Dreux and Ponthieu had told him that they had earned their indulgences and, in spite of the emotional pleas of Simon and his wife, they intended to leave on the following morning. Of the great northern host which had arrived in September, only the bishop of Chartres and his men consented to stay for a few more days.

The agreement was that Raymond de Termes would open the gates to the crusaders the next day. That night, after a prolonged autumn drought, the heavens opened. The defenders awoke to find their storage tanks filled by the heavy downpour, and the besiegers' camp already deserted by the bulk of the northern host. When Simon's marshal crossed the muddy no-man's land to receive the castle's surrender, he was greeted with an outright refusal. Simon sent the marshal back to reason with the garrison and offer them any terms they chose provided that the castle was surrendered for the winter. With him went Bernard de Roquefort, former bishop of Carcassonne, who had been a friend of Raymond de Termes, and whose mother and brother, both Cathars, were among the garrison. Two officers of the garrison who felt that their honour had been committed by the previous day's agreement, agreed to leave the castle, and surrendered themselves voluntarily. But the others were unmoved, and the siege continued. It was mid-October. The bishop of Chartres left at dawn the next morning taking his army with him. The leaves turned to deep brown. The rain became snow, and glacial winds blew it in the crusaders' faces. Shortly the mountain roads would be blocked and the bulky siege machines stranded among the remote peaks of the Corbières. Simon refused to consider raising the siege.

In November, to Simon's intense elation, a large party of crusaders arrived on foot from the German province of Lorraine. He was now strong enough to surround the castle once again. The trebuchets, whose engineers had persistently failed to get the range and height of the ramparts, suddenly found their mark, inflicting terrible destruction on the keep and the upper works of the walls. On 22nd November Simon ordered his men to construct a trench up to the walls, in the hope of finding a weak point which could be mined by his sappers. In spite of the renewed activity of the besiegers, the castle could probably have held out for a considerable time. But dysentery, the scourge of crowded, ill-drained mediaeval castles, had begun to claim victims among the garrison. There was panic at the sight of the sappers approaching the ramparts, especially as the garrison could expect no terms now that they had broken faith with the besiegers. On the night of 22nd November the garrison tried to slip away unnoticed. But in the middle of the escape, Raymond de Termes ordered his men to wait while he went back to fetch something that he had forgotten. While they waited their movements were spotted by a sentry who raised the alarm. The crusaders, roused from their beds, gave chase and killed some of the escapers, but most, lighter of foot, escaped into the dense forest. Raymond himself was found hiding in the undergrowth by a volunteer foot-soldier from Chartres. He was taken back to Carcassonne where he passed the rest of his life in a cell below the tower of the citadel.

Simon's unexpected victory gave a new urgency to the political war that the legates were still waging against Raymond VI. Raymond had been living under the threat of excommunication ever since his conflict with the legate Thedisius at the council of St.-Gilles in July. The legates had had a legal excuse to proceed against him for four months.

All that they needed was the political opportunity. As Simon de Mont-fort marched north in triumph across the Aude to the Tarn valley, receiving surrenders and taking possession of abandoned castles, Raymond invited him to a meeting. The meeting occurred at Christmas, but it was stormy. Simon noticed that the count's entourage included several men whom he believed to have betrayed his interests to the enemy. He protested vigorously. The count was evasive and the two men parted on bad terms.

Simon could afford to quarrel with the count. After the fall of Termes, Peter II of Aragon could scarcely refuse to accept him as his vassal without losing his rights of suzerainty altogether. It had become clear that if Simon was not to destroy the elaborate skein of Argonese interests in the Midi, he would have to be drawn into it as the Trencavels had been. On about 22nd January 1211, while the king was on his way to Montpellier, he was met at Narbonne by all the competing factions: Arnald-Amaury and the bishop of Uzès, the counts of Toulouse and Foix, and Simon de Montfort himself. Arnald-Amaury begged him to accept Simon's homage, and after a decent show of reluctance Peter did so. He went further. He agreed to the betrothal of his four-year-old heir James to Simon's daughter Amicia, and left James in Simon's custody as a pledge of his sincerity. Now that he had magnani-mously acceded to the legates' wishes Peter was in a position to extract concessions in other directions. He wanted Raymond VI to be recon-ciled to the church on reasonable terms. Arnald-Amaury agreed to soften his terms so far as to allow Raymond a proportion of the property confiscated from heretics, provided that he co-operated in their per-secution. In territory directly under his control, the count would be allowed to take the entire property of convicted heretics; elsewhere he would have a third or a quarter. Later the legates were to point to this offer as evidence of the magnanimous treatment that they had always accorded to Raymond VI. They had asked nothing more, they said, than that he expel the heretics from his territory. In reality there were other conditions, but these were not declared at Narbonne. They were held back, to be announced at a council of bishops summoned to Montpellier for the end of the month.

A week later, Raymond duly attended at Montpellier. In the presence of the Argonese king and a crowd of notables, Arnald-Amaury handed him a written list of the legates' demands. They were exceptionally severe. Raymond was to dismiss his mercenaries within twenty-four hours; he was to satisfy the grievances of numerous ecclesiastical landowners; and he was to withdraw his protection from Jews and from all who were designated as heretics by the church. Then followed a number of sumptuary regulations. No more than two meat dishes were to be served at the count's table, and he himself was to wear nothing but good, plain-coloured durable cloth. His castles and strongholds were all to be demolished. And the urban nobility, that strange class, unknown in the north, whose presence made the cities of Languedoc so hard to capture, was in effect to be abolished, for all noblemen of Raymond's principality were to be made to live in the country. Usurers and toll-collecters were to disappear. The army of the crusade was to be entitled to food and shelter from the count and his vassals. Finally Raymond was to enrol himself among the Templars or Hospitallers and exile himself in the Holy Land until further notice.

The count listened in astonishment as his secretary slowly read out this extraordinary document. He beckoned to the king of Aragon and begged him to listen to the 'strange commands which the legates have given me'. The more extreme of these commands may conceivably have been invented by the propagandists of the war which followed. But there is little doubt that the legates had deliberately pitched their terms unacceptably high. They did not wish to see Raymond reconciled. They were conscious of their power, and they wanted to extend it into his principality. In doing so they were prepared to give him a propaganda advantage of which he did not fail to make use. After hearing the terms read out for a second time, Raymond left the room without a word, clutching the document in his hand. He let the legates know that they would have his answer on the following day. But by the next morning he had left Montpellier without so much as taking his leave of them. He had seen a buzzard flying towards the left, it was said, and had taken it to be a bad omen.

# ✠ VIII ✠

## 1211: Triumph and disaster

'An inheritance may be gotten hastily at the beginning, but
the end thereof shall not be blessed.'

PROVERBS XX.21

On 6th February 1211 the papal legates excommunicated Raymond VI
and laid an interdict on the county of Toulouse. Messengers followed
westward in the count's tracks to enforce the traditional irritants:
silent bells, bare altars, locked churches, processions of clergy carrying
the Eucharist out of the gates of towns sullied by Raymond's presence.
In Rome, Innocent III received the abbot of St.-Ruf, who had been
sent to obtain the necessary confirmation. The legates were well aware
that their treatment of Raymond VI grossly contravened the pope's instructions, but they were fortunate in the moment that they had chosen.
Innocent was preoccupied with perils closer at hand than the Albigensian heresy. The emperor Otto, once his creature, had invaded the
papal state. The problems of the church in Portugal and England
clamoured for his attention. And there were other crusades: in the
east, and in central Spain where the conquests of the Castilian crown
were menaced by a new north African invasion. Events were crowding
in on Innocent with a rapidity that taxed his efforts to master all the
details of a complex diplomacy. Ill-informed and ill-obeyed by distant
legates with ambitions of their own, he wearily confirmed the judgement
of Montpellier.

The pope's letters of confirmation were issued in Rome on 17th
April. In Languedoc the war had already begun. Reinforced by a new
army from the north, Simon de Montfort decided at the beginning of
March to deal with Cabaret, the last remaining outpost of resistance in
the viscounty of Carcassonne. The news of his intentions was enough for
Pierre-Roger. His narrow mountain valley was surrounded by Simon's
fortresses, and the more timid of his garrison were already deserting
to make their peace with the crusaders. He summoned Bouchard de

Marly from the dungeon in which he had lain for eighteen months and proposed a bargain. He would make him a personal gift of the castle if Bouchard would undertake to see that he came to no harm at the hands of the crusaders. Bouchard, chained, unshaven, still dazed by the sudden turn in his fortunes, accepted. In a final and characteristic act of largesse, Pierre-Roger had the prisoner's hair cut and his verminous body washed in a perfumed bath before letting him leave for Carcassonne with a chestnut horse and a new suit of clothes, as he had once done, in the days of his glory, to a succession of itinerant *troubadours*. Bouchard kept his promise, for after Simon had taken possession of Cabaret, Pierre-Roger was granted a new fief in low-lying country where he would be less dangerous to the crusade. But Pierre-Roger remained an unrepentant heretic. He died in exile in extreme old age in the Aragonese territory of Roussillon.

The capture of Cabaret left Simon free for greater enterprises. In mid-March, while the abbot of St.-Ruf was still making his way to Rome, he laid siege to Lavaur, an old Trencavel fortress on the frontiers of the county of Toulouse. Lavaur was of no great strategic importance. It occupied a cul-de-sac in a bend of the river Agout, some miles from the nearest bridge. But it was notorious for its strong heretical community, which included the castellan Giraude de Laurac. Her brother, Aimery de Montréal, who was in command of the garrison, was well known to the besiegers, for he was one of those whom the crusade had ruined. In 1209 he had been the most powerful baron of the Lauragais, the seigneur of several towns including Laurac and Montréal. But he had a well-deserved reputation for fickleness, and Simon de Montfort had forced him to exchange his powerful fiefs for humbler estates further from the strategic arteries of Languedoc. After months of indecision, Aimery had finally thrown in his lot with the resistance. But he had chosen his moment badly, for the southern princes were still disorganized and Simon's strength was growing daily. The surrender of Cabaret had been most unexpected and had left Aimery with very little time to prepare his resistance.

Raymond too had been taken by surprise. He had passed the last month in an urgent search for allies. Copies of Arnald-Amaury's extravagant demands at Montpellier were circulating in the major town of his dominions and had found him indignant supporters among his own subjects. Raymond had also sent appeals for help to all the princes of the south, including Savari de Mauléon, king John's seneschal in

Poitou. Their response had been encouraging. The counts of Comminges and Foix had begun to understand that their own fate was intimately bound up with Raymond's. And Savari de Mauléon, although he had no personal interest in the affair, was a man of bellicose temperament, who had been offered a substantial reward for his services. King John, who had been Raymond's brother-in-law, was believed to have instructed him to go to the count's assistance. Whatever their motives, there was every sign, in the spring of 1211, that a formidable movement of organized resistance was coming into being for the first time in two years. Raymond was less warlike than his allies. He still clung to the hope that an open rupture with the crusaders could be avoided. Simon's army included men who had been his friends in milder times, and had marched beside him in 1209. His own cousins, Peter and Robert de Courtenay, were among them. For a while Raymond attempted to support both sides at once. He had furtively sent his seneschal with a company of knights to reinforce the garrison of Lavaur. Yet he allowed the victuallers of Toulouse to supply Simon's army, and even visited the crusaders' camp himself with a contingent of his household knights. He was received coldly. His cousins, far from helping him, lectured him on the duties of a Christian prince. The legates refused to consider lifting the excommunication, and Raymond returned to Toulouse in an ugly temper, taking his knights with him.

Although it was now clear that he would have to fight for his principality, Raymond was not yet master of his own capital. Bishop Folquet had ordered the White Brotherhood to march to the assistance of the besiegers of Lavaur, and Raymond was unable to prevent them from obeying. He rode personally into the Place Montaigon, where Folquet's militia were gathering beneath their banners, and ordered them to disband. They refused and, finding the eastern gate of the city barred by Raymond's knights, crossed to the unwalled suburb on the west and escaped round the back of Raymond's men. The count was more successful in preventing the victuallers' carts and siege engines from reaching the crusaders. But the bishop remained obstinately defiant. On 19th March, Folquet invited him to 'take a stroll' outside the city walls so that he could perform ordinations without breaking the interdict. Raymond replied with an ill-tempered message threatening him with violence if he did not leave Toulouse forthwith. Folquet refused to go and plainly hoped that the count would further strengthen the legates' hand by some rash act. But Raymond had learned that lesson, and wisely left the bishop alone. On 2nd April Folquet abandoned his protracted martyr's vigil and left the city to join Simon at Lavaur. He did not return to it for three years.

Further south, in the upper valley of the Ariège, Raymond-Roger, count of Foix, was completing the muster of his vassals. Sheltered by the truce which Peter II had arranged for him in the previous year, Raymond-Roger had suffered less than most southern princes from the depredations of the crusaders. But this fact had not softened the fierce hatred which this heavy, violent man felt for the crusade. At Narbonne in January, Simon de Montfort had offered him peace on extremely advantageous terms, which the Aragonese king had pressed him to accept. But Raymond-Roger had not accepted them, and he was the first prince to answer Raymond VI's plea for help in February. On 3rd April the truce between himself and Simon expired. A few days later a column of several hundred German crusaders were making their disorderly way from Carcassonne to Simon's camp at Lavaur when they were ambushed in the forest of Montgey by a large force of southerners under Raymond-Roger, and Simon's old enemy Giraud de Pépieux. The Germans defended themselves vigorously, but they were surprised, and heavily outnumbered. They were killed, almost to a man. Raymond-Roger and his men fled quietly to Montgiscard leaving the peasants of the surrounding villages to rifle the clothing of the dead knights and, later to face the vengeance of the crusaders.

Fifteen miles away the garrison of Lavaur, ignorant of what was being done on their behalf, were reaching the end of their resistance. The crusaders had succeeded in filling the moat with earth and brush-wood faster than the garrison could empty it again by night. On 3rd May Simon's sappers mined the wall and the town was taken by storm. The conventions of war placed the ninety knights of the garrison at Simon's mercy, and they paid with their lives for the massacre of Montgey, news of which had reached the crusaders' camp in the closing days of the siege, spiced with the rumour of atrocities common to the propagandists of every war: unarmed men brutally cut to pieces, priests killed with axes at the altars of nearby churches. Feeling was running high in the crusaders' camp. Simon ordered them to be hanged. Aimery de Montréal was taken out first, but the gibbet collapsed as he was attached to it, and rather than waste any more time, Simon had all the prisoners put to the sword. Aimery's sister Giraude was pushed screaming and weeping down a well before an emotional crowd of

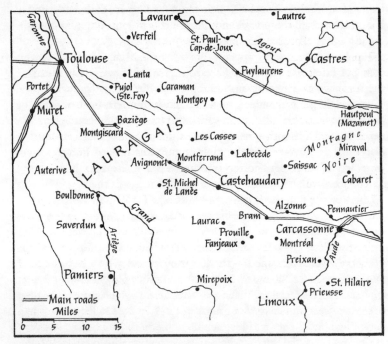

V.   Toulouse–Laurageais–Carcassonne

onlookers, and stoned to death with rocks thrown from the top. As for
the three or four hundred heretics found in the town, they were taken
into a meadow before the walls 'and there we burned them alive with
joy in our hearts'.

The booty of Lavaur was the richest since the fall of Carcassonne.
It included war-horses, valuable armour and rich clothing as well as the
wheat and wine which was found in the garrison's stores. But the
crusaders were frustrated in their hope of riches, for the entire hoard
was made over to Simon's banker, Raymond de Salvagnac. Raymond
was a Christian usurer of Cahors, then the great commercial city of
western France, whose citizens had already acquired the reputation
that was to place them with purses hanging from their necks in the
seventh circle of Dante's *Inferno*. Simon had borrowed considerable
sums from him since the previous summer. In addition to managing
the finances of the crusade, Raymond was responsible for keeping the
revenues of the Languedoc hearth tax. He it was who arranged for them

to be transmitted to Rome through the Templars in Paris, the international bankers to the monarchs of Europe. For these services Raymond received a first charge on the spoils of captured towns and even, when these proved to be disappointing, on fiefs which came into Simon's hands by forfeit. Raymond de Salvagnac was useful and trustworthy, but his trade was disdained in Simon's day, as it was in Dante's. Like many successful businessmen, he redeemed himself through his sons, who were respectable and unenterprising. One of them became a royal clerk to Louis IX; another rose to be a canon of Notre-Dame in Paris; and a third lived to sell to the king in 1261 the fiefs of Pézenas and Torves which his father had received for financing the siege of Minerve fifty years before.[16]

When Lavaur fell, the knights whom Raymond VI had sent to reinforce the garrison were found in the castle. Simon needed no other excuse to declare that the count would henceforth be treated as his enemy. Even so, Raymond hoped to avoid a war. He sent a new offer into the crusaders' camp promising to throw himself and his lands on the mercy of the legates. Some of the leaders of the crusade thought these terms reasonable, and were in favour of accepting them. But Simon's reply was to march on Montgey, which he burned to the ground in retaliation for the massacre of his German reinforcements. At Les Cassès, further south, Raymond VI's garrison surrendered and more than fifty heretics, discovered hidden in a tower, were burned alive. In mid-May, Simon reached the Roman road at Montferrand, a small ill-repaired fortress commanded by Raymond VI's younger brother Baldwyn, which surrendered to him after a short siege.

Baldwyn's role in the crusade was to be greater than the brief defence of an indefensible castle. He was allowed to depart freely with his men, swearing never to fight against the crusade again. But Baldwyn was an impulsive, rootless figure and he had already decided to abandon Raymond's cause and throw in his lot with Simon de Montfort. His defection was a considerable humiliation for Raymond VI and deeply shocking to an age which valued the ties of kinship above all others. But it might perhaps have been predicted, for although he was Raymond's brother, Baldwyn had more in common with the northerners in Simon's camp than with the coarse, cultivated aristocracy of the south. He had been born at the austere court of his uncle, Louis VII, whither his mother had fled from the malice of her domineering husband. The bookish, priestly atmosphere in which Baldwyn had passed his youthful

life could not have been more different from the court of his father
Raymond V, with its loud rumbustuous immorality. He never saw his
father, and did not visit Languedoc until after the accession of Raymond
VI in 1194, when he arrived penniless in the south to claim part of his
brother's inheritance. Raymond VI refused to recognize him as his
brother. When Baldwyn returned a few month afterwards with certifi-
cates from former courtiers of Louis VII confirming his identity,
Raymond took him grudgingly into his service. He sent him to Provence
to conduct a protracted war with the rich, unruly lords of Les Baux.
Baldwyn had distinguished himself in this war and had done grave
damage to his health in doing so. But Raymond had consistently
refused him the only mark of gratitude that he wanted, an adequate
appanage to support his status. Now, in his late forties, Baldwyn had
become resentful and bitter. His piety had always been stronger than
his brother's and his disapproval of Raymond's conduct was certainly
genuine. But there is little reason to doubt that Baldwyn's old ambitions
were in the forefront of his mind when he deserted the cause of the
Midi. If Raymond VI were deposed, he would have a strong claim on
the succession. The future, he judged, lay with Simon and the crusaders.
But, like Simon himself, Baldwyn had misjudged the future and was to
pay for it with his life.

Less than thirty miles of undefended road now separated Simon
from Toulouse. But the greater part of his army had departed for the
north after the fall of Lavaur. Rather than attack a major city with
insufficient forces, he marched north, crossed the Tarn, and occupied
the thickly wooded valleys of the eastern Albigeois in less than a week.
In June, he penetrated as far north as St.-Antonin in the southern
Quercy. Raymond VI looked on helplessly. He had shut himself in the
cliff-top fortress of Bruniquel, a few miles from St.-Antonin in the
gorges of the Aveyron. In spite of the small size of Simon's army, he had
decided to burn the castle and retreat southwards. At this point,
Baldwyn unexpectedly arrived. Raymond disliked his brother, but he
was entirely unaware that he was in league with the crusaders. Baldwyn
asked Raymond to grant him Bruniquel instead of burning it. He had
secretly explained the position to the garrison, who joined in urging
Raymond to agree to his brother's request, professing themselves
willing to serve under his command. Raymond reluctantly consented,
and Baldwyn was duly enfeoffed with the castle. But he did not throw
over his homage immediately. While Raymond departed for Toulouse,

he returned to the crusaders' camp and negotiated favourable terms for his support. Then he made his way to Toulouse in a final attempt to persuade Raymond to submit to all the legates' demands. Raymond adamantly refused. Having satisfied himself of his brother's contumacious disregard of the church's law, Baldwyn could declare his support for the crusade with a clear conscience. He rejoined Simon de Montfort and did homage to him for Bruniquel. In return, Simon promised him a share of his future conquests and a year later actually enfeoffed him with St.-Antonin, the germ perhaps of a small appanage in a rich corner of Quercy.

With most of the territory east of the Garonne in his hands, Simon had only to take Toulouse. A fresh army of German crusaders was approaching the city from Carcassonne under the command of Tibald, count of Bar, a famous soldier of whom much was expected. Simon met the Germans at Montgiscard, twelve miles south-west of Toulouse. He found Tibald eager to advance on the city which, like all northerners, he regarded as the capital of southern heresy. But there was also a deputation of citizens which had come to disabuse him of this notion, and hoped even now to deflect the crusaders from their purpose. They protested that Toulouse had always supported the catholic cause. They had even given the legates hostages for their loyalty. They reminded Simon of the help that they had given him at Lavaur. The legates could not deny that, but they demanded to know why Toulouse still recognized Raymond VI as its count, and they made it clear that only his expulsion from the city would satisfy them. 'Expel the count and his henchmen from the city, renounce your allegiance to him, and accept instead whatever lord the church may appoint in his place,' was their suggestion; 'otherwise we shall crush you and you shall suffer the fate of heretics and their protectors.' The citizens replied that they were bound to Raymond by oath, but their objections went unheard. Bishop Folquet, who was present at the interview, ordered the provost of his cathedral to leave the city with the entire clergy. They did so at once, walking barefoot in procession through the gates, and carrying the Eucharist before them.

The crusaders arrived on 16th June at the river Hers, now a dull straightened canal, then a winding stream some two miles west of the walls, which separated the patchwork of suburban vineyards and vegetable gardens from the open country beyond. Inside the city Raymond had gathered all the strength of his dominions. The counts of

Comminges and Foix had brought large mounted contingents into the city from the south, and from the east had come the frightened, resentful lords of a score of abandoned hill-towns overrun by Simon's army. The garrison, characteristically unprepared, were taken aback by the suddenness of the crusaders' arrival. The work of destroying the bridges over the Hers was only half completed. At the partially dismantled bridge of Montaudran a bloody battle took place which ended in the retreat of the defenders. Raymond's illegitimate son Bertrand, who was captured in the fight, was deprived of his showy armour and ransomed for a thousand livres.

It was an encouraging start to what proved to be a disastrous siege. Toulouse was by far the largest city which Simon had attempted to besiege. After a rash attempt to take it by storm on the first day, the crusaders had to resign themselves to a long siege. For this they were singularly ill-prepared. The walls of Toulouse were nearly three miles in circuit and Simon, in spite of his German reinforcements, did not have the strength to invest the entire city. His army lay huddled before the Château Narbonnais at the southern gate. It was repeatedly attacked by sorties from within the city, which took ungentlemanly advantage of the siesta hour. Within a few days of their arrival, the besiegers had stripped the fruit and grain from every suburban garden, and by the end of the month they were feeling the pangs of hunger. The defenders, far from sharing the hardships of their adversaries, passed freely to and fro across the bridges on the far side of the city to replenish their stores and attack the foraging parties of the enemy. In the crusaders' camp bread was sold at more than twenty times its normal price. On 29th June, after a siege of two weeks, the citizens awoke to find that the crusaders had vanished.

The attack on Toulouse had been a serious mistake, a damaging dent in the reputation which had won lesser towns to Simon's cause without a blow. It had cost Simon a fortnight's use of his precious northern reinforcements, not to speak of the heavy casualties suffered in skirmishes outside the walls. More serious, it had alienated the catholic majority of Toulouse. Simon had affronted their dignity and brutally rejected their claims on his sympathy. They had watched his men tear up their vines within sight of the city walls and cut down workers in the fields, whom their sudden arrival had trapped in the bends of the Hers. They never ceased, thereafter, to be among Raymond's strongest supporters. As for Simon, his army was demoralized, and its members ill-inclined to stay beyond their forty days. Most of the Germans were persuaded to stay on, but the count of Bar, whose lack of crusading zeal had been a great disappointment to the French, left the army in the middle of July to the jeers and insults of his own followers. Simon knew from experience that without a convincing demonstration of power, his towns would throw out their northern garrisons when they heard the news from Toulouse. As soon as the siege was raised, he marched south, deep into the territory of the count of Foix, burning deserted castles and suburbs, and uprooting vines and fruit trees from the neat, terraced hillsides. Having penetrated as far as Foix and spent eight days in laying waste the surrounding country, Simon turned north and marched a hundred and fifty miles to the other extremity of Languedoc. In Quercy, Arnald-Amaury had been active on his behalf. Several of the principal barons of the region had taken part in the abortive crusade of the archbishop of Bordeaux at the outset of the war in 1209, and these were now prevailed upon to renounce their allegiance to Raymond VI and declare their support for Simon de Montfort. Simon himself arrived in Cahors at the end of July. He received the homage of the barons and impressed his presence upon his new subjects by burning the suburbs of Caylus, still held for Raymond VI, and by marching with his army as far north as Rocamadour.

The Midi was only briefly deceived by Simon's brave show of resolution. At Rocamadour he parted company with his loyal Germans and returned to his headquarters at Carcassonne with a tiny rump of soldiers and no knowledge of what reinforcements he could expect from the north. For the first time, Raymond VI had an army to exploit Simon's weakness, and allies to overcome his own timid instinct. In the Toulousain the situation was grave. An enormous southern army, led by the counts of Toulouse and Foix and reinforced by the contingents of Gaston de Béarn and Savari de Mauléon, had already left Toulouse and was moving ponderously down the Roman road towards Carcassonne. Montferrand, the first castle in its path, had been abandoned by its northern garrison. Puylaurens in the north had expelled Simon's officers. Further east, where Simon's marshal had been sent to find help, there were disturbing signs of rebellion. Béziers and Narbonne were unco-operative, and in the entire region of the Aude, only eight hundred men could be found to come to Simon's aid. Many of these deserted on the march. Personal worries crowded in on Simon's military preoccupations. His wife was at Lavaur, now cut off by the treachery of the men of Puylaurens; his son Amaury was seriously ill at Fanjeaux, and his infant daughter was with her nurses at Montréal. None of these towns could be relied upon, and there were hints of treachery among the southerners in Simon's own entourage.

When Raymond's host had reached Montferrand, thirty miles away, Simon held a council of the leaders of the crusade to consider his next action. The prevailing view was that he should hold out against the southerners in Fanjeaux or Carcassonne until help arrived from the north. But this suggestion was vigorously contested by the English crusader Hugh de Lacy. Hugh was a man of strong ambitions and aggressive ways, faults which had already cost him his extensive Irish estates in an unsuccessful rebellion against king John. But he was an experienced soldier who had fought with Simon for longer than most of those present. A prolonged siege, he pointed out, would cut Simon off from his allies and would lose him the initiative. His subjects would interpret it as a defeat and go over to the enemy. His best course was to advance towards the enemy in the hope that they would give battle in open country, where the experienced, heavily armed cavalry of the north would have the advantage. This advice appealed to Simon's instinct, and it was accepted. Leaving a small garrison in Carcassonne, the crusaders marched west and occupied Castelnaudary, on the Roman road eight miles from the van of the southern army. Simon's force, meagrely reinforced with the reluctant conscripts of the Laurageais, amounted to little more than five hundred men. And Castelnaudary could scarcely have been worse equipped to withstand a siege. Its walls had been partially destroyed by Raymond's garrison when they had abandoned it in the spring. It had no internal water supply. Its citizens were overtly hostile to the crusade.

The promised southern host arrived at the beginning of September, 'descending like locusts upon the land and running hither and thither around the town in a show of agitated activity'. The garrison were at dinner when the southerners appeared. It took them several minutes to arm themselves, and in the meantime, the inhabitants of the fortified suburb west of the main town went over to the enemy, swarming over the walls in hundreds and jumping into the fields below. The attackers seized the advantage while they could and burst through the gates of the suburb as the inhabitants were still clambering over the walls. But having penetrated into the streets, they dispersed in different directions, and the garrison were able to drive them back to the gates without difficulty.

Raymond VI's siege of Castelnaudary was a humiliating fiasco. His army certainly outnumbered Simon's, and he very probably had the five thousand men which the best contemporary estimate attributes to him. Nevertheless he was determined to avoid a pitched battle. He did not surround the town, to the amazement of the defenders who were able to water their horses and take in the vintage under the noses of the enemy. Instead he pitched his camp on a hill to the north, and protected it with trenches and palisades so that it was hard, as one observer remarked, to tell who was besieging whom. Even when his soldiers penetrated the fortified suburb, they cut openings in the wall so that they could escape quickly if the garrison retaliated. Simon remained on the offensive throughout the siege. He massed his men outside the gates, waiting for the moment to launch sorties into the enemy's camp. Many of these raids he led in person with a recklessness which appalled his companions. On one occasion he had to be restrained from jumping a trench into the enclosure where Raymond's siege engineers were working their machines under heavy guard.

Simon's recklessness had a purpose. A stalemate, he knew, would be as damaging as a defeat, but Raymond had scrupulously avoided meeting the crusaders in open battle. After several days of indecisive skirmishing, Simon received news that seemed to offer a decisive outcome. Bouchard de Marly and Martin Algai, a Navarrese mercenary in Simon's service, had left Lavaur a few days earlier with most of the garrison and had succeeded in reaching the castle of Saissac, fifteen miles away. They avoided the hostile population of the Lauragais by taking a long, circuitous route through the Albigeois. From Saissac, they made their way down towards the Roman road and there joined forces with Simon's caravan of food-carts from Carcassonne. As they approached Castelnaudary, they found their path blocked by the count of Foix at St.-Martin-la-Lande, a small hamlet four miles from the town. Simon took a calculated risk. He detached forty knights from the garrison, nearly half his cavalry, and under cover of darkness sent them to reinforce Bouchard de Marly at St.-Martin. He warned them to prepare for battle in the morning.

When the morning came, the count of Foix summoned reinforcements of his own. In the crusaders' camp, a Mass was said, and a sermon delivered by the bishop of Cahors. Raymond-Roger of Foix drew up his troops across the road, placing his heavy cavalry in the centre, his light horse (probably dismounted) at one wing, and his infantry at the other, the time-honoured tactical formula of generals who did not know the defensive power of infantry. The crusaders, observing that Raymond-Roger had concentrated his defensive strength in the wings, charged the centre with their entire force. There was a long, sanguinary struggle in which the crusaders, having at first thrown back the southerners by the force of their attack, were slowly driven into retreat by the weight of numbers. Bouchard de Marly attempted to retreat in good order and conserve his forces. But on the other wing, Martin Algai turned and led his men in a headlong flight from the field 'We are lost,' he cried when the bishop of Cahors abused him for his cowardice. The bishop was not long in coming to the same conclusion. Taking the other non-combatants with him, he fled southwards down the Fanjeaux road.

Simon de Montfort had seen the count of Foix and his reinforcements riding out of Raymond's camp towards St.-Martin, and had waited anxiously for the reappearance of Bouchard and his company. They did not come. He consulted his men at the northern gate of the town, but their opinions were divided. Acting on instinct and on a chivalrous preference for battles over sieges, Simon decided to help his men at St.-Martin, even if it meant risking the town. Leaving five knights and most of the infantry to hold Castelnaudary he rode down the Roman road with some fifty horsemen, arriving just as Bouchard's men were abandoning the fiield. Fatally, the southerners had not pursued their beaten enemy. Many of them were mercenaries, probably unpaid, whose appetite for booty was the strongest military instinct they possessed. They were plundering the crusaders' food-train and the bodies of the dead when Simon arrived. Bouchard, seeing Simon enter the field from the west, wheeled round and returned to rejoin the fight from the east. The southerners were taken by surprise from two quarters at once and were routed with much bloodshed. The count of Foix and his son defended themselves superbly until their shields were broken and their swords notched and blunted. On both sides the casualties were heavy. Simon lost thirty of his best men. The southerners were massacred. Some of them, reduced to crying 'Montfort! Montfort!' to save their skins, were taken for crusaders and run through by their own men.

As soon as Simon had left Castelnaudary the southerners had attacked it, led by Savari de Mauléon's Poitevin mercenaries and a force of crossbowmen. They succeeded in reoccupying the suburb, but the

sudden return of the crusaders interrupted the assault and for
to withdraw in haste. Simon was in favour of pursuing them ar
ing the battle into the southern camp. But his men were ti
unwilling to hazard their victory against Raymond's trenches and
palisades. Instead they passed through the gates and dismounted at the
church to sing a *Te Deum*. Training, discipline, and skilful generalship
had won a convincing victory over numbers, and Raymond's morale was
not equal to the strain of pursuing the siege any further. His siege
engineers had reported that the soft local stone was shattering uselessly
on impact with the walls. Boulders had been brought by road from a
distance but even so only two direct hits had been scored in the course
of the siege. Some of Raymond's knights had deserted him on the news
of the defeat at St.-Martin. Others were reduced to sleeping in their
armour for fear of a sudden attack on the camp. On the second night
after the battle the southerners set fire to their siege engines and left.

Yet Simon's cause was far from won. To attempt the conquest of a
quarter of France on an acre of the Toulousain plain was to snatch at
shadows. In the idealized world of the *chansons de geste* kingdoms might
be won by the chivalry of the battlefield but the population of Languedoc
was less easily impressed. There was also a psychological war, and
Simon lost it. The count of Foix, who had taken the direction of
affairs out of the hands of the hapless Raymond, sent messengers
throughout the region announcing Simon's defeat. The French had
been massacred, it was said, and Simon hanged. Hostility to the crusade
turned into open rebellion. Simultaneous risings on the Tarn and the
Aveyron were sparked off by a carpenter of Lagrave, who felled the
captain of the garrison with an axe as he was inspecting some new
water casks. The rebellion spread downstream with the news. This was
a region which Simon had occupied only four months earlier. His power
there was only skin deep, and the northern presence amounted to little
more than the garrison of Bruniquel under Baldwyn of Toulouse.
Baldwyn was at Montégut (now Lisle-sur-Tarn) when the rising
occurred. He marched immediately to Lagrave while the citizens were
repairing their defences. Seeing the golden cross of Toulouse on his
banner they mistook him for his brother, opened the gates to him, and
gave him an excited account of the murder of the garrison commander.
Baldwyn turned on them and massacred them. But while his back was
turned Montégut and St.-Antonin joined the rising and he was obliged
to withdraw to Bruniquel, leaving a small garrison in Lagrave. Further

south, the rebellion had spread to several castles of the Pyrenean foot-hills, and even to Saverdun, one of the first towns which had accepted Simon's rule in 1209.

Simon reacted to the news with a fortnight of frenzied activity. He razed the fortifications of Castelnaudary to the ground and penetrated by forced marches first into the eastern Corbières and then north across the Laurageais towards the Tarn. But before he had reached it, he learned that his cause there was lost. The garrison of Montégut, besieged in the citadel, had surrendered to the citizens. The crusaders turned back and shut themselves in Pamiers while the armed bands of the count of Foix patrolled the valleys around. Simon was saved from further humiliation by a mild winter, and the arrival of a hundred experienced knights recruited by Robert Mauvoisin in northern France. They helped him to recover some rebellious castles in the southern marches of his dominions; but he had lost all the towns which the year's early victories had brought him, except for Lavaur. Like the carpenter of Lagrave, he had come to regard this war as a national war. He no longer believed that the south could be rallied against the Albigensian heresy. In October, he was even deserted by William Cat, a southern knight who had stood godfather to his daughter and fought beside him at Castelnaudary. The blow was said to have left him with a profound hatred and distrust of all who spoke the *langue d'oc*. He did not intend to rely on them again.

# ✠ IX ✠

## 1211–1212: The conquest of the south

'And we took all his cities at that time; there was not a city which we took not.'

DEUTERONOMY III.4

Simon lacked the crust of cynicism that would have shielded others from such disappointments. He was an earnest, introspective man. The oppressive loneliness of his two years in Languedoc easily showed itself in testiness, and intolerance of friends and enemies alike. To his subordinates he was scrupulously correct. He remained with them when they were in danger, consulted them at every stage, and listened to their advice. But he remained distant and taciturn. He had commanded a succession of forty-day armies and had become indifferent to individuals. He had few close friends. Robert Mauvoisin, who had undertaken difficult missions on his behalf in Rome and Paris, was his closest political adviser. But Robert was often away on official business, and his health was failing. Simon came to depend increasingly on others, often priests like Guy, bishop of Carcassonne, who, as abbot of Vaux-de-Cernay near Montfort-l'Amaury, had persuaded him to join the original expedition of 1209. He relied heavily on his family. At Christmas 1211, Simon was unexpectedly joined at Castres by his brother Guy, a man who shared his restless ambition but lacked his earnestness, and came to understand better than Simon the complexity of Languedoc's politics. Guy had accompanied his brother on the fourth crusade, and had shared his disgust at the spectacle of the siege of Zara. Both brothers had made their way to Syria by way of Italy, but Guy had stayed there and had achieved the ambition of many a landless younger son by marrying a lady of greater position than his own, Heloise of Ibelin. Heloise belonged to the royal family of the kingdom of Jerusalem, but the kingdom of Jerusalem in 1211 was little more than a name. Guy no doubt felt that his prospects would be brighter in Languedoc. In this he was cruelly deceived. But his arrival was welcome to Simon, particularly as several towns had surrendered to him on his way from the coast.

After Christmas 1211, Simon attempted to restore his fortune in the western Albigeois, between the Tarn and the Aveyron. The count of Toulouse had spent the entire autumn in this region, and had recovered every stronghold but Bruniquel, which his brother Baldwyn still held for the crusaders. The campaign was a damaging failure. Raymond's army followed Simon everywhere, refusing to give battle but falling on stragglers and foraging parties. Simon's communications caused him difficulties. In a region of steep river gorges, the southerners controlled every crossing of the Tarn west of Albi. Food ran short in the crusaders' camp. The fields were bare in mid-winter, while the food stores of the walled towns were filled with the yield of the autumn harvest. A month was wasted in the fruitless siege of St.-Marcel, an important Cathar refuge north of the Tarn. By Easter 1212, Simon had achieved nothing but the capture of two isolated castles.

The fortunes of the crusade now hung on the eloquence of a handful of preachers who were then completing their winter tour of the northern provinces. But in Spain an unforeseen calamity had occurred which was to jeopardize all their efforts. In the summer of 1211 the Almohade vizir an-Nasir invaded Castile with a huge north African army; in September the fortress of Salvatierra fell after a two-month siege and northern Spain lay open to the Moslems. Emotion ran high in France, for Salvatierra was a fortress of the military order of Calatrava, which had close links with the Cistercians. A Castilian crusade was proclaimed in January 1212. Arnald-Amaury, who had now had himself elected archbishop of Narbonne, undertook to lead the French volunteers across the Pyrenees. The Castilian king, Alfonso VIII, sent his personal physician to recruit crusaders among the nobility of western France, while the archbishop of Toledo actively preached the holy war at the French court. In spite of the indifference of Philip Augustus to the fate of Spain, many of his subjects took the cross against the Moors. Languedoc, it was true, was nearer and less dangerous and its climate more temperate. But Spain was rumoured to be fabulously rich, as any knight who had heard the *Chanson de Roland* knew; and Alfonso VIII openly held out the prospect of a rich booty to those who took part. This unexpected competition can scarcely have been welcome to Simon. Nevertheless his chief military engineer, the archdeacon of Paris, had gone north in October to devote himself to the more spiritual business of preaching the Languedoc crusade. The bishop of Carcassonne was already there, and a number of northern clerks had also volunteered their services, including Jacques de Vitry, the Augustinian canon from the diocese of Liège, whose use of jokes and stories, a technique not yet learned by St. Dominic, represented a revolution in the art of preaching. In time the stories were to become conventional, and collections of them were made which other preachers plagiarized. But they were fresh and entertaining in 1211, and persuasive, for many of those who heard them were later found in Languedoc.[17]

The year 1212 witnessed the last spontaneous outburst of crusading enthusiasm in western Europe. In addition to the official crusades in Spain and Languedoc and the continuing appeal for immigrants in the Latin empire of Constantinople, there was the extraordinary episode of the Children's Crusade to draw attention to the rise of eschatological hysteria among the poor. The Albigensian crusade had its own share of these low-born volunteers with more enthusiasm than training. Their presence was reflected in a higher proportion of foot-soldiers than had been usual in previous years, and in the number of those who arrived without any arms at all. These unarmed hangers-on had become a serious hindrance to the Middle Eastern crusades. Determined attempts, not always successful, had been made to exclude them. But in Languedoc they seem to have been accepted willingly enough. At least one town, St.-Antonin on the Aveyron, was captured by their efforts. Among their superiors, the recruitment campaign was more successful than anyone had anticipated. The preachers were particularly fortunate in Germany, where they did not have to compete with the canvassers of the Spanish crusade. The provost of Cologne cathedral took the cross with his brother, the count of Berg; with them came William, count of Julich, and Leopold VI of Austria.[18] But there were important contingents from northern France as well, petty seigneurs of the Auvergne and an army of Normans and Champagnards who arrived with the archdeacon of Paris in April. Smaller groups appeared at irregular intervals throughout the summer, some of them coming from Italy and the Italian colonies on the Dalmatian coast. Their hardships began long before they reached Simon's camp. They were instructed to go first to the headquarters of the crusade at Carcassonne, whence they were directed to the field of operations. But they had no maps, and even local troops had been known to lose their way in the narrow valleys of the Montagne Noire. Straying crusaders who fell into the hands of the count of Foix were killed or mutilated. Exhaustion, hunger, and the merciless summer heat claimed their own victims. In August, heavily laden recruits were fainting by the roadsides north of Carcassonne. Simon's wife, riding past on the way to join her husband, rescued some of them and carried them pillion into the camp.

At the beginning of April the crusaders captured Hautpoul (now Mazamet), an important crossroads which secured the communications between Carcassonne and the plain of the Albigeois. The garrison fled by night under cover of a thick mountain mist, and the crusaders rose in the morning to find the castle open and empty. It was the turning point of Simon's fortunes. During the next month he was joined by no less than three new armies, from Auvergne, Germany, and northern France, and was able to consider conducting two campaigns at once. Guy de Montfort was placed in command of the Normans and Champagnards and sent south to invade the county of Foix. They took Lavelanet by storm and massacred the population; after this they were able to pass effortlessly through the count of Foix's dominions, wasting the land and destroying the villages and towns which they found abandoned in their path. Simon, accompanied by the Germans and Auvergnats, invaded the Laurageais, the region which he had won and lost in the previous summer. The campaign was a triumphal march. No one dared to resist him. Raymond VI, who had shut himself in the castle of Puylaurens, fled with his army as soon as Simon approached, and his subjects followed his example. St.-Michel-de-Lanès, one of the few towns to offer any resistance, was levelled with the ground.

In May, Simon returned to the Tarn, where Raymond had twice thwarted him. Most of the towns in this region belonged to the count's private demesne, and six of them had been named by the council of Avignon in 1209 as notorious citadels of Catharism. This time, Raymond was not there to defend them. Simon's camp was filled with deputations from towns anxious to submit to him on any terms he chose to impose. A year before, Simon would have accepted these offers at once. Now he had learned that fear was the only guarantee of loyalty in towns that wanted only to be left alone. When the citizens of St.-Marcel came to throw themselves on his mercy he reminded them that they had defied his army for a month, earlier in the year, and refused to listen to them. Later, Simon found the town deserted. He pulled down the fortifications and set fire to the wooden houses. Laguépie, a few miles away, suffered the same fate. At St.-Antonin Simon refused to negotiate with the

garrison. When the barbicans were stormed by a leaderless mob of unarmed poor in the crusaders' camp, he had the commander of the
town taken to his already crowded cells beneath the citadel of Carcassonne. Some townsmen tried to escape by swimming across the Aveyron, but they were caught and killed. The others, who had taken refuge
in the church, would have suffered the same fate had Simon not been
persuaded that a populous town was worth more than a charred wasteland.

Simon left Baldwyn of Toulouse to complete the conquest of the
Aveyron valley. He himself marched into virgin territory in the Agenais
to the west. The Agenais was the most recent addition to Raymond's
mosaic of territories. He had acquired it from Richard Cœur-de-Lion
in 1196 as the dowry of his fourth wife, Joan Plantagenet. Heresy had
never prospered in the provinces of the Plantagenets. Although a
Cathar bishop of Agen had been appointed in 1167, there is no trace
of his activities, and in 1210 Innocent III himself had remarked on the
absence of Perfects. Probably they had fled at the time of the ill-fated
expedition of the archbishop of Bordeaux in 1209. Nevertheless, Simon

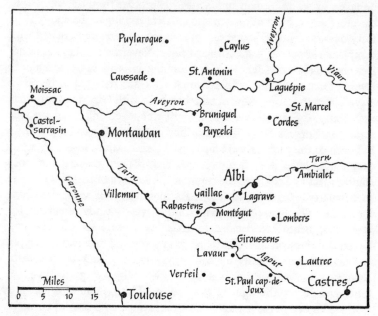

VI.   Albigeois–southern Quercy

had an acceptable excuse for invading the Agenais; it was among the richest parts of Raymond's demesne and the bishop, who was anxious to throw over Raymond's sovereignty, had invited the crusaders to take possession of it.

The Agenais was a region of strong castles, as befitted a territory which had been the frontier between France and England and was to be again. Most of them had been abandoned on the news of Simon's approach, and only one was prepared to put up any resistance on behalf of Raymond VI. This was Penne d'Agenais, a rock fortress on the river Lot whose defences had only recently been modernized by that master of fortification, Richard Cœur-de-Lion. It had a newly drilled well, two forges, a bakery and a windmill, and a commander, Hugh of Alfaro, who had every reason to defy the crusaders. He was a Navarrese mercenary captain of exactly the kind whose dismissal had been demanded by the church; his wife was an illegitimate daughter of Raymond VI. Accordingly he had taken in provisions on the news of Simon's approach, and hired four hundred Spanish mercenaries. The siege began on 3rd June. As soon as it was clear that Penne would not be taken by storm, Simon summoned his brother from the south with the other army. Most of his own troops were coming to the end of their forty days, and polite invitations to stay longer had been greeted with complaints about the state of their health. Nevertheless Simon did not lack men. New crusaders were still coming into his camp and a substantial force under the archbishop of Sens was reported to be on its way. The archdeacon of Paris, who had been with Guy de Montfort in the county of Foix, designed the largest trebuchet which had yet seen service in Simon's army. This machine did some damage to the keep, but even so the garrison were far from the end of their resistance when they surrendered after a seven-week siege. They realized that they could expect no help from the count of Toulouse, and they did not care to be martyrs for a cause which Raymond himself seemed to have forgotten. The great southern coalition was already breaking up. Gaston de Béarn had decided to make his peace with the crusaders. Savari de Mauléon had quarrelled with Raymond and had kidnapped his young son as security for the 10,000 livres of back pay which he claimed was owed to him. The count was obliged to go to Bordeaux to recover his son through the good offices of king John. How much of this was known to the garrison of Penne is unclear. But as mercenaries under the ban of the church they knew that it was wise to negotiate while they still had a strong hand. On 25th July they marched out of the castle under a safe-conduct, leaving the crusaders masters of the Agenais.

Ten days earlier, on the southern face of the Sierra Morena, the army of another crusade had shattered the power of the Almohades at the battle of Las Navas de Tolosa, and turned the destiny of Spain.

Simon had not forgotten the trouble which his own mercenaries had caused him. His first action after the fall of Penne was to march on Biron, the castle of Martin Algai, where a personal vendetta had to be settled. Martin Algai's career could stand for many of its kind.[19] He was a Navarrese, like most of the celebrated mercenary captains of southern France, a man of low birth, little piety, and strong superstitions whose brutal, aggressive reputation had penetrated the songs of the *troubadours* in his own lifetime. Such men made their living by hiring out bands of professional soldiers under their own command to whoever could afford them. Martin's band was not large, but it had brought him wealth and, which he no doubt valued more, social position. In about 1206 he had married into the Gontaut family, thereby acquiring the castle of Biron in western Quercy. And with his new status had come the social obligations which underlined it: Martin became a regular benefactor of the Cistercian abbey of Cadouin and probably intended to be buried there. He had served many masters. He had fought for Richard Cœur-de-Lion in Aquitaine, and served briefly as king John's seneschal in Gascony and Périgord. Then, in 1211, he had joined Simon de Montfort's service, only to betray it by fleeing at the critical moment from the battlefield of St.-Martin-la-Lande. Martin did not have the face to return to Simon's army, so he made his peace with Raymond VI and retired to Biron. Biron was only twenty miles from Simon's camp at Penne. At the end of July the crusaders appeared there in force and almost immediately took the outer wall by storm. Martin's garrison, who had taken refuge in a tower, were glad to deliver up their master in return for their own lives. He was handed over to his erstwhile employer and peremptorily told to confess his sins. Then he was drawn round the walls behind a horse, and hanged from a gibbet at his own gates.

Only two towns of any importance still resisted the crusaders in northern Languedoc, Moissac and Montauban. Both were major road junctions commanding river crossings which Simon would need to control if he was to keep possession of the Agenais. Montauban was the more important of the two, but the long circuit of its walls may have

deterred Simon from attempting to besiege it with his shrinking army.
The crusaders therefore made for Moissac, and arrived there early on
the morning of 14th August, as the monks of the great Benedictine
abbey were emerging from terce.

The journey from Biron crossed the most abrupt dividing line in the
landscape of Languedoc, the fifty-mile stretch of the river Garonne
from Agen to Caussade which separates the great Toulousain plain
from the last outposts of the Massif Central. Mediaeval men were not
insensitive to landscape. A priest in Simon's camp could speak lyrically
of the broad valley of the Lot below Penne, 'the distant expanse of
prairie, the rich mantle of cultivated fields, the luxuriant vines, and the
wonderful invigorating air in plains criss-crossed by beautiful streams
and rivers'. But the love of mountains belongs to another kind of
romanticism. The hills of Quercy mean more to us than they did to an
age which imagined the Garden of Eden as a flat cultivated plain, and
called the gentle valleys of Burgundy 'those terrible places' fit only for
the most austere of all monastic orders.[20] For the crusaders, who had
passed most of the summer in the parched forests of the Causse de
Limogne, the Garonne valley was a promised land. They feasted on
the yield of the orchards and vineyards. Baldwyn of Toulouse dined on
goose and roast capons. Yet this terrestrial paradise was man-made,
the creation of long years of ecclesiastical peace which the church itself
was now violating. Two centuries earlier, most of it had been covered
by thick forest crowding in on scattered islands of cultivation. The
lines of poplars which now hold the banks of the Garonne and stabi-
lize its course, are the contribution of the eighteenth century. The
twelfth century created the open fields, and neat, cultivated terraces.
The religious orders, the Benedictines of Moissac and the Templars
and Hospitallers of Toulouse, had bought out the smallholders,
driven back the forest, and recreated the *villae* of Roman times. Only
the church had the capital and the longevity to complete such ambitious schemes. 'We found this place a deserted wasteland, and it had
been a wasteland for many years,' the Hospitallers declared in 1195 of
the village of Lacapelle. But now it was populous and rich. The explo-
sive increase in the population of the south, which had created a new
class of rural poor, had fed these settlements with rootless immigrants.
Towns expanded from small villages like Castelsarrasin, or arose out
of empty fields like Montauban, founded by the count of Toulouse in
1144. Villages like St.-Nicholas de la Grave, facing Moissac across the

confluence of the Tarn and the Garonne, had been created from nothing by the Benedictines. Its plan, dull and rectangular, with straight, regular streets and houses built on identical plots, still bears witness to the conscious planning which gave birth to it.

Moissac itself was a creation of its abbey, albeit a more leisurely creation. Like Pamiers and Agen, it was owned jointly by the abbot and the count of Toulouse, an unsatisfactory arrangement which was the source of continual disputes at Moissac as it had been elsewhere. Only days before the arrival of the crusaders, the abbot had been on the point of setting out for Paris to take his complaint to the king, when Raymond's men had confiscated his papers and taken away his baggage. The citizens sided with the count. They preferred to be ruled at a distance. They expelled the abbot from the town as the crusaders approached, and replaced him by a force of three hundred mercenaries, who rang the bells of the churches incessantly to demonstrate their contempt for the interdict. Raymond VI had sent some knights to reinforce them, but he himself was still detained at Bordeaux, trying to rescue his son from the clutches of Savari de Mautléon. He made no attempt to relieve the town.

Moissac was built on low ground, but it had high walls and was vigorously defended. Until the crusaders were reinforced, halfway through the siege, they were unable to surround it, a weakness which the garrison put to good use by occupying a hill west of the walls. From here they were able to launch raids on the crusaders' camp and fire bolts into the crowd gathered to hear the bishop of Carcassonne preaching. The arrival of the bishop of Toul with a new army from the north put an end to these activities. But the crusaders failed to take the place by storm. The archdeacon of Paris applied himself to the construction of larger siege engines, and 'cats' were built in the hope of mining the walls. The besiegers suffered heavy casualties from the crossbowmen on the walls. A bolt struck the saddle of the chronicler Peter of Vaux-de-Cernay as he was urging on the siege engineers, to his great indignation. Another killed a gentlewoman in the suite of Baldwyn of Toulouse. Simon himself was injured in the foot while helping to repel a sortie. A nephew of the archbishop of Rheims, who had been captured and taken within the walls, was hacked to pieces and shot out of the town from mangonels. In the camp, priests processed barefoot among the tents, carrying their reliquaries and singing the *Veni Creator Spiritus* 'so loud that it could be heard a league away'.

The siege greatly disturbed the towns of the surrounding region. They wanted only to be left in peace, but they knew that if Moissac fell they would be called upon to choose one of two lords and expose themselves to the fury of the other. Montauban decided to hold out for Raymond and sent raiding parties to harass the crusaders at Moissac. At Castelsarrasin, which was nearer and weaker, the fighting had provoked vigorous debate. Their garrison, commanded by Giraud de Pépieux, had abandoned them to their fate, and they reasoned, according to William of Tudela, that the count of Toulouse was unlikely to recover his towns unless the king of Aragon helped him or the pope called off the crusade. In either of these events they would have to reconsider their position, but meanwhile they were 'anxious not to be massacred'. One of them quoted an adage to the effect that only a fool abandons the safety of the shore to save a drowning man. They sent a deputation into Simon's camp with an offer of submission, and their example was followed in every other town of the region except Montauban.

The news of these happenings set the citizens of Moissac at odds with the garrison. The crusaders' machines had already destroyed part of the wall. An assault was thought to be imminent. The garrison consisted largely of mercenaries who knew what fate they could expect at Simon's hands, and intended to resist to the last man. But the citizens knew that the vintage was approaching and they wanted to take it in themselves. They sent emissaries to offer the town to Simon in return for their lives. These terms were accepted. The townsmen opened the gates to the crusaders and the garrison, including Raymond VI's knights, were all put to the sword. The abbot, who had been in the besiegers' camp for most of the siege, received his reward. His rights were confirmed and those of the count of Toulouse were transferred to Simon de Montfort. But the abbot came to think no better of the new lord than he had of the old. The citizens had paid Simon a hundred gold marks to protect their houses from pillage, but the abbot had not been a party to this transaction and the crusaders had no compunction about sacking the monastery. No sooner had Simon left than the abbot wrote a bitter letter of complaint to Philip Augustus.

Moissac had held out for long enough to save Montauban. The son of the count of Foix had now entered the town with a hundred knights, and the preparation of the defence was well advanced. It was clear that a major siege would be required, and the middle of September was too late in the year to undertake one. Moreover, Simon had other plans. He was being pressed by the abbot of Pamiers to march on Saverdun, a town which had expelled the crusaders a year before and had taken to raiding the abbot's lands. He also hoped to complete the isolation of Toulouse before the onset of winter by invading the county of Comminges in the upper valley of the Garonne.

Simon's sudden reappearance in southern Languedoc after an absence of nearly a year gave a sharp jolt to the local garrisons. He arrived to find that Enguerrand de Boves, his commander in the region, had already taken Saverdun with the help of some German crusaders who had recently arrived. The counts of Toulouse and Foix had been in the town, but they had fled on Enguerrand's approach. The collapse of resistance in Comminges was equally rapid. Muret, the northern gateway to the county, was strong enough to hold out until the arrival of reinforcements from Toulouse, only twelve miles away. But no reinforcements came, and the inhabitants fled after setting fire to the wooden bridge over the Garonne. Simon swam the Garonne with a few companions and extinguished the fire. A characteristic incident revealed the uncommon powers of leadership which had already won him so much with such small armies. Although the river was in flood, the bulk of the army, including almost all the cavalry, had swum across by nightfall. But the others were unable to swim, and pitched their tents on the opposite bank where they were in danger of being attacked by raiding parties from Toulouse. Most of them were lightly armed foot-soldiers and camp-followers of little consequence. But Simon, overruling the strong objections of his marshal, swam back across the river and waited with them until the bridge could be repaired. Several days were lost. But the delay cost Simon little. Before he left Muret the bishops of Comminges and Couserans arrived to welcome him. They had arranged for most of the baronage of Comminges and Béarn to meet Simon at St.-Gaudens and transfer their homage to him. Without striking a blow, Simon had achieved the ambition of every count of Toulouse in two centuries. He had reduced the petty Pyrenean kingdoms of Foix and Comminges to a handful of remote fortresses in the southern highlands.

All Languedoc was now in Simon's hands except for the large but isolated cities of Montauban and Toulouse. As a conqueror, he had found his strongest ally in the anarchy of Languedoc; as a ruler he intended to bring it to an end. He had already enfeoffed many of his northern followers with the castles abandoned or lost by the enemy. But their status, like Simon's own, remained uncertain, and their obligations to their subjects and to Simon himself had yet to be defined. Arnald-Amaury had known from the beginning that the Midi would need to be recast in a northern mould. This lesson had not been lost on Simon. In November at the close of the campaigning season, he summoned a 'parliament' to meet him in the hall of his castle at Pamiers. Who attended this parliament is not recorded. But we may assume that Simon's enemies were not included and therefore that the southern nobility were under-represented. The southern bishops, however, were there in force, and so were the representatives of the towns. The outcome of the meeting was the appointment of a commission of twelve, whose task it was to draw up a new code of laws. The twelve were carefully chosen. They included four ecclesiastics, four crusaders, and four southerners (two knights, and two bourgeois). What part Simon himself played in their deliberations cannot now be known, but the Statute of Pamiers, which he solemnly approved on 1st December 1212, reveals on every page the fine balance of interests on which he would depend for his control of Languedoc.

The church was handsomely rewarded for its support. It received a guarantee of its many immunities and privileges, and the promise of effective action against heresy. The punishment of heretics was the business of the church itself, but the secular power undertook to deliver up those who were caught and to confiscate the property of those who were not. Even repentant heretics were to be excluded from public office and could be required to live in a place designated by Simon himself. Attendance at Mass on Sundays and feast-days was made compulsory, particularly in the case of the seigneur and his wife who might be fined if they absented themselves. As for the bourgeois of the towns, they were equally favoured, for the petty nobility, still implacably hostile to the crusade, could scarcely be destroyed without their support. Serfs were to be free to emancipate themselves by migrating to the towns, a privilege unthinkable in the north but one which the south had long accorded them in theory. Other clauses gave effect to principles on which the church and the towns had long been agreed: justice to be administered free, recent toll-gates to be removed, seigneurial taxation to be severely curtailed.

Those southern landowners who remained in possession of their fiefs were permitted to observe the uses of the Midi as they had always done. But for others, the uses and customs of the region of Paris were to prevail. This meant that there were to be limits to a landowner's freedom to divide up his property on his death or alienate it to the church. Such limits were essential if Simon's power was not to be eroded as the power of the Raymonds had been. The church cannot have been pleased by the restrictions on alienation in mortmain, but doubtless it swallowed its objections in the face of military necessity. Military necessity was indeed the essence of Simon's problem. The Raymonds had been unable to extract knight service from their vassals and had been driven to employ mercenaries instead. Simon, however, required his vassals to attend when summoned and to furnish him with the number of knights which was specified for each fief. Moreover, for the next twenty years, these knights were to be northerners. If their castles passed into the hands of their widows or daughters, then those ladies were to marry northerners, or at least southerners who met with Simon's approval. Simon's followers had come as conquerors, not as immigrants. They were a tiny minority in a conquered land, and they had already taken on the enclosed mentality of a beleaguered garrison.

# 1212–1213: Muret

'There is no king saved by the multitude of an host; a
mighty man is not delivered by much strength.'

PSALMS XXXIII.16

Simon de Montfort had conquered Languedoc, but he had not proved
his right to rule it. The legates wanted to make him count of Toulouse,
and his heirs after him, and they had been pressing Innocent III to
sanction the change ever since the formal excommunication of Raymond
VI in 1211. But there were difficulties. Raymond was a vassal of the
French crown; only the king of France could sanction his removal,
and Philip Augustus had shown no inclination to do so. He had always
distrusted the crusaders, and when they invaded the county of Toulouse
in 1211 he wrote testily to the pope to point out that he did not propose
to let the church choose his vassals for him. Innocent replied with
soothing evasions, but instructed his legates that the territories conquered from Raymond VI were on no account to be assigned to anyone
else. They were to be held in trust for 'whoever shall be found entitled
to them', a purposely vague phrase which Innocent persistently refused
to clarify. The following summer, he went further. While Simon's army
was sweeping unopposed across northern Languedoc, Innocent
addressed to his representatives a short lecture on canon law. Raymond,
he reminded them, had not yet been convicted of heresy, still less of
murdering Peter of Castelnau. And even if he had been, it would be
necessary to prove some crime against his heirs before the principality
could be transferred to another dynasty. The existence of the son destroyed whatever hopes Simon may have had of replacing the father.

The rights of the young Raymond found other defenders, for his
uncle was king John of England, and his wife was a sister of Peter II of
Aragon. Peter returned from the campaign of Las Navas de Tolosa in
the autumn of 1212 to find the count of Toulouse waiting for him with
the news of his brutal expropriation. Peter was Raymond's kinsman,

but ties of kinship alone would not have persuaded this shrewd and ambitious politician to intervene in the county of Toulouse. The reduction of Raymond's principality to Toulouse, Montauban, and a handful of highland fortresses threatened to put an end to Aragonese influence on the northern slopes of the Pyrenees. Particularly infuriating was Simon's invasion of Foix, Comminges, and Béarn, for all these territories were fiefs of the Aragonese crown. So long as the crusade had remained a pious venture, Peter had tolerated it, albeit with ill grace. But now it had become a private war to create a principality for Simon de Montfort. As one of the victors of Las Navas, Peter felt that he had some claim on Innocent III's sympathy. At the end of the year, he despatched the bishop of Segorbe and one of his royal notaries to Rome to remonstrate with the pope and persuade him to suspend the crusade.

After Christmas 1212, Peter crossed the Pyrenees. Having worked closely with Arnald-Amaury on the Las Navas crusade, he had high hopes of an agreement. But Arnald-Amaury was not encouraging. He promised no more than that if Peter reduced his demands to writing, the council of bishops which was about to meet at Lavaur would consider them. Peter framed his demands with studious moderation. He hoped, he said, that the bishops would have mercy on Raymond VI, who was ready to undergo any penance that might be required of him, even a penitential crusade in Spain or the Holy Land. But if they could not bring themselves to be merciful, then let them at least recognize the rights of his son. In the case of the counts of Comminges and Foix and the viscount of Béarn, Peter was on firmer ground. As their suzerain he demanded the restoration of their lands. Somewhat disingenuously, he denied that they were heretics, or even protectors of heretics; but if anything could be proved against them, he undertook to see that they made restitution and submitted themselves to the penance of the church.

The council of Lavaur considered these requests and replied with an uncompromising refusal. They rehearsed the story of the legates' dealings with Raymond VI, omitting, it is true, the controversial matter of their demands at Montpellier. Against the count of Comminges they could find only the vaguest grounds of complaint. But they had no difficulty in proving that the other two, if not actually heretics, were certainly sympathetic to heresy and violently anti-clerical. Only a few months earlier, some mercenaries in the pay of Gaston de Béarn had sacked

Oloron cathedral and conducted a vile parody of the Mass from the high altar. If the three Pyrenean princes submitted to the church and sought absolution, they would 'receive justice', but what that justice would be, the fathers of Lavaur were unwilling to say. Peter II continued to negotiate with the bishops until it became clear that they had no intention of allowing any of the southern princes to remain in possession of their dominions. He asked them to agree to a truce until Easter or Whitsun. But the bishops would not hear of it. They were afraid that the news of a truce would dampen the enthusiasm of the fresh crusaders who were now being recruited in the north. Having obtained nothing from the legates Peter had to decide whether to defy them or admit that his demands had been mere bluff, a decision made the more difficult by the fact that his six-year-old son James was still in the hands of his prospective father-in-law, Simon de Montfort. Nevertheless, he broke with the crusade. Brushing aside a ringing warning from Arnald-Amaury, he returned to Toulouse and formally took Raymond's territories under his protection. In February he returned to Spain to raise an army, leaving a small guard of Catalan knights in Toulouse. His last action before leaving was to 'defy' Simon, a formal act of great legal consequence which indicated that the relationship of lord and vassal was now at an end. Simon's messenger, sent to remonstrate with the king at Perpignan, was arrested and thrown in prison. It was a declaration of war.

At Lavaur, the assembled bishops were nervously composing a letter of self-justification to the pope. The legates knew that Peter was in high favour at the Lateran, and they had not forgotten how Innocent had humiliated them in 1210. They lauded the achievements of the crusade so far, but they emphasized how much remained to be done. They thundered against the faithlessness of the citizens of Toulouse. They added new accusations to Raymond's already formidable catalogue of sins, even alleging that he was in league with the emperor Otto and the Almohade king of Morocco. They begged the pope not to be persuaded by specious arguments to throw away the triumphs of the crusaders 'achieved by the shedding of so much Christian blood'. Individual bishops added pleas of their own. The archbishop of Arles and his suffragans compared Toulouse to Sodom and Gomorrah. The bishop of Béziers associated the young Raymond with all the sins of his father. All these letters, together with a bundle of *pièces justificatives*, were confided to the legate Thedisius, the archdeacon of Paris, and three others, to be carried to Rome. Before they left, the legates were approached by two emissaries of Raymond VI with a new offer of submission. But they were not prepared to be side-tracked. They replied that the count had already had opportunities enough to justify his conduct. He could state his case to the pope. In the middle of February, Thedisius and his companions left for Rome.

Events had already overtaken the slow machinery of mediaeval diplomacy. Peter II's ambassadors reached Rome first, and had already secured an audience with the pope while the bishops assembled at Lavaur. Both ambassadors were experienced and persuasive diplomats. They explained the military situation to the pope, and pointed out that heresy had long ago ceased to be the principal target of the crusade. Instead the holy war had been turned into an instrument of Simon's ambition and greed. Raymond of Toulouse had been denied absolution in scandalous breach of ecclesiastical law solely in order to excuse the invasion of his dominions. Béarn, Comminges, and Foix, Simon's latest conquests, were catholic territories: did Simon not recognize as much himself when he accepted the homage of their populations, 'unless by that act he intended to make himself a protector of heretics'? The ambassadors insisted that the spiritual objects of the crusade had been achieved; heresy had been eradicated. Any further military operations could only be at the expense of good catholics, and of the other crusades in Spain and the Holy Land. Innocent was persuaded. 'You, archbishop,' he wrote to Arnald-Amaury, 'ought to have been content with the spoliation of heretics, instead of which you have robbed loyal catholics of their land and . . . unashamedly usurped the domain of the count of Toulouse.' To 'our chosen son', Simon de Montfort, he was equally brutal. 'The king of Aragon has informed us that you have turned the crusade against the faithful, shedding the blood of innocent people, . . . and appropriating the lands of his vassals while he was fighting the Infidel.' Since Peter II was minded to continue the war against the Moors, Simon was to desist from attacking his territory in future and was to restore everything that had already been conquered in Béarn, Comminges, and Foix. As for the count of Toulouse, the legates were to canvass the opinions of the bishops and magnates of Languedoc, and send their conclusions to Rome for his personal decision. Meanwhile, there were more urgent tasks for Christian chivalry than the subjugation of Languedoc, and the crusade was accordingly suspended.

The pope's pronouncement was received with jubilation at the Aragonese court. The bishop of Barcelona was immediately sent to Paris to carry the news to the French court where, it was hoped, Innocent's bulls would have a sobering effect on the preachers of the crusade. Paris was still ignorant of the pope's decision. The bishops of Toulouse and Carcassonne had been active on Simon's behalf throughout the winter. In spite of the French king's unconcealed dislike of crusades, they had persuaded his eldest son Louis, now twenty-five years old, to lead an expedition to the Midi. The favour of the heir to the throne was worth more to an ambitious knight than that of an ageing parsimonious king, and Louis found an army of volunteers almost at once. On 3rd March 1213 the two southern bishops attended a meeting of the royal council in the capital, at which the departure of the expedition was fixed for 21st April. The euphoria of the French court was interrupted by the arrival of the bishop of Barcelona and his attendants. But the bishop was not as successful as his master had hoped. Unfortunately no authenticated text of Innocent's bulls had been available at the time that he had left Spain, and so he had had to make do with some letters from various Catalan bishops, vouching for their existence. These were circulated at court but did not have the impressive aura of the originals. It was king John who saved Raymond in 1213 as he had done in 1207. Philip Augustus suddenly decided in March to exploit John's difficulties by invading England. He proposed that Louis should lead the invasion and receive the conquered country as an appanage. The muster planned for 21st April was therefore transferred to Rouen and the army of Languedoc directed to the Channel ports. A small force of crusaders was raised by the bishops of Orléans and Auxerre, but any hope that they would be followed by others was dashed by the unexpected successes of king John and his ally the count of Flanders. In May the French failed to take Ghent and their armada was burned by the English at Damme. Philip gave orders that none of his vassals were to go to Languedoc. Shortly afterwards the English-born cardinal Robert Curzon arrived from Rome to preach a new crusade in the Holy Land. The preachers of the Albigensian crusade were peremptorily instructed to devote their talents to the liberation of Jerusalem. The heretics of the Midi were forgotten.

The result of this succession of misfortunes was that Simon de Montfort was left with no more than his small permanent army, and was unable to lay siege to either Toulouse or Montauban. Guy de

Montfort besieged Puycelci in June with the small contingent brought by the bishops of Orléans and Auxerre, but when their forty days were done, the siege had to be abandoned. Simon wandered aimlessly through the Toulousain with the rest of his army, levelling abandoned castles, uprooting fruit trees, and destroying the crops. Toulouse itself was crowded with hungry, embittered refugees. Disarmed mercenaries, landless aristocrats, and the peasant farmers of fields of charred stubble blocked the streets with their cattle and carts full of belongings. By night they slept out in the cloisters of the abandoned monasteries of the city. By day they raided the outlying country, falling on isolated groups of crusaders with the ferocity of men who had nothing to lose. At the end of June the citizen militia stormed the small castle of Pujol, ten miles from Toulouse, where three of Simon's knights had established themselves. The knights took refuge in a tower, and were offered their lives if they surrendered, but when they were brought back to Toulouse an angry mob broke into their prison, dragged them through the streets from the tails of horses, and hanged them from gibbets outside the city gates.

On 24th June the crusaders gathered at Castelnaudary to witness the knighting of Simon de Montfort's eldest son Amaury. For Simon, this was a moment of more than passing importance. The desire to found a dynasty was very strong in his nature, as it had always been in those rootless societies founded by the knightly adventurers of Simon's world: Outremer, Sicily, Norman England. Heredity was a symbol of permanence, treasured most by newcomers. The dubbing of a knight marked more than his admission to a military caste; it associated him with the conduct of his father's affairs, affairs which would one day be his own. Therefore that retentive autocrat Philip Augustus had postponed his son's knighthood until his twenty-second year and even then had imposed a variety of niggling conditions. But Simon needed his son. He also had an eye to the propaganda value of the ceremony, a solemn assertion that knighthood was an order of the church, and that the war in Languedoc was a holy war. He had tents erected for the spectators in a meadow outside Castelnaudary and an altar placed in an open pavilion at the summit of a hill. Here the bishops of Orléans and Auxerre stood, splendidly robed, while Amaury was led before them by his father and mother to be presented with his sword and belt from the altar. The surrounding clerics broke into the *Veni Creator Spiritus*. Amaury turned to receive the homage of the crusaders as his father's heir. Peter of Vaux-de-Cernay, who watched the ceremony and wept, thought its religious overtones a wonderful innovation. In reality it marked another stage in the process which was transforming knighthood into an institution whose significance was ceremonial, not military, another instrument in the propaganda of war. Amaury was abruptly immersed in the duties of his status. Simon enfeoffed him with the lands beyond the Garonne, and ordered him to conquer those which still held out.

The lands which Simon granted to his son were among those which the pope had ordered him to restore to their southern lords. But exactly a month before, Innocent had revoked his bulls in language as stern as that which he had earlier addressed to Simon and Arnald-Amaury. Simon had a diplomatic triumph as well as a family occasion to celebrate at Castelnaudary. The five emissaries of the council of Lavaur had arrived in Rome in March and had been accorded a frosty audience by the pope. Peter II's ambassadors were still in the city, and it is a measure of their influence that Thedisius and his companions took nearly two months to change Innocent's mind. They protested that he had been misled. The work of the crusade, they pleaded, was far from done. Toulouse and Montauban and the mountain fastnesses of the Pyrenees still sheltered defiant communities of heretics, subjects of the southern princes whom Peter II was now protecting. The Aragonese ambassadors vigorously denied this and an acid debate continued throughout the spring against the background of Rome's grandiose Easter festivities. Both sets of ambassadors were repeatedly summoned to the pope's presence and the issue was discussed at length in the college of cardinals. The impossibility of conducting such a delicate political exercise at a distance was never more obvious, but Innocent eventually decided to believe Thedisius. In a curt letter, which even omitted the customary opening greeting, he accused Peter II of deceitfully playing on his ignorance. 'We are astounded to learn of the lies by which your ambassadors obtained bulls from our hand in favour of the counts of Comminges and Foix and Gaston de Béarn.' If those princes had really been faithful catholics they would have sought absolution and reconciliation with the church; but none had done so. Therefore the threat of dispossession must remain over their heads. Protectors of heretics, the pope declared, were more dangerous to the faith than heretics themselves. Innocent forbade the Aragonese king to interfere with the crusade, but he did not give Simon all that he wanted. Although the pope refused to restore their lands to the counts of Toulouse, Comminges, and Foix, he would not grant them to Simon de Montfort either. Instead he announced that he would shortly be sending a new legate—there were already five—to consider the grievances of the southern princes, and impose a political settlement on the province. This was a major, and to Simon an extremely unwelcome, concession to Peter II. Moreover, having suspended the crusading indulgences at a particularly damaging moment for Simon, Innocent would not now restore them. He hinted at the possibility of new indulgences in the future, if the Cathars continued to defy the crusade. But of these nothing more was to be heard. Since Simon had conquered almost all of Languedoc, Innocent no doubt felt that he could make do with the troops that he already had. The pope was too absorbed in the preparations for a new Middle Eastern crusade to allow a rival to flourish in France. In September, as Peter II was marching on Muret, Innocent was writing to the dean of Speyer cathedral instructing him to divert all potential crusaders from Languedoc to the Holy Land.

Only one thing was clear after the pope's repeated changes of mind, and that was that the king of Aragon was forbidden to interfere with the crusade on behalf of the dispossessed princes of the Midi. As soon as Simon received the full text of the bull, he sent two priests to Spain to bring it to the attention of Peter II and to enquire whether he proposed to comply with it. Peter was evasive, but his intentions were obvious. He had reinforced his small garrison in Toulouse and summoned his vassals to meet him in arms. His shrinking demesne, already heavily mortgaged to Jewish and Moorish bankers, was further encumbered with debt. Everywhere, active preparations were being made for the invasion of Languedoc. The Midi was tense. Peter was rumoured to have an enormous host of mercenaries at his disposal. Messengers from the count of Toulouse arrived in most of the walled towns summoning the citizens to throw out their garrisons. Some of them did so. In Toulouse, the dwindling band of *troubadours* who still clung to the faded court of Raymond VI wrote *sirventès* in honour of the king whom they expected 'to fill the fields with helmets and hauberks, lances and fluttering banners; to raise the pride that has perished at the hands of the French freebooters; for justice is our companion and destruction shall be theirs.'

In the first few days of September Peter II crossed the Pyrenees by the narrow defile of the Venasque pass. Simon had withdrawn all his garrisons from the district west of the Garonne, and the Aragonese were fêted in every town they came to. Volunteers flocked to join their ranks. A few miles from Toulouse they joined forces with the smaller armies of the counts of Comminges and Foix, and with an enormous mob of militiamen from Toulouse. These last were not highly regarded as soldiers, but they had brought with them provisions, arms, and six siege engines in a fleet of barges which they towed upstream from Toulouse. On 10th September, the entire horde arrived beneath the walls of Muret where thirty French knights and a small force of foot-soldiers were holding the citadel for Simon de Montfort. The strength of the southern army gave rise to the customary hyperboles, particularly among northern chroniclers who were anxious to demonstrate beyond doubt that God had supported his own in the battle which was to come. But spread across the marshy flats before Muret they certainly looked more impressive than they were. The great majority of them were infantry whom snobbery and military incompetence combined to exclude from active participation in the battle. Peter II's Spanish cavalry numbered eight hundred, and a further two hundred were expected imminently; the Languedoc contingent cannot be estimated but may possibly have included six hundred horse. The total mounted strength of the southern coalition was therefore about twice that of the crusaders assembled forty miles away at Fanjeaux. Of the Spaniards many were veterans of Las Navas, and they had no doubt of success. But the citizens of Toulouse were less confident. They knew Simon's resilience and they were terrified of his vengeance.

Simon was well informed of his enemy's movements. One of Peter II's messengers, carrying a suggestive letter to a lady of Toulouse, had been intercepted by his men. Simon was already on his way to Muret with some seven hundred horse when a rider brought him news that the southern host had besieged the town. His original intention was to ride through the night to reach the beleaguered garrison by morning. But he was restrained by his men, who were tired, and by a strong clerical contingent—seven bishops and three abbots—who hoped that Peter II might still be persuaded to abandon his allies. The prelates insisted on waiting at Saverdun while a request for a safe-conduct was sent to the king's camp. But Peter's reply was that priests who travelled with armies did not need safe-conducts; and the optimistic plans of the bishops had to be abandoned. The crusaders rose at dawn on the

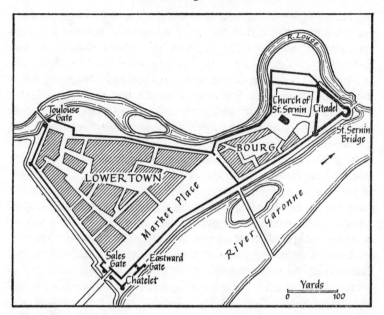

VII.  Muret in 1213

following morning, 11th September. The seven bishops gathered in the darkness of the castle chapel and solemnly pronounced the excommunication of the leaders of the southern army, by the flickering light of their candles. Below the walls of the castle, the army was forming up in three battle squadrons, a precaution against ambushes.

The delay at Saverdun almost cost them Muret. On the afternoon of the 11th, the southerners decided to assault the walls. The Toulousain militia, who had pitched their camp by the Garonne, west of the walls, bombarded the lower town from the west and north until the tiny garrison were forced to withdraw to the upper town. The Toulousains assaulted the battered walls and invaded the lower town, furiously pursuing the crusaders through the streets and killing several of them. In the midst of the chaos, Simon's army appeared on the Saverdun road, on the far side of the Garonne. Panic seized the ill-trained militiamen. From where they were they could easily have held the wooden bridge over the Garonne. But instead they withdrew in confusion to their camp, and Simon crossed into the town without resistance. For the lack of an adequate chain of command, an opportunity had been lost, but the Toulousains did not fail to give their retreat a strategic excuse. Peter II, it was said, wanted to allow Simon into the town so that he would be trapped and captured there with his entire army.

Yet this hasty rationalization of an undignified flight came near to being justified by events. The southerners did not know that there was only one day's food in the citadel. The town, for all its natural strength, could not have survived even the shortest siege. Simon knew that he had only twenty-four hours to defeat in battle an army vastly stronger than his own. The bishops saw another escape. They had no confidence of victory in battle against the hero of Las Navas de Tolosa, and they proposed another attempt at negotiation. As a good catholic, Peter II might be moved by the words of the legates; the Toulousains, they thought, might be persuaded by their bishop, Folquet, who was with the crusaders in Muret. Two priests were found to act as ambassadors, but they obtained nothing more than respectful platitudes from the Toulousains, and the king dismissed them from his presence. The two priests passed the entire night in the enemy camp and returned to the town before dawn the next morning, 12th September. They found the bishops installed in the priory of St.-Germer, in a state of extreme agitation. The king had refused to allow a truce for further negotiations. But the bishops, in desperation, resolved to send a new party of priests barefoot into his camp to beg him to abandon God's enemies. The priests left at dawn. The Toulouse gate was left open for their return in the belief that Peter would not dishonour himself by attacking an open town in the hour of negotiations. But this belief proved to be unfounded. No sooner had the priests left than a party of southern knights crept up the walls and briefly erupted into the lower town, while the Toulousains let loose a hail of boulders and arrows against the north-west corner of the walls. Some of the boulders landed in the priory of St.-Germer, where Simon was conducting an anxious conference with the bishops. They wanted to wait for the return of the barefoot ambassadors; but Simon was impatient to attack the Aragonese while they were still unprepared. The bishops gave way, and the barefoot ambassadors were abandoned to their fate.

The crusaders had been reinforced in the night by the viscount of Corbeil, who had brought a handful of northern knights from Carcassonne. Their total strength now amounted to about eight hundred horse and an insignificant number of foot-soldiers. Simon ordered them to muster in the market place, in the south-west corner of the town, and await his instructions. He himself returned to the castle to arm himself. In the castle church, the bishop of Uzès was saying Mass. Simon lingered briefly in the darkened church and then walked out on to the castle terrace in full view of the besiegers, where an equerry was waiting with his horse. A stirrup strap broke as he mounted, and there was a cacophony of whoopings and jeerings from the other side of the river Louge. In the market place, the bishop of Toulouse, dressed in robes and mitre, was haranguing the crusaders. He promised the glory of martyrs to those who fell in battle, and held up a crucifix for their adoration. Simon de Montfort's oration was more prosaic. He ordered his men to charge in compact lines, and not to dissipate their strength in hand-to-hand fighting. Three squadrons were to be formed, the first under William of Contres, the second under Bouchard de Marly, and the third a reserve under Simon's own command. The army filed out through the Sales gate and round on to the path that led east along the bank of the Garonne. Crossing the Louge by the St.-Sernin bridge, they found themselves facing the lines of the Aragonese army across a mile of flat scrubby plain.

In the southern camp all was not well. The leaders of the coalition had risen early and attended Mass. But Peter II, a notorious womanizer, had passed the night with one of his mistresses, and was so exhausted that he was unable to stand upright during the reading of the Gospel. There had been an acrimonious council of war at dawn. Simon's intentions were unknown. Raymond VI wished to avoid a battle altogether. He proposed to fortify the camps with palisades, as he had done at Castelnaudary, and repel the crusaders with crossbows if they attempted to force a battle. Simon could be starved out at leisure. The Aragonese knights in Peter's suite guffawed at this plan: 'Is the king of Aragon to dishonour himself by the kind of cowardice which has brought you to your present pass?' Peter rejected Raymond's suggestion as unworthy of a knight. Raymond retired, humiliated, to sulk in his tent, while the king and the count of Foix drew up their troops in the north of the plain. Peter chose a strong position at the summit of a gentle rise, with his right flank protected by a stream, and his left by a broad marsh. A sound tradition placed the commanders of armies in the reserve, so that their men would not be left leaderless at the first charge. Simon had respected it. Peter did not. He exchanged his distinctive armour for that of an ordinary knight and placed himself immediately behind the front line. It was a pointless vanity, but a common one, which fifty years later was to destroy the cause of Manfred of Hohenstaufen on the battlefield of Benevento.

Peter had the advantages of numbers and terrain, but he exploited neither of them. Each knight was allowed to place himself in the line, with his equerry and mounted sergeant. A confused mass of horsemen, without infantry, without orders, waited for the French charge. The result was a rout, not a battle. Simon's first squadron charged a mile across the plain and struck the Spanish cavalry with overpowering

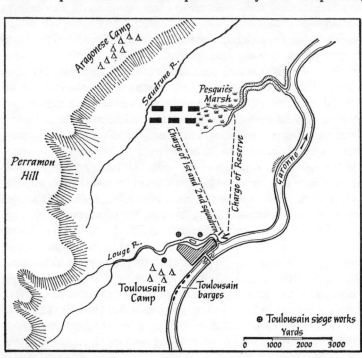

VIII.  Battle of Muret

violence. The Catalans were thrown aside 'like dust before a gale', and as they fell back on the second line, another northern squadron hurled itself into the gap. The young Raymond, watching from the Perramon hill, remembered many years later a noise like the hewing of a forest of trees, mingled with the confused war-cries of 'Comminges!', 'Aragon!', and 'Montfort!' Peter II was trapped in the thickest of the fighting and was struck to the ground, crying out 'I am the king!', but too late to be spared or taken alive. By now Simon himself had joined the mêlée with the reserve, picking his way along a path across the marsh and falling on the Spanish left. In the midst of the fighting Simon's stirrup strap broke again but he held off his assailants with his fists for long enough to recover his balance and the use of his sword. The entire Spanish line had broken up, and as the news of Peter's death spread, they turned and fled headlong towards the Perramon hill, pursued by most of the French army. The battle had lasted scarcely twenty minutes. The French foot-soldiers, who had stayed behind to hold the town, swarmed across the plain to finish off the wounded and plunder the dead. Simon sought out the body of Peter II and found it already stripped naked by pillagers.

The militia of Toulouse, serenely ignorant of the massacre of their allies, had launched an assault on the western wall of the town. Bishop Folquet, who had seen the rout from the citadel, sent a messenger to warn them to submit before the victorious crusaders returned from the battlefield. He gave the messenger his cowl as proof of the authenticity of the message. But the Toulousains could not believe that they were lost; they snatched the cowl and beat the messenger out of the camp with it. The bishop's news was confirmed too late by the sudden appearance of Simon and the reserve. The Toulousains fled in all directions but were easily caught and run through by the mounted crusaders. Many flung themselves into the river and were drowned in the fast current. A handful of them reached the barges moored by the Garonne, and they were almost the only survivors of the great host of militiamen which had left Toulouse three days earlier. For the city, it was a political and a social disaster. Nearly every household mourned a member of the militia. The consuls had to set up special tribunals to hear the mass of litigation between the heirs of so many unexpected dead.[21] For Aragon too the defeat was a terrible blow. Their king had been killed fighting against a French crusade only a year after leading a Spanish one to victory. Peter had been sacrificed to the northern ambitions of his dynasty at a time when the defeat of the Moors had opened up unparallelled opportunities in the south, to be exploited by an energetic leader; but Peter's heir was only six years old and he was a hostage of Simon de Montfort in the citadel at Carcassonne. Simon himself had reached the height of his fortunes.

On the day after the battle, the bishops addressed a circular letter to all Christendom, hailing it as a miraculous victory against over-whelming odds. It was true that the southern army had been vastly larger than the French, but the battle of Muret was not a miracle. Peter had dispensed with the services of almost all of his infantry, and his cavalry probably outnumbered the crusaders by no more than two to one. He had refused to wait for the two hundred horse under Nuño Sanchez and Guilhem de Moncada, whose arrival was expected within a few hours. He had not even waited for Raymond VI's contingent, which had therefore taken no part in the battle. The despised militia of Toulouse were confined to their camp, at the far end of the plain.[22] The battle was that rare perfection imagined by the authors of the *chansons de geste*, a conflict on flat ground between opposing lines of cavalry. It was a fine feat of northern horsemanship, but it went far towards demonstrating the uselessness of such feats in all but the most artificial conditions. The impressive strength of massed infantry as a defence against cavalry charges had been repeatedly demonstrated in the Middle Eastern crusades, and in Anglo-Norman battles such as the famous victory of Henry I of England at Brémûle in 1119. Forty years before Muret, the infantry of Milan had succeeded in repelling for several hours the heavy German cavalry of Frederick Barbarossa, after their own cavalry had fled. Renaud of Boulogne was to prove the same point at Bouvines in the following year. Peter would have done well to learn this lesson. But to the audiences of the *chansons de geste*, Milan was a synonym for wealth, not tactical wisdom. Mediaeval armies did not study battle plans. They did not attempt to absorb the experience of the past, or even of their own contemporaries. The troops may often have been professionals, but the commanders never were. The age of the professional career general begins in the fourteenth century, and in Italy, not France. Their predecessors were men of limited vision and no learning, stronger on strategy than tactics, and inclined to erect snob-bery into a military virtue. Their limitations should warn those who seek to make a 'science' of mediaeval warfare on the basis of lessons learned and mistakes corrected.

# 1213–1216: Judgement in Rome

*'Surely the land on which thy feet have trodden shall be thine inheritance.'*

JOSHUA XIV.9

The body of Peter II was carried back to Toulouse after the battle, to find a temporary resting place in the priory of the Hospitallers of St. John. Raymond VI had already fled to the safety of the city walls, and he was followed at a short distance by the dejected refugees of the battlefield, including the counts of Comminges and Foix. But Simon de Montfort did not pursue him. Why he failed to follow up his victory by marching on Toulouse is far from clear; but his force was small, and the true extent of his victory may have taken some time to dawn on him. The opportunity, once lost, could not be regained by negotiation. The bishops in the crusaders' camp offered to reconcile the city to the church in return for the surrender of two hundred hostages, but the Toulousains, having offered sixty to begin with, finally recovered their nerve and refused to deliver any hostages at all. Instead they joined with the counts of Comminges and Foix in throwing themselves on the mercy of the pope, in the hope that he would be more lenient than his legates.

They were not disappointed. Innocent had no intention of allowing the chance of the battlefield to disturb the due processes of law. To the evident irritation of his legates in France, he appointed Peter of Benevento, an Italian cardinal and a canon lawyer of no political experience, as his special emissary in Languedoc. Peter was the sixth legate to be appointed since the beginning of the crusade, and Innocent was determined that he should not become one of Simon de Montfort's partisans, as all his predecessors had done. He was therefore given the most precise instructions. In them, Innocent announced that he intended to lay the whole Albigensian imbroglio before the ecumenical council which he had summoned for the following year. Meanwhile

Peter of Benevento was to absolve all the southern princes and the citizens of Toulouse, but he was strictly forbidden to make any permanent arrangements for the province. The most that he might do was appoint a temporary administrator of the conquered territory. Toulouse itself was to be placed under the protection of the Holy See, and 'on no account to be molested by Simon de Montfort' until the decision of the great council was made known. In effect, Innocent wanted the various contestants to freeze their positions exactly as they were on the eve of Muret, until the complexities of the legal position could be resolved.

Peter of Benevento followed his instructions to the letter. In April 1214 the archiepiscopal palace at Narbonne was the scene of an orgy of contrition as the counts of Comminges and Foix, followed by the cities of Narbonne and Toulouse and Raymond VI himself, came forward to renounce their evil ways and receive absolution at the new legate's hands. The counts of Comminges and Foix each surrendered a castle as an earnest of good faith, and the count of Comminges also offered one of his younger sons as a hostage. Raymond VI surrendered the Château Narbonnais of Toulouse, and promised to go into temporary exile abroad while his claims were considered by the church. Meanwhile, the southern princes were left with nothing but the hope of mercy from an ecumenical council which had yet to meet.

Since Simon was in physical control of the province, this was probably as reasonable a compromise as could be attained. But there was one class of men whom no compromise could satisfy. The *faidits* were the large petty aristocracy whom the crusade had dispossessed and replaced by northern fiefholders. At each advance of the crusading army, these men had either fled to Toulouse or held out in their fortified hill-villages, waiting for help that never arrived. Either course lost them everything they had, as Simon's invincible army reduced every pocket of resistance between the Tarn and the Pyrenees. Their large families of co-owners, dependants, courtiers, and hangers-on followed them into penury. A thousand noblemen were condemned to wander penniless across a land which they had once ruled, sang an unnamed *troubadour* bewailing the death of Raymond-Roger Trencavel in 1209; and a thousand nobles, the poet added, meant a thousand ladies, a thousand tradesmen, and a thousand courtiers ruined. 'Ah Lord! How low we have fallen.' Of the four munificent courts to which Raimon de Miraval had directed his accompanist, Saissac and Cabaret now belonged to

Bouchard de Marly, a petty seigneur from the Ile-de-France who was related to Simon's wife; Minerve had seen its proud independent lords 'resettled' on low-lying land near Béziers; the fourth, Aimery de Narbonne, had saved his skin only by allying himself with the crusaders; and the *troubadour* himself had lost his castle at Miraval and fled to the protection of Peter II of Aragon, who was now dead. Simon could make no concessions to these men without dispossessing his own followers. All that Peter of Benevento could do for them was to allow them to wander in peace, on condition that they bore no arms, rode on cobs not coursers, and kept out of walled towns. Even so, they formed a dangerous, irreconcilable class whose strength was by no means spent.

In February 1214 they had scored a notable triumph. On the night of the 17th, as Baldwyn of Toulouse was sleeping in his own castle of Lolmie in Quercy, his bedroom was quietly locked from the outside. Traitors opened the castle gates to a force of mercenaries gathered beneath the walls under the command of a local *faidit*. The small northern garrison was surprised and overpowered. Baldwyn, who was found asleep in bed, was seized and carried off in triumph to Montauban to await the count's pleasure. Raymond had his brother hanged. The sentence was carried out forthwith by the count of Foix in person, assisted by his son and an Aragonese knight who had not forgiven the death of Peter II. It was Raymond's last act of revenge for the blow which fate had dealt him, for now he had himself become the most august of the *faidits*. After his submission to Peter of Benevento in April, his once great principality had been reduced to nothing. Even his palace in Toulouse, the Château Narbonnais, was held for the church by bishop Folquet. The count lived for a while in the house of a rich citizen of Toulouse, with his son and their respective wives, both Aragonese princesses. Shortly afterwards they all fled to England where they lived in such penury that Innocent had to pay the count's expenses in travelling to Rome for the ecumenical council.

Innocent's intention in sending Peter of Benevento to Languedoc was to call a halt to Simon de Montfort's conquests. Now that the southern princes had been reconciled at Narbonne, he saw no reason why peace should not return to the province after five years of continuous warfare. Simon thought otherwise. He wished to present a *fait accompli* to Innocent's great council which would make it impossible to restore Raymond VI or his son to any part of their dominions. Innocent was far away. During the winter, the bishop of Carcassonne and the arch-

deacon of Paris had suborned Robert Curzon, the legate responsible
for preaching the Middle Eastern crusade in the north. Setting aside
the pope's instructions, Robert permitted Jacques de Vitry and others
to revive the preaching of the Albigensian crusade. The armies of
northern crusaders began to reappear, not perhaps as large as the great
hosts of 1211 and 1212, but large enough to secure Simon's grip on the
Midi. The first of them was led by Robert Curzon in person, who
passed the summer in Simon's camp presiding over a succession of
sieges and burning heretics found in the keeps of captured castles.

Simon was now in practice count of Toulouse, even though he
might style himself 'controller' (*dominator*) in the official documents.
As such he inherited the ambitions and the problems of his predecessors. At least one of the ambitions was gratified in the summer of
1214, when his son Amaury married Beatrice of Burgundy, the heiress
presumptive of the rich province of the Dauphiné, north of Provence. If
Simon could consolidate the scattered rights of the house of Toulouse
in Provence, he would be well on the way to becoming one of the
strongest territorial princes in France. The problems were less tract-
able—bands of unemployed mercenaries, rebellious barons, self-
governing towns. The count of Valentinois had fought in the original
crusade of 1209, but he was no more inclined to submit to Simon's
authority than to Raymond VI's. The count of Rodez was trying to
transfer his homage from the house of Toulouse to the king of England.
In Périgord, Bernard de Cazenac and his terrible wife, 'that new
Jezebel', terrorized the middle valley of the Dordogne, raiding monasteries and exacting protection money from villages by the threat of
wholesale mutilations.

These were old problems, only briefly abated by Simon's arrival.
Bernard de Cazenac might be dispossessed in 1214, but he had recovered his smaller castles within a year, and by 1218 he was able to
bring a small army to the assistance of Raymond VI. Government by
continuous show of force was clearly unsatisfactory, and if the flow of
crusaders were to dry up, would become impossible. Simon's larger
plans depended on the use of the considerable territorial power of the
church as a counterpoise to the strength of the baronage. Innocent III
certainly helped him by ruthlessly removing bishops whose hearts were
not in the cause. In one year, 1211, Innocent dismissed two archbishops
and three bishops, replacing most of them with Cistercians or northerners.
The aged bishop of Carcassonne, whose relatives had fought Simon at

Termes and Toulouse, was summarily replaced by Guy of Vaux-de-Cernay, a Cistercian abbot fromthe Ile-de-France, friend of Simon de Montfort, and uncle of the venomous official historian of the crusade. Arnald-Amaury himself replaced the archbishop of Narbonne. The legate Thedisius became bishop of Agde. Three successive bishops of Béziers were associates of Simon de Montfort. The new bishops proved to be invaluable auxiliaries. It was the bishop of Rodez who had invited Simon to intervene in the Rouergue, just as the abbot of Pamiers and the bishops of Cahors and Agen had earlier invited him into their own dioceses. And it was to the bishop of Rodez that Simon confided the castle of Sévérac which he had captured from some *faidits*. This was a shrewd policy which Simon followed on other occasions. The Château Narbonnais at Toulouse was garrisoned by the bishop; the castle of Foix was assigned to the abbot of St.-Thibéry, who in turn entrusted it to one of his martial nephews. Elsewhere Simon earned the favour of the bishops by recovering for them the rights which lay landowners had usurped in more than a century of southern anarchy. Fifteen lay seigneurs restored impropriated tithes to the bishop of Béziers in the first six months of 1211 alone. Such acts, which filled the record-books of the region while Simon ruled it, represented a major shift of the balance of power in Languedoc. In the independent minded, self-governing towns, the bishop could be a terrible scourge of the consuls, and was far more likely to have Simon's interests at heart. Nîmes refused to recognize Simon as the successor of Raymond VI and closed its gates in his face; Simon replied by granting his rights over the town to the bishop.

Half a century earlier, the same policy had been attempted, without much success, by Raymond V. One reason for its failure then was that the bishops had had quarrels of their own with the counts of Toulouse. Simon may have felt that his status as the church's 'chosen son' protected him from such squabbles, but he was quickly disillusioned. He found his claim to the duchy of Narbonne disputed by none other than Arnald-Amaury, who asserted that the duchy belonged by right to the archbishop, and claimed it for himself. The citizens of Narbonne, who had only submitted in 1209 in order to escape the fate of Béziers, were delighted to exploit this division in the ranks of their northern conquerors. When Simon tried to enter the city with his army in the spring of 1214, he was briskly repelled by the militia, a humiliation from which he was still smarting a year later. All of this must have made it plain to Simon that as commander of the crusade, he could claim the loyalty of catholics, but as ruler of Languedoc he could not.

The gravest threat to his power in 1214 came from the western marches of his territory bordering on the still-powerful empire of the Plantagenets. In 1214 king John had been reconciled to the church and the five-year interdict which had dislocated his dominions had been lifted. His principal concern was now to recover Normandy from Philip Augustus, and with this in mind he had constructed a formidable coalition of Philip's long-standing enemies, including the count of Boulogne and the emperor Otto IV. John landed at La Rochelle in February 1214 and planned to march on the Loire provinces, while Otto was simultaneously to invade France from the north. John's preparations, however, were considerably further advanced than Otto's. Why not employ his spare time restoring the count of Toulouse to his possessions? The young Raymond was, after all, John's nephew, while Simon was a northerner who had demonstrated his loyalty to Philip Augustus, and lost his English estates in consequence. The title 'earl of Leicester', which Simon still employed in official documents was a continuing reminder of his old quarrel with king John. Another was Simon's occupation of the Agenais, over which John claimed special rights. The Agenais had been an English territory until 1196, when it had been ceded to Raymond VI as the dowry of his fourth wife, Joan Plantagenet. John felt that it should pass to the issue of the marriage, the young Raymond, and not to a northern freebooter whose closest links were with England's enemies. No doubt his irritation had been fanned by Raymond's ambassadors, who are known to have been active at John's court since 1212. But how closely Raymond was involved in John's coalition is impossible to say. All that is known is that John was paying subsidies to Raymond even before his flight to England, and that he had actively encouraged the barons of the Agenais to rise against Simon de Montfort.

Simon was well aware of the threat and passed the spring and summer of 1214 cautiously shadow-boxing with the English king. In April, John marched to La Réole on the marches of Aquitaine. Simon's frontier fortress of Marmande, only twelve miles away, promptly went over to him, and was reinforced by a small English garrison under John's chamberlain Geoffrey Neville. Six miles upstream, another frontier fortress at Mas d'Agenais expelled its northern garrison; boats made their way from La Réole, to prevent Simon from fording the river, to retake it. At this point Simon was summoned to the presence of the legate at Narbonne. By the time he returned in June, the rebellion had spread throughout the frontier area and had found powerful allies among the local baronage. But John himself, the principal pillar of the rebellion, had gone north to coerce Philip Augustus's vassals in Poitou; his chamberlain, who was ill-prepared for a siege, hastily withdrew. Leaving a new garrison in Marmande, Simon turned north to besiege Casseneuil on the Lot, a powerful fortress-town whose defenders had been promised help by the English king. John appeared menacingly near Périgueux with an army that included several of the Languedoc *faidits*, and the crusaders waited apprehensively for his descent. But the king hung fire. He informed the legate Robert Curzon of his rights over the Agenais. But before Robert could reply, John's attention had been diverted to the north, where prince Louis was threatening his position in the Loire valley. Simon proceeded in peace with the siege of Casseneuil. On 18th August he bridged the moat with a huge wooden belfry tower, and took the town by storm in the eighth week of the siege. By this time the threatening situation in France had suddenly been transformed. John's Poitevin allies deserted him early in July, thus forcing him to withdraw in fury to La Rochelle.[23] Two weeks later Philip Augustus inflicted a crushing defeat on Otto's Anglo-German army at Bouvines in Flanders. The fate of the English in France was sealed for more than a century. As far as Simon was concerned, the discomfiture of king John meant that he could conduct an autumn campaign on the Dordogne without interference from the west. For the rest of Languedoc, Bouvines was an event of incalculable moment. It ended any hopes that Raymond VI may still have entertained of being replaced on his throne by an outside power. And it ensured that the ultimate beneficiary of Simon's labours would not be his own descendants, but those of Philip-Augustus.

Simon's chief concern in the autumn of 1214 was to have his conquest of Languedoc formally recognized by the church. However, Peter of Benevento had strict instructions to make no permanent dispositions of the conquered territory until the forthcoming ecumenical council. In July 1214, while Peter was away in Spain, Simon persuaded the other legate, the pliable Robert Curzon, to grant him all the northern provinces of the principality of Toulouse together with 'other territories yet to be conquered'. What Peter thought about this when he returned in the autumn can only be imagined. But his position was a difficult one. All the southern bishops were ardent Montfortists, and it was clearly wise to make some concession to them. In January 1215 five archbishops, twenty-eight bishops, and a host of lay magnates met at Montpellier to elect a 'temporary' count of Toulouse, pending the meeting of Innocent's council. The delegates elected Simon by acclamation, but the citizens of Montpellier gave him a pregnant reminder of the limits of his powers. On Peter II's death they had thrown over the suzerainty of Aragon and declared themselves an independent city-state. For all their ardent catholicism, they would not allow a man as ambitious as Simon de Montfort within their walls. He had to await the news of his election in the Templars' house outside the gates. When he slipped into the town to signify his acceptance of the honour, the citizens mustered in arms and broke up the session of the council, forcing both Simon and his electors to take to their heels.

In April 1215, prince Louis arrived in Languedoc with a formidable army, to fulfil, two years late, the vow he had made in Paris in 1213. Simon was delighted. Now he would have an opportunity to coerce Narbonne and Toulouse, both of which had submitted to the legate Peter of Benevento but not to him. The legate was less than delighted, for Toulouse was under the protection of the Holy See; while Narbonne, he was uncomfortably aware, could not be taken without an open breach with Arnald-Amaury. Peter of Benevento nervously confronted Louis's army at Vienne, but he was prevailed upon to fall in with Simon's plans as so many other legates had been before him. The combined army, accompanied by the legate, arrived outside Narbonne early in May, and the archbishop found himself standing in alliance with the passionately anti-northern citizens against the crusade of which he had once been the leader. Doubtless the irony of the moment escaped him. Unfortunately the citizens had weaker nerves than their defiant archbishop, and, rather than face a siege, they agreed to demolish their own walls under the supervision of two of Louis' knights. While they were at this melancholy work, the same penalty was imposed on Toulouse. Broad gaps were made in the walls at strategic places. The fortified houses and towers of the nobility were razed to the ground, and the chains kept at each street corner for building barricades were removed. The Château Narbonnais was detached from the fortifications of the town so that it could hold out against the citizens as well as an outside enemy; it was surrounded by trenches and palisades and a new gate was pierced in it facing away from the town, thus enabling Simon to come and go unmolested. 'At last the pride of Toulouse was humbled,' Peter of Vaux-de-Cernay observed with satisfaction. Innocent III was furious. The attack on Toulouse he was prepared to overlook, but the destruction of the walls of Narbonne was outrageous. 'You have tried to usurp the duchy of Narbonne from the man to whom you owe everything, . . . sullying your reputation with the stain of ingratitude,' he wrote to Simon; 'take care that you do not give him just cause for complaint at our ecumenical council, . . . or else we shall punish you in whatever manner we shall think fit.' The threat was scarcely veiled, but Simon does not seem to have been greatly perturbed by it. Louis returned to France at the end of May leaving him unchallengeable in the Midi, except perhaps by the great council for which bishops and abbots through the Christian world were at that moment preparing their departures.

The council which Innocent had been planning for two and a half years opened in the cavernous gloom of the old Lateran basilica on 11th November 1215. Four hundred bishops, eight hundred abbots, and a mass of lay magnates, ambassadors, and officials sang the *Veni Creator Spiritus* in a crush so intense that at least one bishop was suffocated. The greatest of all the ecclesiastical councils of the middle ages had an immense agenda of which the Albigensian crusade was but a small part. But the presence of almost every participant in the great struggle for Languedoc ensured that it would be vigorously debated. Eighteen southern bishops attended, and among the northern bishops present, twelve had taken part in the Albigensian crusade at some time in the past six years. Raymond VI, the young Raymond, the count of Foix, and several of the more important *faidits* had appeared in Rome for the occasion. But the vultures had also gathered for pickings from their forfeited dominions. Simon de Montfort was represented by his brother Guy. King John had asked two English prelates to press his claims on the Agenais. Representing his own interests was Raymond VI's son-in-law, Pierre-Bermon d'Auduze; he hoped to acquire the principality of Toulouse for himself, but he played little part in the council and his claims do not appear to have received serious attention.

In the midst of this maelstrom of conflicting ambitions, Innocent III made his own views clear. He wished to leave Simon de Montfort in possession of the old Trencavel dominions, but restore the rest of Languedoc to Raymond VI. This 'counsel of Achitophel', as Peter of Vaux-de-Cernay called it, found a few supporters among the bishops.

But the vast majority of the council were roused to indignant protest. Raymond-Roger of Foix was called upon to speak for the southern princes. He vigorously justified their conduct and accused Simon of masking his ambition with shallow pieties, wreaking murder and destruction on an innocent catholic population. The bishop of Toulouse angrily replied with a list of Raymond-Roger's own enormities, mentioning his massacre of the crusaders at Montgey and the notorious heresy of his sister Esclarmonde, who was at that moment presiding defiantly over a Cathar court in the impregnable mountain fortress of Montségur. Raymond-Roger denied that Montségur had ever formed part of his dominions. 'Am I to be ruined for my sister's sins?' As for the victims of Montgey, they were no pilgrims but 'brigands, traitors, and perjurers come to destroy me under the sign of the cross'. One of Raymond VI's counsellors went further, shouting out that there would have been more such 'pilgrims' with pierced eyes and severed noses, if he had known that the matter would be raised in Rome. There was a murmur of disapproval among the audience. The count of Foix launched into a violent diatribe against Folquet of Toulouse, that renegade monk, former *troubadour* and notorious libertine, 'singer of songs whose sound is damnation'. Raymond de Roquefeuil broke in with a plea for the *faidits* and particularly for the son of Raymond-Roger Trencavel, 'condemned to wander in penniless exile' for the supposed sins of his father. 'Friends,' Innocent announced; 'we shall do what is just,' and he withdrew into the Lateran palace.

The pope retired to the palace garden, to collect his thoughts in peace. But some of the southern bishops, fearing that he was about to undo the work of six years, followed him and gave vent to bitter recriminations against the southern princes. 'My lord, if you restore them to their lands we are done for,' one of them cried. Innocent protested that he could not lawfully deprive local catholics of their territories; Simon was entitled to the confiscated possessions of proven heretics, but he could find no legal justification for giving him more. Folquet of Toulouse openly called this a 'tortuous piece of sophistry'. 'How can you bring yourself to dispossess Simon de Montfort? He is a faithful servant of the church, entirely devoted to your cause. He has put up with hardship and exhaustion, thrown himself into the battle against heretics and mercenaries.' To fob Simon off with the confiscated property of heretics was mere hypocrisy if the pope then proceeded to declare that the counts of Toulouse and Foix were not heretics. He might as well openly dispossess Simon and have done with him. Folquet's words had the force of a *fait accompli*, as the others did not fail to point out. They made it clear that they would not have Simon dispossessed, and would encourage him to hold his conquests by force if need be. Raymond VI had his champions. The archdeacon of Lyon, a man who three years later was to be dismissed for showing favour to heretics,[24] leapt to Raymond's defence; and so, ironically, did Arnald-Amaury, who in his new capacity of archbishop of Narbonne had come to see a greater menace in Simon's strength than in Raymond's weakness. The pope agreed with them. He chided Raymond's enemies for their lack of Christian charity; they were 'preachers of suffering and discord'. Even if Raymond was guilty of heresy, which he was not, why should his heir, the young Raymond, be dispossessed? When the crusade had begun, he was only twelve years old. The archbishop of York added, on behalf of king John, that even if it was right to deprive the young Raymond of his father's inheritance, it could not be right to deprive him of the Agenais, which was his mother's. 'I can do no more,' Innocent wearily replied, 'the bishops are against me.' Since Simon controlled the land, he told the council, no power of his could take it away from him: 'but let him guard it well, for if he loses it, he will not have my help in getting it back.'

The council's decision was published on 14th December 1215. Raymond VI, on account of his 'inability to govern his dominions in accordance with the faith', was to lose everything that the crusaders had occupied. He was to live in exile, out of Languedoc, on his wife's dowry and a pension of four hundred marks a year. Those of Raymond's lands which the crusaders had not conquered were to pass to the young Raymond as soon as he was of age: in practice this meant only the marquisate of Provence on the eastern side of the Rhône. As for the count of Foix, Innocent ordered two commissaries to investigate the allegations made against him and to report within three months; if the report vindicated him, then he would have his castle at Foix restored to him.

Innocent's concession to the count of Foix was but a small cloud on Simon's horizon, for the council had accorded him almost everything that he could ask for. When the news reached him from Rome, he left for the north to do homage to Philip Augustus for the county of Toulouse. The king received him at Pont-de-l'Arche with unexpected warmth. Few remembered his earlier coolness. Through the northern provinces Simon conducted a magnificent progress from town to town, fêted everywhere with chanting processions singing 'Blessed is he who comes in the name of the Lord.' Enthusiastic mobs crowded round to touch the hem of his garment. In the Midi, another deliverer was receiving the honours of his people. The young Raymond, accompanied by his broken father, had landed in April at Marseille to be mobbed on the quay by excited supporters. The citizens of Avignon had massed at their gates to greet him with patriotic harangues and shouts of 'Toulouse'. An army of *faidits* had flocked to his standard at Orange. Simon was still receiving the plaudits of the north when a messenger despatched by his brother Guy brought him the disquieting news that the young Raymond had laid siege to Beaucaire. The lower town had already fallen. In the citadel the northern garrison were approaching the end of their resistance.

# ✦ XII ✦

## 1216–1218: The turning of the tide

'The son shall not bear the iniquity of the father.'
EZEKIEL XVIII.20

The austere ruins of the castle of Beaucaire stand on the edge of a steep cliff which rises abruptly from the west bank of the river Rhône, the last imposing natural feature before the valley flattens out into marsh and moorland. The river, which now runs in narrow channels some three hundred yards away, covered the base of the cliff in the thirteenth century. A lacework of paths, bridges, and staircases led down to the water's edge, where a privileged corporation of Rhône boatmen carried passengers for an exorbitant fee across the river to the twin town of Tarascon. Beaucaire was the heart of a region which the counts of Toulouse had always preferred to their older territories in the west. Raymond V had held his famous court here in 1174, when gold coins were said to have been ploughed into the ground amid scenes of unmatched extravagance and ostentation. The land was poor, parched by the summer heat and fierce winds of the Rhône valley. But life held delights which were exotic luxuries in other parts of France, the luxuries for which poor land is often famous: wine, honey, limes, and olives. The essentials of life were imported by river, an indulgence which rich commercial cities could afford. Few other towns of Raymond's dominions could have matched the feast with which Avignon celebrated his return from Italy; 'a rich banquet where every variety of fish was served flowing with delicate sauces and washed down with red, and rosé wine, scented with cloves, while jugglers and musicians, singers and dancers performed for their delight.'

The Rhône towns had savoured the pleasures of independence while their masters had been fighting against the crusade in the west. Some, like Marseille, had turned themselves into veritable republics, dominated by aggressive popular associations. Raymond VI had never been a particularly effective ruler in the Rhône towns. His instinct had always been to buy the loyalty of upstart town councils with privileges and immunities, so that he could concentrate on his enemies among the baronage. Simon had very different ideas. Like most northerners, he disliked and suspected autonomous towns, and often tried to govern them through the bishops, those implacable enemies of communal self-government. After two years of Simon's rule, the Rhône towns were ready to welcome Raymond VI back with a warmth that must have taken him by surprise. Marseille, Avignon, and Tarascon were able to provide him almost overnight with a substantial army, which which was joined in the next two months by most of the baronage of Provence.

A double invasion of Languedoc was planned. The young Raymond would attack Simon in the Rhône valley; while his father would raise a new army in Spain and cross the Pyrenees to threaten Simon's rear. The latter part of the plan took rather longer to organize than had been anticipated. But the young Raymond began his allotted task immediately. He crossed the Rhône at Avignon in late April and laid siege to Beaucaire.

In spite of the noisy preparations of the past two months, their arrival was a terrible surprise to the northern garrison. The citizens had been forewarned. They were ready to open the gates to the young Raymond, and had mustered in the streets to repel the garrison's expected counter-attack. But the garrison were still arming themselves, and the Provençal knights were already charging through the gates by the time they arrived. Braving a hail of arrows and stones, the crusaders fought their way through the northern quarters of the town until they were forced by heavy casualties to withdraw. Although the Provençals were in control of the town, the crusaders still held the castle immediately outside the walls, and the Redorte, a large triangular tower overlooking it to the north. The Redorte did not survive for long. Before the garrison had had time to recover their strength, the southerners had set fire to it. By the evening it had surrendered. Overlooked by the Redorte on the north, hemmed in by the town on the south, and cut off from the Rhône by a fleet of boats from Tarascon, the garrison of the castle looked out on a powerful southern army barring the road to the west. The prospects of resistance seemed small.

Nevertheless, they held out for more than four months. During much of this time there was no sign of help from the main body of the crusading army. It was dispersed among scores of garrison towns when

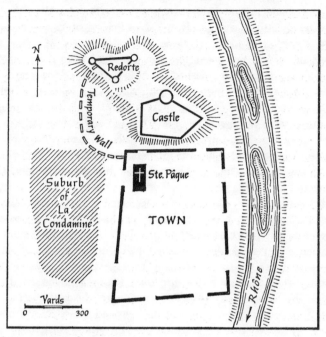

IX.   Beaucaire in 1216

the news of Raymond's attack arrived, and its commander was four hundred miles away in the north. Not until the first week in June was Simon able to gather his troops before Beaucaire and by this time the besiegers were in well-entrenched positions on the hill. They had built a wall round the western side of the castle, so as to bring it within the fortified enclosure of the town. The result was that the defenders could not make sorties into the besiegers' ranks, and neither could the main body of the crusading army get close enough to relieve them. The Provençals showed no inclination to abandon their strong position and they declined Simon's invitation to a pitched battle. On 5th June, therefore, the crusaders settled down to besiege the besiegers. This, as Peter of Vaux-de-Cernay remarked, was like besieging all Provence, for Raymond's troops were well supplied by river from Avignon, while Simon's had to rely on heavily guarded food convoys from Nîmes and St.-Gilles. The defenders of the castle were reduced to eating their horses.

The crusaders made several attempts to storm the walls of the town or batter them with mangonels, but each time vigorous resistance and steep escarpments defeated them. The Provençals were far more successful with their own siege engines. From within the town, their trebuchets gradually demolished the upper works of the keep. They constructed a huge battering ram with which they began to smash the castle's outer walls. The defenders resisted with superb courage, raining missiles down on their attackers and suffocating sappers with smoking braziers let down from the walls. At one point they even succeeded in seizing the head of the battering ram with a kind of lasso. But their morale was low. Quarrels had broken out among them. There was no contact with Simon's army. Below them, in the vineyards of the town, the decaying corpses of captured crusaders could be seen hanging from olive trees. Despairing signals were raised above the highest turret of the castle, first a black flag of distress, then a few days later, an empty napkin and bottle. Finally, in the middle of August, one of them succeeded in escaping through the siege works of the southerners to tell Simon that they could hold out no longer. On 24th August Simon accepted terms. The defenders of the castle were allowed to leave with full honours, taking their arms and possessions with them. Simon withdrew with his army, leaving the young Raymond in possession of Beaucaire.

The impossible compromise of the Lateran council had been torn in shreds, but the Vicar of Christ did not hurl forth his thunderbolts as many had expected. The author of the epic Song of the Crusade, a passionate partisan of the southern cause, believed that Innocent III had actually blessed Raymond's resort to force, during the young prince's final audience in December. In a man as conscious of legal proprieties as Innocent, such duplicity is scarcely conceivable. But whether Innocent would have turned a blind eye to the war in Languedoc cannot be known, for on 16th July 1216, a month before the fall of Beaucaire, the great pope died at Perugia. He probably never knew of the savage battle by the Rhône which was to lose Simon de Montfort in two years what he had gained in six. The dead pope was quickly forgotten. Jacques de Vitry, who had so often preached the Languedoc crusade in the days of its triumphs, happened to pass through Perugia on the day after Innocent's death, and found the body unattended in one of the churches of the town, stripped by thieves of its precious vestments and left naked and rotting in the close summer heat. The cardinals and curial officials were more interested in his successor, Honorius III. He had been Innocent's chancellor, and he adopted almost all of Innocent's policies. But Honorius was a milder man, and he was already very old at the time of his election. He lacked the fierce energy as well as the political shrewdness of his predecessor. His one consuming ambition was to recover the holy places of Palestine and to that ambition most of his other policies took second place. Languedoc was an irritating distraction. Honorius might listen, scold, encourage, admonish, but he did not actively interest himself in the Albigensians until it was too late.

It was several months before the significance of the fall of Beaucaire was appreciated. Strategically, the loss of the castle was not a disaster. But its psychological impact was considerable. Not the least of Simon's difficulties during the siege of Beaucaire were the mutterings of rebellion which mounted with each passing week of failure. His supply trains were harassed by guerillas. Toulouse had not even waited for Simon's capitulation before intriguing behind his back with Raymond VI, now recruiting soldiers in Spain. Simon would have been wise to recognize that he could not fight two wars at once. He would either have to appease the aggrieved citizens of Toulouse or abandon the Rhône valley. Instead he was considering ways of extending his power into Provence at one end of his territory and towards the Atlantic at the other. Hubris had followed Simon's earlier victories. He remained entirely convinced that his destiny was in God's hands and he would not countenance any compromise. Others were less certain. 'How fascinating to watch the workings of divine providence,' an inquisitorial notary was later to recall; '. . . as soon as the crusaders forgot the laws of Christ, by whose aid the land had been won, and instead became slaves of their own passion, ambition, and greed, the Lord made them drink from the cup of His anger.'[25] Certainly the young Raymond's greatest gain at Beaucaire had been the destruction of his enemy's morale. That wonderful self-confidence from which so much courage had been born, and so much territory conquered against all the odds, now suddenly evaporated. Henceforth, discord and self-doubt followed in the crusaders' steps. Only Simon himself remained confident, and his confidence was to lead him into a succession of disastrous misjudgements.

The first misjudgement followed immediately upon the defeat at Beaucaire. Simon had convinced himself that the citizens of Toulouse were responsible for all his troubles. He was also seriously short of money to pay his soldiers' wages. Both problems, he decided, could be solved by making Toulouse pay for its treachery. Riding at fifty miles a day across the length of Languedoc, he reached Montgiscard on 28th August. The next day he was at Toulouse. A distinguished delegation of citizens met him apprehensively at the gates, and a brief but angry interview followed. Simon charged them with betraying him. They denied it. Simon's answer was to arrest them and shut them in the Château Narbonnais, while the bishops and the abbot of St.-Sernin rode through the streets summoning the citizens to a general meeting outside the walls. As the great mass of people crowded through the southern gate at Simon's bidding, armed bands of crusaders passed through the streets breaking into aristocratic houses, carrying off coins and jewellery. But the plundering of Toulouse was singularly mishandled, for most of the inhabitants had not yet left the city when they realized what was happening behind their backs. Within minutes the entire city was in arms. The plunderers found themselves attacked in the streets by furious bands of Toulousains armed with axes and blunt weapons. Those that could, took refuge in the bishop's palace, the bell-tower of the cathedral, or the town house of the count of Comminges; but many others were lynched. At the eastern and southern gates the main body of the crusading army tried to fight their way into the city to rescue their companions. But the citizens' anger had lent them strength. After fighting through the night the crusaders withdrew to the plain outside, setting fire to the wooden houses as they did so, and destroying much of the south-eastern quarter of the city.

Simon's demolitions of the previous year had not been thorough enough. There were large gaps in the walls, but enough had been left standing to enable angry mobs to keep the crusaders at bay for a considerable time. And to besiege the city now would mean consigning to their deaths the crusaders still holding out in the bell-tower and the hôtel de Comminges. Simon therefore resorted to deception. On the following morning he summoned another general assembly of citizens to meet him under safe-conduct in the suburb of Villeneuve, just outside the cathedral gate. He promised an amnesty to all but a handful of ringleaders, and even these would be allowed to exile themselves from the city. Bishop Folquet met the leading citizens beforehand in the town hall and gave them his personal guarantee that these promises would be kept. Then, as soon as the trapped crusaders had been allowed to leave the city, the leading patricians in the assembly were seized and thrown in prison. Simon's vengeance was terrible. Toulouse was occupied in force. Prominent citizens were arrested in their homes, and obscurer ones were picked out at random in the streets and sent to join the others in the cells of the Château Narbonnais. The prisoners, some four hundred of them, were dispersed in small groups among the various castles of Languedoc to be held as hostages for the city's good behaviour. Next, the urban knights, a class which the northerners had always distrusted, were rounded up, deprived of their arms, and expelled from the city to live on the land, like their northern peers. Their property in Toulouse was forfeit. Those who remained were allowed their liberty but they paid dearly for it. Although Toulouse had long ago been exempted from direct taxation, a tallage of 30,000 silver marks was now imposed, and enforced by a programme of ruthless sequestrations. Houses were marked with crosses if their occupants had not paid, and demolished unless the default was remedied. The consulate was abolished. The fortifications of the *bourg* were allowed to stand, but those of the *cité* were destroyed yard by yard. 'Towers and tall houses, walls, vaulted chambers, and crenellated mansions were all smashed. Shopfronts, balconies, ceilings and painted walls, vaults, doorways, pillars all came down. The din was terrible. Everywhere the sun shone in thin rays through the heavy clouds of dust thrown up by furiously busy demolition workers.'

Even before Simon had left Toulouse, messengers from the city were crossing the Pyrenees to urge Raymond VI to hasten his preparations for the invasion of Languedoc. Their mission was certainly assisted by Simon's next folly. Simon had long had designs on the Pyrenean principality of Bigorre, a fief of the Aragonese crown which was ruled in her own right by its countess, Petronilla. In November 1216, he married his younger son Guy to Petronilla. She was many years his senior, but the middle ages never considered that to be any impediment to a dynastic marriage. A serious objection was that the lady was already married to Nuño Sanchez, a cousin of the young king of Aragon. Simon persuaded the archbishop of Auch to annul this inconvenient union; it was an act of somewhat questionable legality, but Simon's strategic interests were at stake, and the objections of the nobility of Bigorre were brushed aside. As soon as the marriage had been celebrated at Tarbes, Simon invaded the county and installed the bridegroom there by force. He failed, however, to take Lourdes, the strongest fortress of the region, from which Nuño Sanchez continued to control the southern highlands of the county. The rest was occupied without resistance, but it can scarcely have been worth the indignation which was aroused in Aragon, where Raymond VI was at that moment seeking allies.

Almost as foolish was Simon's treatment of Raymond-Roger, count of Foix, who, for all his cynicism and brutality, was one of the few really able military leaders among the southern aristocracy. Since the Lateran council Raymond-Roger had scrupulously abstained from aiding Simon's enemies, Innocent III had promised to restore him to his possessions, provided that he could satisfy a special papal commission of his orthodoxy. While the commissioners were at work, Simon repeatedly harassed the castles still in the count's possession, in the hope that he would blacken his reputation by retaliating. Raymond-Roger complained to the new pope, who ordered Simon to justify his conduct. Simon replied with various procedural devices intended to draw out the cumbrous workings of papal justice. Nevertheless, the papal commissioners completed their investigations with unaccustomed speed, and Honorius III announced his decision in November 1216. Raymond-Roger was declared to be orthodox and the abbot of St.-Thibéry, who was holding the castle of Foix in the name of the church, was ordered to restore it to him. Simon was stunned. He refused to accept the verdict. Ignoring the protests of the papal commissioners, he occupied Foix in February 1217, strengthened its fortifications, and replaced the abbot of St.-Thibéry's garrison by his own. He then besieged Raymond-Roger's son for six weeks in the nearby castle of Montgrénier, forcing him to capitulate for lack of water at the end of March.[26] Strangely, Honorius does not seem to have been particularly disturbed by this flagrant act of contempt. He was not Innocent III.

In the spring of 1217, Simon felt strong enough to return to the Rhône valley where his troubles had begun. The pope had sent him a new legate, Bertrand, cardinal of St. John and St. Paul, who had already installed himself at Orange when Simon arrived. Bertrand's principal purpose was to settle the embarrassing quarrel between Simon and Arnald-Amaury, who had now gone so far as to excommunicate the church's 'chosen son' for infringing his rights over the duchy of Narbonne. But Arnald-Amaury's petulant act does not appear to have been taken seriously in the south, and Bertrand had already turned to graver matters. From the moment of his arrival he had been harassed on the roads and virtually blockaded in Orange by the allies of the young Raymond. Crossbowmen had fired random shots at him. One of them had wounded a papal courier in his suite. The Rhône towns refused to recognize his authority, and when their consuls came to meet him at Châteauneuf, they answered his protests with vigorous abuse. As a result of this experience the new legate had been turned into an ardent partisan of Simon's cause even faster than his predecessors. The recalcitrant towns were excommunicated. When the legate met Simon for the first time at Pont-St.-Esprit in July, he commanded him to cross the Rhône into the Provençal territory which the Lateran council had allotted to the young Raymond. Simon complied with alacrity. He had already crushed all opposition to his rule on the west bank, except at Beaucaire; and Beaucaire would soon surrender once its Provençal allies had been conquered. In Provence, the main champions of the southern cause were the young Raymond, who had established his capital at Avignon, and the count of Valentinois, a long-standing enemy of Simon's. Neither was prepared for an invasion but they were relying on Avignon's river fleet to prevent the crusaders from crossing the Rhône. Simon had anticipated this problem. He marched north to Viviers, where the bishop had already assembled a fleet of his own and thrown a bridge of boats across the Rhône. The Avignonese arrived too late, and the crusaders descended without warning on the startled garrisons of the east bank. Most of them abandoned their strongholds in Simon's path or surrendered after a nominal siege. Simon had good reason to be satisfied with the summer's campaign. By September much of the northern Rhône valley was in his hands, and the count of Valentinois was suing for terms. But before the terms had been signed, the ground had collapsed beneath Simon's feet in the west.

In mid-September, Raymond VI launched his long-awaited invasion of Languedoc. His force was small—some volunteers recruited in Aragon, the counts of Comminges and Couserans with their contingents, and a good number of the Toulousain aristocracy whom Simon had expelled from the city the year before. But by keeping to the minor valleys and crossing the Garonne at fords, not bridges, they retained the advantage of surprise to the last. They were within twenty-five miles of Toulouse before they met any resistance. By the time the news of their coming reached the garrison in the Château Narbonnais, Raymond was already in the city. He had entered by the ford of the

Bazacle, riding past the lines of moored water-mills under cover of a thick autumn fog. His supporters were well prepared. Crowds gathered quickly, and welcomed Raymond's army with almost hysterical enthusiasm, before turning to the gratifying business of revenging themselves on the crusaders and collaborators. Those that could be found were massacred in the streets. Others fled in terror to the sanctuary of the churches or ran for the gates, bringing the first news of the rising to the startled northerners in the Château Narbonnais. 'Who are these rowdies who have taken over my city?' Alice de Montfort was said to have asked, on observing the fracas from an upper window; 'Alas!' she remarked when she was told that Raymond VI was their leader, 'yesterday everything was going so well.' With only a skeleton force in the castle, Alice could do nothing until reinforcements had arrived from Carcassonne. But Carcassonne was nearly sixty miles away. By the time that Guy de Montfort had arrived with a hastily assembled force of garrison troops, the Toulousains had barricaded the streets at the entrances to the city, and Guy's men were repelled with heavy losses. Towards the evening the noise of celebrations could be clearly heard by the demoralized tenants of the Château Narbonnais. The crusaders captured in the afternoon's battle were being dragged behind horses to the gallows.

Alice's messenger found Simon beyond the Rhône at Crest, engaged in delicate negotiations with the count of Valentinois. Simon did not lose his nerve. He ordered the courier to keep quiet and look contented, and then continued with his negotiations as if nothing had happened. As a result he did not reach Toulouse until 1st October, nearly three weeks after Raymond's return. The Toulousains had made good use of this precious respite. Simon had efficiently destroyed nearly every yard of wall in 1216, but the churches had been left intact and these were now converted into fortresses. Crossbowmen were lodged in the towers and pinnacles of the cathedral and the abbey of St.-Sernin. On the edge of the city volunteers worked day and night to construct makeshift fortifications around the vulnerable south-eastern quarter. When Simon arrived with the crusading army, a continuous line of walls and trenches extended from the Garonne to the cathedral, a distance of more than a thousand yards. Behind these home-made defences stood an army which was growing daily in strength. The crusaders, surrounded in the Château Narbonnais, had been unable to prevent Raymond from reinforcing his small force with contingents from Spain and the mountain principalities. A horde of *faidits* had arrived from throughout the province. But the citizens themselves were the backbone of the defence. For the duration of the siege, Toulouse became a totalitarian state. Those who were not fighting at the walls were directed to watch-duty or trench-digging. Rich merchants and civic dignitaries hauled rubble through the streets. Women worked the siege engines. Heavy taxes were imposed to pay the wages of the professional soldiers, and the property of known Montfortists was sequestered. Faint-hearts, shirkers, traitors, and tax-evaders were arrested and deprived of their property; some of them conjured up important business or vows of pilgrimage and slipped out of the city to wait on events in safety.

In his destructions of the previous year, Simon had forgotten the barbicans which guarded the bridgeheads on the west bank of the Garonne. This proved to have been a costly omission, for across these bridges there now flowed an unending stream of reinforcements and supplies. To stop this, Simon devised an ambitious plan. West of the suburb of St.-Cyprian, across the roads leading into Gascony, he proposed to build a new town and populate it with fresh immigrants. While the siege lasted it would strengthen his positions and supply his army. And then, when Toulouse had been conquered, emptied of its inhabitants, and levelled with the ground, Simon's town would replace it, a new Toulouse, conceived without sin.[27] This decision, the classic resort of despots in all ages, proved hard to execute in practice. Leaving half his army on the east bank under Amaury's command, Simon crossed the Garonne on rafts with the other half and attempted to seal off the suburb of St.-Cyprian. But in spite of his efforts the count of Foix succeeded in slipping across the bridges by night with a substantial army, to be welcomed into the city with torches and tambourines. Although the suburb was unfortified, Simon met unexpected resistance there. After several weeks he had achieved nothing, while on the opposite bank Amaury was having difficulty in repelling determined sorties from the town. Simon was forced to abandon the west bank in November, leaving the forlorn footings of New Toulouse behind him.

The crusaders passed the rest of the winter wretchedly huddled before the home-made fortifications on the south side of the city. They beat off the persistent sorties of the defenders, but not once did they succeed in penetrating into the streets. Their morale was low. They were cold and wet while the Toulousains, for all their anxieties, had meals and warm homes to return to. The crusaders had their head-quarters in the Château Narbonnais, a huge, rambling unutterably gloomy Roman fort which the counts of Toulouse had with good reason visited as infrequently as possible. Simon had once hoped to overawe the city from this monument. But for this purpose it was entirely unsuitable. It had been built to resist an attack from the south, and its vulnerable north face, pierced with windows and galleries, was rapidly demolished by trebuchets fired from the town. The chapel was hit while the cardinal-legate was saying mass in it, and one of his chaplains was killed by falling masonry.

The fragility of a thousand-year-old fort was the least of Simon's

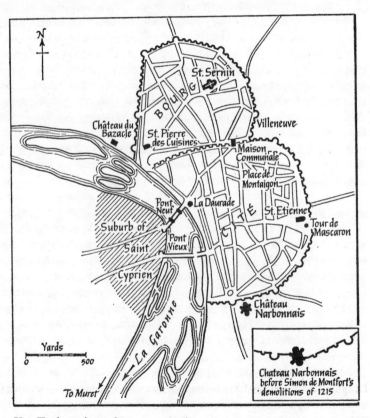

X.  Toulouse in 1218

worries. He had no money and his paid troops were threatening to desert him. Some of them were Gascon levies who made no secret of their sympathy for the Toulousains. Simon never ceased to look over his shoulder, where murmurs of rebellion grew daily louder, and reinforcements were being obstructed and even murdered on their way to his camp. Inside the Château Narbonnais, close friendships were becoming strained. Alan de Roucy and Guy de Montfort had opposed the coercion of Toulouse in 1216 and they insisted that Simon had only himself to blame for their rebellion. This was true but unhelpful, particularly as rumours of these disagreements had reached the ears of the enemy in Toulouse. Even more humiliating was the behaviour of the cardinal-legate. He repeatedly accused Simon of cowardice and military incompetence, reproaches which were scarcely deserved, for he had done as much as he could with his small army, and had thrown himself with his accustomed recklessness into every battle. Simon consoled himself with black thoughts of revenge on the city which had so often thwarted him. New Toulouse was taking shape in his mind, though not on the abandoned patch of land west of the Garonne. There would be no quarter when the city fell. No sanctuary would be respected. Nothing would be left to provide shelter for another generation of rebels and heretics.

No negotiated surrender could be expected on these terms. Simon had already begun to rest his hopes of victory on the preaching of another crusade in the north. However, the situation in Europe did not favour such plans. The great Middle Eastern crusade which two popes had planned for the past five years seemed at last to have become a reality. One expedition was already in Syria. Another was about to depart. The aged pope regarded this as the climax of his life and he was in no mood to welcome a distracting side-show in southern France; it was as much as he would do to write testy letters to the leaders of the rebellion. In December he reminded the young Raymond of the 'bounty and compassion' which the Holy See had always shown to him, and peremptorily ordered the southern cities and the count of Foix to submit to Simon de Montfort. Other letters were addressed to Philip Augustus and the French bishops, who were beseeched to do all they could for Simon, short of diverting crusaders from the Holy Land. In Languedoc the cardinal-legate had already decided on more abrasive measures. The bishop of Toulouse was sent to Paris to plead with Philip Augustus, and then to join Jacques de Vitry in a preaching tour of the north. Alice de Montfort travelled with him, and endeavoured to persuade her large well connected family to come to her husband's assistance. She was empowered to offer them rich lands in Quercy when the rebels had been defeated. At the same time, emissaries of the cardinal-legate called on French abbeys to demand financial contributions. Mercenaries were hired with the proceeds. All this bustle was good for the besiegers' morale, and it produced results surprisingly quickly. The first reinforcements arrived in January 1218. In May bishop Folquet and Alice de Montfort returned in triumph with a fresh army including Michel de Harnes, one of the heroes of Bouvines, and Walter Langton, brother of the archbishop of Canterbury. They were followed within a few days by a second army under the count of Soissons.

Toulouse had also been reinforced. Recruiting officers scoured Périgord and Quercy, where Simon's generous offer to his wife's relatives cannot have added to his popularity. Bernard de Cazenac, whom Simon thought he had crushed in 1214, was raising an army on the Dordogne; the viscount of Turenne, whom Simon had set to keep an eye on him, contributed to it. Volunteers continued to arrive from the Rhône valley and from Spain.

Whatever advantage Simon gained from his reinforcements was quickly wiped out by Raymond's. In spite of the host which Folquet had brought from the north, he was unable to reoccupy the west bank of the river in May. After taking half his army twelve miles upstream to cross the Garonne, he found that the Toulousains had dug a deep moat around the suburb of St. Cyprian which the crusaders' horses, weighed down by their heavy chain armour, were unable to jump. Simon's troops were driven back and forced to pitch their tents at a safe distance, a humiliation which was keenly felt by their leader. Suddenly the weather, so often Simon's enemy, came to his assistance. At the end of May there was a terrible rainstorm. For three days the deluge continued, flooding the streets and cellars of the city and flattening the bedraggled tents of the besiegers outside. The Garonne broke its banks, carrying away both of the bridges of Toulouse, and destroying the water mills on which the city depended for its flour. The trenches round the suburb of St.-Cyprian were filled with slime and debris. Simon's work had been done for him. He immediately occupied the suburb, summoned a fleet of boats which was being held in readiness downstream, and prepared to launch an amphibious assault on the city.

The Pont-Neuf of Toulouse was a bridge of the kind which can still be seen over the Lot at Cahors. It was built on five piles of masonry sunk into the river bed, from two of which rose tall stone portcullis towers blocking the passage of the bridge. With the wooden carriage-ways broken by the flood, these towers were left standing isolated in mid-stream. Their garrisons were cut off from both banks, but they were still capable of raining arrows down on Simon's boats and they constituted the principal obstacle to his plans. They would need, how-ever, to be kept supplied from the town. With superb courage, one of Raymond's Spanish equerries succeeded in linking the east tower to the city with a fragile rope-bridge, across which its defenders were brought weapons and food. But the west tower was untenable. At first it was supplied by drawing baskets along ropes stretched between the two towers; but Simon's siege engines had already begun to batter it from the west bank. At each hit, great blocks of masonry slid into the water. The defenders suffered heavy casualties and they were soon forced to abandon it to Simon's men.

Before the crusaders could assault the east tower, an untoward incident forced Simon to return to the opposite bank. In spite of the strength of his forces there, Bernard de Cazenac had succeeded in entering the city by the north with five hundred men, and he was followed a few days later by the young Raymond leading the contingents of Provence. The church bells and fanfares which rang out to welcome them were a clear warning to Simon not to overstretch his army. Another warning came a few days later. While Simon was still on the east side of the city, a force of Toulousains crossed the river in barges, reoccupied the west bank, and began to assault the pilgrims' hospice where the crusaders had established their headquarters. Throughout the night and for most of the next day, the two sides fought tenaciously for control of the river. Simon, with a body of picked knights, stormed the east tower from boats and succeeded in holding it for several hours until they were dislodged. Meanwhile the Toulousains, together with a force of German mercenaries, tightened their grip on the west bank. The crusaders retreated in disorder. Several of them fell into the river, where they were drowned in their heavy armour.

It was now mid-June, the ninth month of the siege. The western arm of Simon's planned double assault had had to be abandoned. But the eastern arm was still taking shape. His carpenters had spent a month building an enormous wooden 'cat', a mobile shelter which enabled an assault party to approach the base of the walls in safety. However, as this monster approached the walls, a trebuchet, fired blindly from inside the city, scored a direct hit against it. The intricate carpentry was smashed, and several of the assault party inside were killed. Then, on 25th June, the Toulousains launched a sudden sortie from two points against the carpenters' compound, where the 'cat' was being repaired. Many of the crusaders were at mass. They were taken by surprise. Simon waited until the elevation of the Host, and then ran to the spot, where the battle was already in progress. His brother Guy had been wounded and his horse killed by crossbow bolts. Simon gathered some troops and tried to block the gate in the city walls, through which the Toulousains were still pouring out into the mêlée. From a platform behind the walls, the women of the *Bourg* were firing heavy blocks of masonry from a trebuchet. They were firing at random into the confused mass of soldiers. But one of their missiles struck Simon on the head and killed him.

# ✠ XIII ✠

## 1218–1224: The liberation

'Therefore the children of Israel could not stand before their
enemies, but turned their backs before their enemies;
because they were accursed.'

JOSHUA VII.12

The news of Simon's death was received in Toulouse with indecent
rejoicing. Church bells rang out. Happy processions of citizens danced
through the streets to drums, cymbals, and trumpets, as Simon's
relatives and chaplains gathered up the mutilated remains of his body
and carried them back to the Château Narbonnais. Simon was hailed
there as a saint and a martyr. 'But as for me,' observed the jaundiced
*troubadour*, 'I have no doubt that if Christ is served . . . by burning
towns and . . . butchering women and children, then Simon is even
now seated in glory in Paradise.' Only Raymond VI stood aside from
the general mood of execration. Simon, he told the chronicler William
of Puylaurens, had had all the qualities of a great prince, courage,
foresight, and remarkable perseverance. Those qualities needed no
better illustration than the speed with which his work was undone
under his successor. On the day after his death, the crusaders met in the
Château Narbonnais under the presidency of the cardinal-legate, and
unanimously elected Simon's eighteen-year-old son Amaury to succeed
him. Amaury is a distant, insubstantial figure in the history of the
crusade. His life was passed under the shadow of his great father.
What little is known about him suggests that he had Simon's courage
and resourcefulness, but none of his personal charisma and, more
significantly perhaps, none of his fanatical self-righteousness. He
began his reign under poor auspices, the heir to a humiliating defeat
which was to hang over the rest of his years in Languedoc. The only
charismatic figure in the politics of the Midi after Simon's death was
the young Raymond, twenty-one years old, extravagantly admired,
and the heir through his mother to the energy and ability of the
Plantagenets.

*199*

The leaders of the crusade had cast a heavy burden on Amaury's shoulders, but few of them were prepared to help him bear it. The count of Soissons announced that his forty days were drawing to an end. Amaury's southern vassals slunk off to their estates to await events, and even his father's northern companions began to return to their homes. The old hopes, long sustained by Simon's defiant optimism, were now gone. Toulouse remained unconquered. The last crusaders were withdrawn from the west bank. The great 'cat', which Simon had died defending, was abandoned, and gleefully burned by the Toulousains. Amaury ordered a last, desperate assault on the walls, and when this had failed, he raised the siege. On 25th July the crusaders burned their siege engines and returned to Carcassonne taking the remains of their dead leader with them. There, Simon was buried in a chapel of the old romanesque cathedral of St.-Nazaire. A chaplain and a perpetual lamp were endowed by his widow, and miracles were shortly recorded at the tomb. The crusaders paid their respects, and then left.

Two months passed before Honorius III was informed of Simon's death. The news was a terrible shock to the aged pope who, for all his earlier tepidness, had never seriously supposed that the crusaders were in danger of being defeated. But that prospect seemed real enough now to warrant a new crusade, in spite of the fact that reinforcements were desperately needed by the army of John of Brienne, fighting the Infidel in the Nile Delta. On 11th August, Honorius proclaimed a plenary indulgence to all who would go forthwith to Amaury's assistance. 'The people of Israel are oppressed by Pharaoh,' he declared with unconscious irony to the bishops of France and Germany, urging them to raise volunteers in every parish. But Honorius was a realist. He knew that although a general appeal might raise a few enthusiasts, no expedition would succeed without the active support of Philip Augustus or his son. He addressed impassioned letters to both princes, imploring them to intervene in the Midi. But neither was in a mood to listen. Philip had always regarded the Albigensian crusade with misgivings. He did not share the church's detestation of the Raymonds, and he was not interested in Amaury's thankless inheritance. Louis was equally unenthusiastic. He had recently returned from an exhausting and unsuccessful attempt to conquer England, which had left him with a marked distaste for distant adventures. Accordingly, when Alice de Montfort and three southern bishops visited the royal court in early

August to plead her son's cause, they met with a discouraging refusal. Philip's vassals asked him for permission to go, and he gave it, with evident reluctance; but he added that he had 'no intention of getting involved in it himself'.

What changed Philip's mind was a characteristically devious manœuvre on the part of the legate Bertrand, who offered the leadership of the expedition to Thibault IV, count of Champagne. Thibault was seventeen years old, recently knighted, and extremely ambitious. He was also, through his mother, the heir presumptive to the kingdom of Navarre. Philip was appalled by the prospect of the young count adding Languedoc to Navarre and combining them with his huge fief of Champagne. He ordered his son to take command of the expedition himself, and Louis took the cross in November in a sulking mood which contrasted markedly with the enthusiasm of his earlier crusading vow, five years before. Honorius expressed his hope that the expedition would leave as soon as possible. But Louis was not to be hurried. His departure was fixed for Ascension Day of the following year.

The delay had disastrous consequences for Amaury. The death of Simon, and the disappearance of much of his army, was the signal for mass defections among the southern towns. Lombers, Nîmes, and Castelnaudary lost no time in recognizing the Raymonds and many lesser places followed their example. William of Les Baux, who had been Simon's principal ally in Provence, was captured by the Avignonese and savagely tortured to death. There was even evidence that some churches, in spite of the mass replacement of bishops by Innocent III, were rediscovering their ancient links with the southern aristocracy. Pamiers was delivered into the hands of the count of Foix by an obscure conspiracy in which two Cistercians of Boulbonne were found to be involved. Another Cistercian was punished by the general chapter of the order helping Raymond VI to raise mercenaries in Poitou. The abbot of Lagrasse was accused of 'many crimes' in November 1218, including showing favour to local *faidits*. Those incidents, scarcely important in themselves, were indications that the southern nobility were returning to their lands and their influence. The church took them very seriously. When some *faidits* recaptured the town of Lescure, the bishop of Albi, the saintly William Peire, was accused of aiding and abetting them, and threatened with deposition. Three years later, Honorius was to order an enquiry into the treachery of certain bishops and priests, ominously instructing his legates that the privileges of the Cistercians and the military orders were not to be allowed to impede their investigations.

Amaury's military position in the winter of 1218–19 was scarcely more satisfactory. As soon as the siege of Toulouse had ended, the young Raymond reoccupied much of the Agenais, while the count of Comminges invaded his own lands south-west of Toulouse, which Simon de Montfort had awarded to one of his southern followers called Joris. Joris, aided for a while by Amaury, put up a stiff resistance. He besieged Cazères, taking it after a short siege and putting the entire population to the sword. But at Meilhan, he was less fortunate. His small army, caught between the rebellious inhabitants of the town and the army of the count of Comminges, was massacred and he himself captured. By this time Amaury had already left to stem the tide of defeat in the Agenais, committing the fatal mistake that his father had always avoided, of dispersing his forces in small pockets which could be picked off one by one by the vastly stronger southern coalition. Strategic folly may have had less to do with this decision than Amaury's very serious disciplinary problems. His youth did not command respect. His vassals, who had trembled at his father's name, had come to underestimate the southerners and the hatred which their own arrogance provoked. Even the disaster at Toulouse had not chastened them. With Simon's strong hand removed, they plundered and murdered at will, and according to William of Puylaurens publicly flaunted their concubines and ill-gotten luxuries. The exaggerations of this straitlaced notary must be treated as such, but they were certainly symptoms of a profound malaise in the crusading army. Several of its most experienced captains had gone off on adventures of their own, and Amaury did not have the authority to recall them. Two of them, John and Foucaud de Berzy, turned their troop into a roving band of brigands looting towns and stealing cattle in the villages around Toulouse, until, early in 1219, they were decisively defeated at Baziège by the young Raymond and the count of Foix.

These brief encounters, the last pitched battles in a war more notable for its sieges, were of little strategic importance. But they struck at Amaury's prestige, and the loss of men killed or captured was a grave blow to his cause. Most of the crusaders who fought at Baziège were killed, while the young Raymond's army reported only one equerry lost. These figures (like the eight crusaders and several thousand southerners killed at Muret) may owe something to the exaggeration of propagandists. But they are by no means absurd. Though French knights did not yet ride into battle encased in metal plate, a century of contact with the Turks and the Greeks had brought their armour to the point where it was proof against most weapons other than the terrible Gascon *dard*. Beneath the chain mail which covered the whole of their bodies, they wore a thick cloth quilt sewn onto a leather backing, called a hacqueton (from the Arabic *al-qutun*, cotton) like the 'alcottonis, a light garment impenetrable by sharp weapons' which Saladin had presented to Richard Cœur-de-Lion at the end of the third crusade. The head was protected by a steel helmet. Judging by the delicate line drawings which illustrate the only manuscript of the song of the crusade, the crusaders still wore the old-fashioned conical helmet with an extension covering the nose. More fashionable, though heavy and cumbersome, was the pot-helmet encasing the whole head, which Raymond VI is shown wearing on his official seal. Armour of this kind served its purpose well. Formerly, William the Breton remarked in his account of the battle of Bouvines, men had fallen by the ten thousand, but now victories were won with only slight casualties.[28] It was the defeated who were massacred: helpless unhorsed knights and lightly armoured foot-soldiers left on the field like the Toulousains slaughtered at Muret. The young Raymond's knights were followed into battle at Baziège by foot-soldiers whose task it was to capture distinguished prisoners for their ransoms and to finish off the others. 'For this is what a battlefield looks like when the fighting is over,' sang the *troubadour*, 'blood and spilt brains covering the ground, eyes and limbs, feet, legs, and arms scattered about.'

The news of his losses was brought to Amaury at Marmande in the Agenais, which he had been besieging to no avail since December 1218. His army was too small to cut off the town's supplies and he was looking anxiously to the north where Louis's preparations were ponderously proceeding. So was the young Raymond. His emissaries were at the French court, trying to persuade the king to recognize Raymond VI as count of Toulouse and call off Louis's expedition. They were also active in England, where they succeeded in arousing fears that Louis might attack English Gascony while he was in the Midi. At one point these diplomatic efforts came close to success, for Philip toyed with the idea of recognizing Raymond, and had to be recalled to the path of political propriety by a stern letter from Honorius III.

Louis's expedition left Paris on 16th May, and arrived early in June before the walls of Marmande. It looked impressive. Apart from some twenty bishops and a sea of Cistercians and Benedictines, it included thirty-three counts with an enormous throng of knights and foot-soldiers, provoking the usual hyperboles among contemporaries who attempted to count them. There were also sizeable German and Flemish contingents, and a troop of French volunteers who approached from the west under the command of the bishop of Saintes. Marmande, which had defied Amaury for nearly six months, was quite unable to resist this new horde. The outer defences were almost immediately taken by storm and the garrison, remembering perhaps the fate of Béziers, threw itself on Louis's mercy. The commander of the town was Centule d'Astarac, a former crusader who had turned his coat after 1216, and there were voices among the bishops that he be burned as a heretic or hanged as a traitor. It was decided, however, that he could more usefully be spared and exchanged for prisoners in Raymond's hands. The punishment planned for him was visited instead on the wretched inhabitants of the town. They were slaughtered to the last man, woman and child, and the town left in flames as the army continued its march towards Toulouse.

Toulouse was making feverish preparations. The municipality had been taking in supplies for several weeks. The walls and barbicans had been strengthened. A large garrison had been gathered by the young Raymond. In front of the altar of St.-Sernin the canons had displayed the body of St. Exupéry, one of Toulouse's earliest bishops who was believed to have protected the city from the Vandal invaders of the fifth century. Louis arrived from the north-west on 16th June. His army, unlike Simon's a year before, was large enough to encircle the city and the citizens, for all their courage, can hardly have been confident of the outcome. They beat off the first assault, and watched for six weeks as Louis's host sat encamped before the walls. Then on 1st August, forty-five days after his arrival, Louis suddenly burned his siege engines, released his prisoners, and marched away with his army. The defenders were astonished. Contemporaries were at a loss to explain Louis's behaviour. It was due, William of Puylaurens thought, to the valiance of the garrison who had beaten off all his assaults. Others, particularly northerners, offered dark hints of treachery and betrayal. It was probably true that some of the army, having served their forty days, had decided to return home, and others were no doubt demanding payment which Louis could not afford to give them. But the fault almost certainly lay with Louis himself. He had taken the cross under duress and he abandoned it as soon as he decently could. He left two hundred knights with Amaury for a year; but he had achieved nothing. It was a curious episode which Honorius and his legates, perhaps wisely, enveloped in a discreet silence.

The two hundred knights, welcome as they were, could do little to stop the cascade of defections which followed Louis's departure. John and Foucaud de Berzy, who had been released by the young Raymond in exchange for the commander of Marmande, began to terrorize the Toulousain once more with a series of well-publicized atrocities. But they were recaptured during the winter and their heads impaled above the gates of Toulouse. Puylaurens, held for the crusaders by Foucaud's wife, was captured a few weeks later. Servian fell in the spring of 1220. Lavaur was taken by storm and its garrison massacred except for a few who swam to safety across the Agout. The crusaders made several attempts to recover the initiative, but all ended in embarrassing failure. Amaury besieged Castelnaudary for eight months without recapturing it, and suffered heavy casualties before he was forced to withdraw; among the dead was his younger brother Guy, 'handsome, faithful, and valiant in arms', who was killed in one of the first assaults. A few weeks later, Alan de Roucy, a famous paladin and one of Simon de Montfort's closest companions since 1211, died defending Montréal, which surrendered to the southerners shortly afterwards.

In countless towns, the citizens faced the difficult decision which side was likely to triumph, knowing that on such fine judgements their future would depend. Most of them threw in their lot with the young Raymond, but without enthusiasm. They had seen false dawns before. The difficulties of the citizens of Agen were those which all Languedoc experienced. They were almost equally divided on the issue, though it was the Montfortists who had been in the ascendant between 1212 and 1221. This, however, had not prevented Raymond's supporters in the city from going to the assistance of Toulouse in 1217, and in the summer of 1221 they were plotting to open the gates to the young Raymond's army. They spread disquieting rumours to the effect that Amaury was planning to take hostages for their loyalty and confiscate their goods. Amaury was quick to deny that he had any such plans. He sent them an ingratiating letter, full of praise for their loyalty, and promised that he would let them come to no harm. The consuls, apparently reassured, undertook to admit Amaury's officials and close their gates to his enemies. But the young Raymond offered them better terms, an amnesty for the city's Montfortists and the promise of a garrison strong enough to resist the crusaders. Three weeks later Agen submitted to the house of Toulouse.

In Rome Honorius III made frenzied efforts to turn the apparently irresistible tide of defeat. After the fiasco of Louis's crusade Bertrand was recalled and replaced as papal legate by Conrad of Urach, cardinal-bishop of Porto and former abbot of Cîteaux. Conrad was a German, the son of the count of Zahringen, and a man of great personal holiness as well as an outstanding papal diplomat. However, his appointment came too late. He arrived in the spring of 1220 to find most of the province in Raymond's hands, and Amaury dispirited and bankrupt. On entering Béziers he was expelled by a mob and forced to flee by boat to Narbonne. Having taken the measure of the enemy, Conrad attempted to organize a military order, the Order of the Holy Faith, which was to be modelled on the Templars and would, it was hoped, provide Amaury with a standing army for the defence of his dominions. Funds were raised and a master was appointed. The pope's formal approval was given in June 1221. But thereafter the Order of the Holy Faith disappears from view. The reason was almost certainly a shortage of recruits at a time when the holy war was taking on all the character-istics of a political squabble for secular ends.

Undeterred by this failure, Honorius III directed a succession of jeremiads at the young Raymond and his allies. He threatened Toulouse, Nîmes, and Avignon with the suppression of their bishoprics, a calcu-lated blow to their prosperity as well as their prestige. In June 1220 he gave the young Raymond a month to submit to the church or lose the lands which the Lateran council had awarded him beyond the Rhône. 'Do not congratulate yourself on the ephemeral victories you have already won,' Honorius warned him; 'do not imagine that you can defeat God and defend your territories once we have deprived you of them.' A year later Honorius repeated the threat, this time giving the young count two months to submit. Raymond was unmoved, and in October 1221, he was solemnly declared stripped of all his dominions. It was an empty menace, as both sides knew. Honorius proposed to enforce his sentence by proclaiming a fresh crusade, and set about collecting another 5 per cent tax from the hard-pressed French church. The yield of this tax was spent on hiring mercenaries on Amaury's behalf, for volunteers showed themselves most reluctant to come forward. The archbishops of Rheims, Sens, and Bourges preached in vain throughout the winter, and the townsmen of France, whom Honorius invited to 'surge forth in unison and cover themselves with temporal and spiritual glory' were resolutely uninterested. Some of them, Honorius complained, were under the mistaken impression that Raymond VI was the legitimate count of Toulouse. Nonetheless, the pope remained fervently optimistic and serenely unaware that the enthusiasm of his contemporaries was spent. The fifth crusade, after two exhilarating years in which it had come close to destroying the Ayubites, ended in disaster in September 1221. Contemporaries advanced a variety of explanations for God's humiliating refusal to help his own. Many of them blamed the Albigensian crusade for diverting money and men away from the ill-fated Nile expedition. The *troubadours* directed a barrage of propaganda against the 'false crusade' which ravaged the homes of French Christians while the Nile delta was abandoned to the sultan, and this sentiment, originally confined to the embittered supporters of the Raymonds, was now gaining ground in the north. Weariness and cynicism had smothered both the violence and the idealism of earlier crusades.

Honorius was no more successful with Philip Augustus. 'These humiliations are a shaming reproach to both of us,' he wrote to the king in June 1221. Philip did not agree. He turned a deaf ear to the pope's appeals and did nothing to help the three archbishops in their search for recruits. At the end of the year the legate Conrad made a bold appeal to Philip's self-interest. He persuaded Amaury to offer his dominions to the French king and withdraw from Languedoc in favour of the Capetian monarchy. Since Amaury's dominions were by now reduced to Carcassonne and a handful of widely scattered castles, this surrender did not involve much sacrifice on his part; but it offered Philip the prospect of an expansion of his domain almost as spectacular as his annexation of Normandy in 1204. In the spring of 1222, Conrad travelled to Paris to persuade him to accept it, and Honorius added his own pleas in May. The pope offered him another 5 per cent tax on church property as well as the normal plenary indulgence if he would invade Languedoc and annexe it to his crown. It was an offer which Philip could scarcely refuse. Nevertheless, he refused it. His reasons are not recorded, but he was doubtless aware of the strength of anti-French feeling in the Midi, and he may well have felt that so long as the

Plantagenets remained the strongest power south of the Loire, he would be unwise to add to the number of his enemies.

In July 1222 Raymond VI died in Toulouse after a reign of twenty-eight years during which only the energy of his son had saved his dynasty from complete disaster. The church pursued him to the grave. Although he had died in the habit of the Hospitallers, with the absolution of the abbot of St.-Sernin, and in spite of the numerous pious bequests which filled his will, the church held that as an excommunicate he could not receive a Christian burial. His coffin stood for many years outside the priory of the Hospitallers while Raymond VII pleaded with successive popes to allow him to be buried in the chapel. It was still there in the fourteenth century. But by the sixteenth, rats had destroyed the wooden coffin and Raymond's bones had disappeared.

The church's vengeance was confined to the dead. Raymond VII, who had long ago succeeded his father in fact if not in name, took Moissac in the spring of 1222 and then swept unopposed across the Minervois and the Narbonnais. Early in the following year he rounded off the conquest of the Agenais by besieging Penne. Amaury made a supreme effort to relieve the town, gathering the largest army that he could muster and marching towards it accompanied by the legate and the bishop of Limoges. The besiegers withdrew on his approach, and Amaury briefly savoured his first victory. But with his mercenaries on short contracts, there was little that he could do to exploit it. His position continued to deteriorate. 'Here at Béziers we are surrounded by the might of the enemy and expecting to be killed at any time,' Conrad and his episcopal colleagues wrote to the king in May 1223; '. . . on bended knee . . . we implore you to help us, unless you wish to see the heretics so strong and numerous that they will burst out to engulf your entire kingdom.'

No help was forthcoming. Indeed Honorius had already begun to recognize defeat. With the power of possession behind him, Raymond had addressed tactful letters to both pope and king asking to be recognized as count of Toulouse and hinting that he would be ready to make concessions to the church. For a number of reasons, the pope was disposed to listen to these overtures. The prospects of dispossessing Raymond seemed remote, especially as Amaury wanted nothing more than to renounce his burdensome inheritance and Philip Augustus could not be persuaded to take it up. Moreover, Honorius had high hopes that the emperor Frederick II was about to lead a new crusade to the Holy Land, and his earlier attempt to conduct two crusades at once had not encouraged him to repeat the experiment. A truce was concluded in the summer of 1223. Raymond VII visited Amaury at Carcassonne and the two men were seen joking and talking happily together. But a peace conference at St.-Flour in Auvergne revealed irreconcilable differences. It had to be adjourned to Sens, where Philip-Augustus promised to take the negotiations personally in hand. The conference resumed at Sens in July, but before the matter of Languedoc could be raised, Philip Augustus died and the assembled dignitaries dispersed. Conrad returned to Rome to report to the pope. Raymond and Amaury rushed south to resume the war.

Louis VIII, who now succeeded to the French throne, was to have much to do with Languedoc in his brief reign. He was a small, lean man, cold and unemotional, rather delicate in health, and prematurely aged at thirty-six. Like his father he had unbounded ambitions for his dynasty, but unlike Philip he was a man of very profound piety with a genuine horror of heresy. One of his first acts was to take 10,000 silver marks from the sum assigned to pious works in Philip's will and send it to the impecunious Amaury for the defence of his few remaining castles. But this, as he politely explained to the legate Conrad, was as much as he could do until he was securely established on his throne. A change of reign was always a delicate and dangerous moment in the history of a mediaeval state. Honorius reminded the new king that Amaury's offer to surrender his claims to the king was still open, and urged him to invade Languedoc without delay. But circumstances forced Louis to treat these requests as his father had done. He expressed his regrets, and these were probably genuine.

Louis's regrets did little to help Amaury. The 10,000 marks paid his soldiers' wages for a few weeks and enabled him to beat off a determined attack on Carcassonne by the counts of Toulouse and Foix. But an attempted counter-attack was less successful. Amaury briefly besieged one of Raymond's castles, but his supplies ran out and incessant rain turned his camp into a sea of mud. The bedraggled army returned to Carcassonne, where almost all Amaury's soldiers deserted him and fled to the north, running the gauntlet of Raymond's troops on the way. Amaury was left in the city with less than a hundred knights, a large crowd of frightened women and children, and no stores.

In Narbonne, five southern prelates gathered in the archbishop's palace, surrounded by a hostile populace who were already negotiating with the enemy. By Easter, they hoped, the king might appear in the province, or perhaps some new crusading army would be raised. Carcassonne had to be held until then; but Amaury was bankrupt and mercenaries were refusing to serve on promises. The bishops went to desperate lengths to raise money. They mortgaged their estates and even offered themselves as hostages for repayment. From Rome, Honorius ordered the archbishop of Sens to borrow 5,000 marks and arranged to extract new taxes from the northern abbeys. Amaury himself offered his own person and his ancestral domains at Montfort-l'Amaury as security for a loan of 3,000 marks. It was all in vain. No one would lend them a single penny. In the citadel of Carcassonne, Amaury pleaded with his few remaining knights to accept his northern estates as security for their wages until Easter. Twenty of them agreed to do so, including Amaury's uncle, Guy de Montfort, and Simon's old marshal, Guy de Levis. The others refused. So, on 14th January 1224, Amaury came to terms with the counts of Toulouse and Foix. He surrendered Carcassonne, Minerve, and Penne d'Agenais, and in return the two counts promised that five other places held by the crusaders would not be attacked for two months. Amaury did not abandon his claim to be count of Toulouse, but he undertook to withdraw to northern France, and to indicate before Whitsun on what terms he would be prepared to renounce the titles which his father had won on the battlefield. It was as honourable a surrender as four years of humiliating defeats would allow. The viscounties of Béziers and Carcassonne were immediately awarded to the sixteen-year-old son of Raymond-Roger Trencavel; he had been two years old when his father had been brutally dispossessed in 1209.

On 15th January, Amaury left the great fortress city which for fourteen years had been the headquarters of the crusade, and returned to his family's estates in the forest of Rambouillet. He brought with him the bodies of his father and of his younger brother Guy, sewn up in ox-hides. They were buried a few weeks later in the priory church of Hautes-Bruyères, which the Montforts had founded a century before. Amaury himself did not have the brilliant future which his father intended, but he was not forgotten. He distinguished himself in the service of the crown, becoming constable of France in 1230, a position which the modest income of his family estates was never enough to support. The church paid off his debts in 1239, and he joined the ill-fated crusading expedition of the count of Champagne. In Palestine he fought with a reckless courage worthy of his father, which made him a hero in Europe but resulted in his capture by the Arabs. After eighteen months in a Cairo prison his health was broken, and he died at Otranto on his way back to France in 1241. For many years his tomb could be seen in St. Peter's in Rome.

Amaury was not the only member of his remarkable family to find a grave far away from the forest of Rambouillet. Simon's brother Guy returned to Languedoc and defended the fiefs which the crusade had won him until January 1228, when he was killed by an arrow outside the castle of Vareilles. His descendants were lords of Castres until the beginning of the fourteenth century, but few of them lived there. Guy's son Philip, nephew of the great 'athlete of Christ', followed Amaury to the Holy Land in 1239 where, unlike Amaury, he settled, marrying the heiress of Toron near Tyre and becoming one of the most formidable barons of Outremer. He was assassinated by an agent of sultan Bibars in 1270. Simon de Montfort's youngest son, also called Simon, knew the most dazzling fortune of all. He made his way penniless to England in 1231 and exercised his powerful charm on Henry III. Having recovered his ancestral earldom of Leicester and married the king's sister, he turned against his benefactor to lead the great baronial rebellion which ended only with his death on the battlefield of Evesham in 1265. Two of Simon's sons, grandsons of the crusader, were captured at Evesham, but they escaped in 1266 and sought their fortunes in Italy, where Charles of Anjou was opening up a new field for French adventurers. One of them, Guy, became the governor of Tuscany and Florence, and married into the Aldobrandesca family. In 1271 he avenged his father's death by murdering the English king's cousin, Henry of Almain, in a church at Viterbo. The event shocked Europe and led briefly to Guy's imprisonment. But he lived to fight new battles on foreign fields. He was captured at sea in 1287 and died shortly afterwards in a Sicilian prison. A hundred years after his death, Simon de Montfort's descendants had lost Languedoc but they had planted their lion banner on castles from Syria to the marches of Wales, upholding the adventurous tradition of the family which an English chronicler had called, with unmerited contempt, the 'race of Ganelon'.[29]

# ✠ XIV ✠

## 1224–1229: The crusade of Louis VIII

'I have raised up one from the north who shall come.'
ISAIAH XLI.25

The truce which protected Amaury's last castles in Languedoc expired on 14th March 1224. On 7th April, Palm Sunday, Raymond's officials took possession of Agde, marking the change of lordship with the ceremonial which legal tradition required, a banner flown from the citadel and a cry of 'Toulouse! Toulouse! Toulouse!' from an open window. There was no resistance. Across the Midi similar ceremonies marked the restoration of scores of castles to a generation of *faidit* owners and the return of the southern princes to the positions of 1209. A Trencavel ruled in Carcassonne and a count of Foix in Pamiers. The sons of the lord of Cabaret held court there once again. Toulouse had replanted its vines and rebuilt its bridges. The crusade was a murderous, soon forgotten interlude.

Amaury had not forgotten it. His first ambition, on returning to the north, was to find a champion to avenge the defeated crusade. The king of France was the only possible choice. Now that he was securely installed on his throne, Louis VIII had leisure to perceive what his father had ignored, that the new opportunities of the Capetian monarchy would lie not in the north but in the Midi, with its commercial wealth and political weakness, and a strategic position which would one day enable his successors to turn the flank of the Plantagenets. In February, Amaury repeated his offer to surrender his rights in Languedoc to the crown, and Louis accepted it. The pope's co-operation was essential, but no difficulties were foreseen on this score; Honorius had for some months been urging him in terms of waxing hysteria to invade Languedoc. Three French bishops had already been sent to Rome with a list of Louis's terms. In effect the king was asking Honorius to place the wealth and moral authority of the church at his disposal. He and his army were to enjoy the indulgences of crusaders. His enemies were to be excommunicated as were those of his own vassals who failed to march with him or send substitutes. The cost, Louis pointed out, would be heavy and the church would be expected to contribute to it; a sum of 60,000 livres a year for ten years was mentioned. Anticipating a favourable reply, Louis set about preparing the expedition. He wrote to the citizens of Narbonne urging them to hold out against Raymond VII for a few months longer, and promising them that relief would not be long delayed. He expected the army of invasion to muster in May.

He was astonished and embarrassed to receive a letter from Honorius at the end of April, rejecting his terms and announcing an abrupt change of plan. The pope's *volte-face* should not have been entirely unexpected. Honorius's thoughts on Languedoc had veered from one extreme to the other in the past year, and the continuance of the crusade after the humiliating defeat of Amaury de Montfort was beginning to seem increasingly pointless. There was also the matter of the Middle Eastern crusade, which the emperor Frederick II had repeatedly promised to lead and repeatedly postponed. His departure was now announced to be imminent. In late March, Honorius made up his mind. He recalled the legate Conrad, who was on the point of setting out for France, and gave him new instructions. Instead of agreeing to all that Louis asked, the pope declared that the Albigensian crusade would have to be postponed. But, Honorius added with singular naïvety, he hoped that the king would maintain his menacing pose for as long as possible, so as to encourage Raymond VII to submit to the church's terms. Louis was furious. On 5th May, the day which had been fixed for the departure of the expedition, he summoned Conrad before an assembly of prelates and barons in Paris and publicly washed his hands of the whole affair. Never again, he told the wilting legate, was the subject to be mentioned in his presence.

The pope's decision was a brutal disappointment to Amaury. Since the projected crusade had come to nothing, he was entitled to resume his claims on the county of Toulouse, and in the course of the summer he made strenuous attempts to sabotage Raymond VII's negotiations with the church. Bitterness and resentment certainly played its part in Amaury's behaviour, but even he cannot have expected to be restored to his father's conquests on the crest of a new wave of crusading enthusiasm. There is little doubt that he was acting on behalf of the French king who did not intend, in spite of his angry words, to be thwarted of his prey.

In July, he wrote to the southern bishops assembled at Montpellier, and urged them in the strongest possible terms to make no peace with Raymond VII. When the bishops ignored his pleas, and drew up a provisional treaty with Raymond, Amaury carried his protests to Rome. A royal embassy was despatched to the Lateran at the end of the year. Its members included Amaury's uncle, Guy de Montfort. They produced a profound effect on the vacillating old pope, and the English ambassadors noted in December that urgent business was being postponed while the college of cardinals were locked in debate. What the majority of the cardinals thought is unclear, but the two English agents were under the impression that the *sanior pars* favoured Raymond VII, an impression which, if it had ever been correct, had certainly ceased to be so by the opening of the new year. The college's reasoning was somewhat opaque, even at the time, but its change of heart seems to have been the work of a vociferous minority of southern bishops. They strongly objected to Raymond's reconciliation principally, it seems, because they feared that they would lose the ample properties which they had gained as a result of the crusade. They alleged that Raymond had not ceased to persecute the clergy and appropriate ecclesiastical property. Scandalous broadsheets circulated in which the archbishop of Arles, Raymond's principal champion among the southern bishops, was accused of having taken bribes. Since the archbishop, together with other emissaries of the count, had been obliged to leave Rome in December after two fruitless months in the city, there was no one to gainsay these calumnies. By February Honorius's mood had wandered back to where it had been at the beginning of 1224. A year had been lost, but it was not too late to revive a project so obviously dear to the French king's heart.

Since Conrad of Urach was in Germany, a new legate was required. In February 1225 Honorius appointed Romano Frangipani, cardinal of St. Angelo, 'a man of high birth and probity, conscientious and persevering, . . . in whom we have every confidence.' The pope's opinion was just, but Romano was not a peacemaker. Unlike his predecessors, who had often been bureaucrats or lawyers, he was a member of one of the great noble families of Rome, an ecclesiastical *grand seigneur* of harsh, authoritarian ways. Within a few weeks of his arrival, he had provoked a serious riot in Paris by breaking with his own hands the seal of the university, whose masters had displeased him. Yet in spite of his remarkable capacity for making enemies, Romano was an invaluable auxiliary of Louis VIII. He became an honorary member of the royal family, following the king on his travels, closely involving himself in the political concerns of the monarchy and acquiring considerable influence. In Rome, his persuasive voice recruited two successive popes as allies of the Capetians against the Plantagenets. This forceful individual did not take long to decide that Languedoc ought to be annexed by the French crown.

In the autumn of 1225 Romano summoned both Amaury and Raymond VII to appear before a council at Bourges on 30th November. Six archbishops, together with bishops and abbots from nine provinces, assembled in the hope of seeing the dispute decisively resolved, and they were not disappointed. Raymond spoke first. He promised to satisfy all the grievances of the clergy and to restore everything that he was accused of taking from the church; heresy would be uprooted from his dominions, and the authority of the church re-established everywhere. Indeed, he would accept any conditions that the pope might choose to impose on him, if the council would agree to his reconciliation with the church. Amaury replied by producing the decrees of the Lateran council and the letters in which Innocent III and Philip Augustus had recognized his father as count of Toulouse. There followed an acrimonious debate between the partisans of either side. Each member of the assembly then submitted his opinion in writing and the legate, after perusing their advice for a considerable time, pronounced that the council had found against Raymond. He had 'failed to obey the orders of the church in the manner expected of him'. Having found the juridical pretext that he needed, Romano called on the king with a delegation of prelates and offered him attractive terms for leading an invasion of Languedoc: indulgences for himself and all his followers, a truce with England enforced with ecclesiastical sanctions, and a 10 per cent tax on the revenues of the church. On 28th January 1226 the legate publicly renewed the excommunication of Raymond at a royal council in Paris, and Amaury de Montfort unconditionally made over his rights to the king. Two days later, Louis took the cross. From Rome, Honorius sent his exultant congratulations: 'Praise be to the Lord Jesus Christ who has fired the souls of our son Louis and the bishops and barons of his kingdom with the fervour of his faith; now we can hope to see the perfidy and obstinacy of the heretics confounded.'

The muster was fixed for 17th May at Bourges. The preaching of the crusade began immediately, but the army which gathered to invade

Languedoc was not a crusading army in the sense that the host of 1209 had been. It was the royal army in the service of the church. The king's rights of feudal knight-service had been enforced to the limits of legal precedent, and those who could not or would not come were made to pay for mercenaries to fight in their place. The size of Louis's host was impressive, but there was more than the tartness of a francophobe English chronicler in the remark that fear of the king, not faith in God, had brought it together. Bouchard de Marly and Savari de Mauléon, who had fought on opposite sides at Castelnaudary in 1211, were both present. So were Guy and Amaury de Montfort. The counts of Brittany and Champagne arrived late and left as soon as they could. The river of bishops and abbots, always large on expeditions of this kind, was swollen to an uncontrolled flood by the offer of exemption from the 10 per cent tax which had been made, perhaps unwisely, to those who appeared in person. The lame, the halt and the blind, and an army of women and children, attended with the rest. They had been drawn by an older tradition which made the crusade a form of mass-pilgrimage, and they hoped to claim their indulgence as camp-followers. But the legate dispensed them from their vows and sent them home.

In the Midi, Raymond VII was borrowing money, and the commune of Toulouse were endowing perpetual lamps at the shrine of St. Exupéry. Neither saint nor sinner could match the resources of the Capetian monarchy, and the count had begun to bargain for English help even before hearing the decision of the council of Bourges. The English king, Henry III, was sympathetic. He had recently lost Poitou and La Rochelle to the armies of Louis VIII, and he was intoxicated by the prospect of recovering them while Louis was caught in the Langue-doc imbroglio. A secret treaty was drawn up in the summer of 1225. Ambassadors were exchanged, and Henry's brother, Richard of Corn-wall, was sent to Gascony with an army. Honorius was alarmed. With only days to go before the muster at Bourges, he addressed a stern letter to Henry III, reminding him of his clear duty to avoid any action jeopardizing the success of the crusade, which was a holy war, fought at the church's command against an excommunicate and a notorious protector of heretics. Henry himself was unimpressed by this epistle and 'thirsted ardently to cross the sea in force'. But his council was more cautious, and perhaps more respectful of ecclesiastical authority. Encouraged by an optimistic report from Richard of Cornwall, it advised that an expedition launched from England was unnecessary and unwise. A court astrologer was consulted. His opinion was that Louis, if left to conduct his crusade in peace, would die on the expedition and leave his kingdom in chaos. Henry looked forward to this prospect, and he agreed to leave Raymond to his fate.

Thrown back on his slender resources, Raymond intended to resist to the last. But his subjects did not. They were weary of unending war and disinclined to ruin themselves in what appeared to be a hopeless cause. Toulouse and Agen were loyal, and so was the count of Foix. The others deserted him in indecent haste. 'We long to rest under your protective wings and live under your wise government,' the seigneur of Laurac informed Louis, more than a fortnight before the army had even left Bourges. He was by no means the first. A host of petty towns and seigneurs had addressed humble letters of submission to the king since the beginning of March, and by early May they were joined by many of the great magnates and cities who should have been Raymond's natural allies. Among these were the citizens of Avignon, once Raymond's firmest allies, and masters of the only bridge across the lower Rhône. Their sole desire was to preserve themselves from an ambitious king and an undisciplined army; and to this end they were ready to allow Louis a free passage of the Rhône provided only that the main army did not pass through the city itself. Louis himself might enter the city with a small retinue. The others were to go round the walls. In their eagerness to placate the king, the Avignonese sent a second embassy under their chief magistrate to meet Louis at Montpellier, and a third to welcome him at Pont-de-Sorgues. Here they handed over hostages for their good behaviour and surrendered Beaucaire, which Raymond had mortgaged to the commune for a large loan. But Louis was not to pass the Rhône unopposed. Before he had travelled the last six miles from Pont-de-Sorgues to Avignon, an obscure misunderstanding had transformed the extravagant humility of the citizens into armed defiance.

The sequence of events was much disputed. But it was clear that the citizens were not prepared to let the main army cross the famous stone bridge of St.-Bénézet, since it could only be approached through the city itself. They therefore built a temporary bridge of rafts upstream of it and invited the French to pass over that instead. The advance guard did so. But when the next column approached, banners flying, under Walter of Avesnes, the Avignonese suddenly burst screaming and blaspheming from the gates and fell on them, showering them with missiles and killing several. Finding their retreat cut off, the survivors ran for the bridge thus effectively cutting the royal army in two. Louis was outraged. He demanded an explanation and summoned the citizens to abide by their promises. The citizens released some prisoners that they had taken, but they insisted that Louis himself had broken the treaty and they barred his passage of the Rhône. The victuals which Louis's purveyors had already bought in Avignon were withheld, together with the purchase money. The reason for this sudden rupture cannot now be known. It is possible that the citizens mistook Walter of Avesnes's column for an assault party and concluded that they had been betrayed. But according to the crusaders, who addressed an elaborate letter of self-justification to the emperor Frederick II as suzerain of Provence, the Avignonese hostages were found to be fewer than had been agreed, and their status insufficiently exalted; the citizens, it was alleged, had closed the gates without warning or provocation in Louis's face. Wilder rumours attributed to the Avignonese a plot to assassinate Louis and the legate as they passed with their small retinue through the streets of the city. This, though probably the most popular theory, is the only one that can safely be dismissed, for the Avignonese would not have surrendered Beaucaire to an army whose leaders they proposed to murder. Nor is it consistent with the curious fact that negotiations between the two sides continued for three days after the attack on Walter of Avesnes. More probably, there was a dispute over the route by which Louis and his personal retinue were to cross the city. The citizens insisted that the royal suite leave by a minor gate, and approach the wooden bridge by a narrow path passing directly beneath the rock walls on the Rhône side. Louis thought this undignified and dangerous. Doubtless there were other points of dispute, but events which were obscure enough at the time will not be illuminated across seven centuries. All that is certain is that on 10th June 1226, Louis laid siege to the city and swore not to withdraw until it had been conquered.

It was as a crusader, not as a king, that Louis besieged Avignon, for the city was part of the imperial county of Provence and its ultimate suzerain was the emperor Frederick II, with whom Louis was on cordial terms. The emperor's authority, however, was of a somewhat nominal kind, and Raymond VII's was scarcely less nominal. In practice Avignon was an independent republic which governed itself on strikingly Italian lines with a *podestà* recruited in Bologna, Milan, Pavia, or Genoa. It even possessed a modest *contado*.[30] The Avignonese were disliked in Provence, and many of their enemies actively assisted the French army. But the city was rich enough to afford a substantial mercenary garrison and a double circuit of walls whose two great gate-towers, Quiquenparle and Quiquengrogne, were proudly displayed on the communal seal. Such a city was not to be taken by assault. Louis settled on the slower course of starving it into surrender. Trenches were dug round the walls, and troops were posted on both banks of the Rhône, linked to each other by a bridge of boats.

Louis's cautious decision condemned the bulk of the army to a summer of unrelieved tedium. Only the siege engineers were busy. A large siege train had been brought down the Rhône on barges, but even constant bombardment from several sides failed to make a noticeable impression on the walls. The Avignonese succeeded in burning several of the machines, and Louis's chief engineer, Amaury Copeau, was killed at an early stage by a well-aimed stone. Inside the city, food was dear, but it was dearer still in Louis's camp, for Raymond VII had wasted much of the surrounding country and supplies had to be brought in at enormous cost by river. The summer was particularly hot. The corn was roasted in the fields and the harvest was a disaster. Dysentery, spread by huge black flies, took a heavy toll of Louis's troops, whose bodies festered in open pits until the king ordered them to be thrown into the Rhône. Discontent mounted in the royal army, and added to Louis's other anxieties. More than half the campaigning season had passed; Richard of Cornwall had attacked La Rochelle; several of the barons in the camp were suspected of plotting against him. On 8th August, Louis was persuaded to order an assault. It was a failure. The assault party, led with great courage by the count of St.-Pol, was subjected to a murderous cross-fire from the towers on either side of them, and the count himself was killed by a stone. The defeat was generally ascribed to the treachery of some of Louis's barons, particularly Tibald count of Champagne, that quixotic figure who might have led the crusade of 1219 but had only joined that of 1226 under duress. He had relatives inside Avignon and appears to have remained in constant contact with them throughout the siege. When the assault of 8th August failed, Tibald left the camp without leave and returned to Champagne. The army's morale could not have been lower.

Fortunately for Louis, the Avignonese did not realize how grave his situation had become. They too were suffering from hunger, and at the end of August they asked for terms. The negotiations were protracted, a clear indication that the Avignonese had strength to spare. But on 9th September they surrendered the city and a hundred and fifty hostages to the French king. The papal legate entered the gates and liberally distributed absolutions in streets that had stood under an interdict for most of the past decade; and the commune effaced its reputation for protecting heresy by promising to pay the expenses of thirty crusaders in the Holy Land. Avignon was spared the horrors of a sack, but every other indignity was heaped upon it. Louis took all their arms and siege engines and an indemnity of 6,000 silver marks. The famous fortifications were levelled to the ground, while on the French side of the Rhône, above the abbey of St.-André, an enormous royal fortress was begun at the city's expense. Two weeks after Louis's departure, the citizens had the bitter experience of watching the Durance flood the site of the royal camp, and of knowing how close they might have come to defeating them.

As it was they had saved Raymond VII from destruction in spite of the treachery of his own vassals. The nobility of Languedoc arrived in Louis's camp in an uninterrupted stream, bearing letters of submission, some of which touched oriental depths of servility. Sicard de Puylaurens, a former *faidit* who had fought against Simon de Montfort at Castelnaudary and defended Toulouse against Louis himself in 1219, now confessed to being 'drunk with delight' at the king's arrival. He 'rolled in the mud to kiss the toe of your glorious majesty. We bathe your feet with our tears, illustrious lord and we crave the privilege of being received as slaves beneath your protective mantle.' Such expressions are a better guide to the strength of Louis's army than the computations of contemporary chroniclers or nineteenth-century generals. Most of Languedoc had submitted before the fall of Avignon. Nîmes had made preparations to resist but in fact surrendered at the beginning of June. The young count of Comminges, son of Raymond's most steadfast ally, promised to place all his forces at the king's disposal. Even Jordan of Cabaret joined the torrent of defectors, but he had the misfortune to fall into Raymond's hands while on his way to greet Louis in person, and he passed the remaining two years of his life in prison. Such men had been shattered by the sudden revival of the war after two years of false peace. They were not prepared to become *faidits* again and even if they had been, their vassals would probably have defied them. The garrison of Carcassonne delivered up the fortress in June regardless of the fulminations of Roger-Bernard of Foix, who held it as the guardian of the young Trencavel. Abandoned by his men, Roger-Bernard would have been glad to follow their example. He came into Louis's camp at Avignon and offered his son as a hostage, remaining with the royal army until the end of the siege; but Louis would not accept his submission and the count fled empty-handed when the king struck camp in September.

Louis's march through Languedoc was a triumphal progress. Arnald-Amaury, now a very old, somewhat mellowed man, went ahead of the army receiving surrenders. The king was fêted at Béziers and Carcassonne, and welcomed at Pamiers with meat, bread, and wine, the gift of the bishop of Toulouse. The opposition evaporated. The count of Foix remained in safety at Limoux until the end of September, and Raymond VII, though his movements cannot be precisely traced, seems to have shut himself in Toulouse. Louis had brought his siege engines from Avignon with the intention of besieging Toulouse, but the approach of winter (it was late October) brought second thoughts, and the siege was put off until the spring. Instead, he repaired to Pamiers where a council of prelates and barons had assembled to consider the government of the conquered territories. Louis appointed a seneschal of Beaucaire, and probably another for Carcassonne. Beneath them, a hierarchy of officials was to administer the extensive lands which Louis had confiscated from the new *faidits*, and enforce the scores of trivial legal rights which together formed the foundation of royal power. In the last days of October, the royal retinue marched north, passing at Castelnaudary and Lavaur the battlefields on which Simon de Montfort had laid the real foundations of Capetian rule.

Louis was the first king of his dynasty to enter Languedoc as a conqueror. The propagandists who had seen in the battle of Bouvines the first fruits of a patriotism that was French, not regional, did not allow this triumph to pass unnoticed. In the bombastic verses of Louis's court poet, Nicholas de Brai, the king became a 'reborn Alexander', a transformation as gross as the one which, in Racine's hands, made elegant courtiers of the heroes of the *Iliad*. Parallels with Charlemagne had more to be said for them. The legends of the *chansons de geste* had served as royal propaganda in many parts of France. They were particularly appropriate in a region where memories of Charlemagne were the only emotional link with the Ile-de-France whence Louis had come. Thirty miles from Avignon lay the famous Roman cemetery of Aliscamps, where tradition asserted that Charlemagne had buried the peers of France and heroes of Ronceval. If the most famous casualty of Avignon, the count of St.-Pol, was buried there as a contemporary asserts, then these emotions may not have been confined to flatterers and *literati*. Louis himself was well aware that he had left no more than a thin crust to hold down a sea of political venom, but he had every intention of returning in the spring. Whether his kingdom would have been equal to the strain of another major campaign, the third in three years, must remain an open question. Like the real Alexander Louis died at the height of his achievement. He was already very ill when he left Albi at the end of October, and he died at Montpensier in Auvergne on 8th November, of excessive chastity thought William of Puylaurens, of dysentery more probably. The siege of Avignon had taken a heavy toll on his delicate health and the citizens, in holding out for three months, may have done Raymond VII a greater service than they realized.

Louis's heir was a twelve-year-old child, Louis IX, whose power was exercised in his name by the queen mother Blanche of Castile, and the legate Romano Frangipani. The achievements of a century of effective royal government were suddenly assaulted by a succession of aristocratic cabals. The government defended itself with astonishing and unforeseen success, but at great cost. Languedoc had to be relegated temporarily to the background. The crown was represented there by a handful of officials and a military governor, Humbert of Beaujeu, with a force of some five hundred knights. Humbert was a young man of conspicuous courage and ability who was beginning a distinguished career in royal service. But his role in the Midi was inevitably a defensive one. Louis's unwise decision to reject the submission of the count of Foix had forced Roger-Bernard to conclude a close alliance with Raymond VII, of which the first fruit was the recapture of Auterive, within a few weeks of the king's death. By the spring of 1227, a provincial council meeting at Narbonne was lamenting the desertion of numerous towns which had surrendered to Louis VIII in the panic of the previous year. Humbert replied by besieging Labécède in the Laurageais and putting most of its garrison to death. But in spite of isolated successes, the royal troops were forced to yield ground throughout the next two years. The year 1228 brought a disastrous spring campaign marked by the loss of Castelsarrasin, and the defeat of the French with heavy casualties.

Nevertheless it was Raymond, not Humbert, who sued for peace, and there were sound reasons for his decision. With the power of the Capetian monarchy in reserve, the French could afford to lose a battle, unlike Simon de Montfort who had always known that a single serious defeat might sweep his rootless dynasty away. Humbert of Beaujeu held the valleys of the Rhône and the Aude, including Carcassonne which was for all practical purposes impregnable. His army was small, but no smaller than Simon de Montfort's had been, and its losses were made good by a steady trickle of fresh men from the north. And Humbert made up in political acumen what he lacked in armed strength. If he could not capture Raymond's towns he could at least inflict misery and ruin on their inhabitants, who were becoming increasingly war-weary and mutinous. Toulouse had seen its suburbs methodically destroyed and its vines pulled up for the fourth time in fifteen years, a task which Humbert of Beaujeu had been able to pursue at a leisurely pace throughout the summer of 1228. Time was on his side. Sooner or later, it was clear, the crown would prevail in Languedoc as it had in every other part of France.

Some of Raymond's leading captains thought so; one of them, Oliver of Termes, defected to the French in November. His eyes, like Raymond's, were turned to the north, where Blanche of Castile had proved to be a ruler of the first rank, and the prospect of a chaotic royal minority had failed to materialize. An aristocratic rebellion, sedulously fostered by the English, had been suppressed with ease, and the possibility of another royal expedition to Languedoc could no longer be ruled out. The new pope, Gregory IX, had been calling for one since June 1228. He had made direct appeals to several French noblemen, and had already arranged for the Cistercians to preach a crusade. It was this menacing atmosphere that the abbot of Grandselve found when he arrived at the royal court in November 1228 with an offer of surrender from Raymond VII. The count declared that he 'longed with all his heart to be restored to the fold of the church and the service of his lord the king'. A truce was declared at the beginning of the following month, while most of the *dramatis personae* gathered at Meaux, east of Paris, to discuss the terms of a permanent peace.

The negotiations continued in Meaux and Paris for more than three months. The outcome showed that Raymond's superb tenacity had not been entirely in vain, for the terms, though personally humiliating, were certainly more favourable than those that Louis VIII would have offered him. Raymond remained count of Toulouse, but he was in effect reduced to the status of a life tenant. His only child, Joan, was betrothed to the king's nine-year-old brother, Alphonse of Poitiers, and on Raymond's death, his dominions were to pass to their issue, regardless of the rights of any male line of the house of Toulouse. The principality was much reduced in size. All its eastern provinces were annexed to the French crown, including most of Raymond's extensive possessions in the Rhône valley. The marquisate of Provence was forfeited to the church (which kept it until 1234). The Trencavels were disinherited for the second time in a generation and their small state, once the sharpest thorn in the flesh of the house of Toulouse, also passed to the Capetians. Raymond was left with most of the diocese of Toulouse and the northern Albigeois together with Quercy, the Rouergue, and the Agenais, about half the empire over which Raymond VI had reigned in 1209.

Contemporaries regarded the terms as harsh, as no doubt they were intended to. William of Puylaurens thought that they could scarcely have been worse if Raymond had been captured in battle. But the harshness was more apparent than real. Most of the territory which Raymond surrendered had formed part of the Trencavel state, and as such had never been more than nominally subject to his ancestors. Indeed the final removal of the Trencavels had arguably increased the power of the house of Toulouse in the dominions which were left to it. Effectively Raymond's territorial losses amounted to Nîmes, Beaucaire, and St.-Gilles, together with a few rich and important properties on the right bank of the Rhône. The *faidits* were treated mildly. Those who were not heretics were permitted to return to their own, and many did so. Even the count of Foix, who had been unable to obtain any terms at all from Louis VIII, was allowed to retain almost all of his county with the exception of Foix and two other castles, which were temporarily surrendered to the king in return for a pension of 1,000 marks a year.

The church had not pursued its vendetta for twenty years solely for the benefit of the French monarchy. The treaty commanded Raymond to restore everything that he was accused of taking from the clergy, although their ownership was often the subject of genuine legal doubts. He was required to pay an indemnity of 10,000 silver marks to the church and to spend 4,000 marks on endowing religious houses for the salvation of his soul. A further 4,000 marks was to go towards the foundation of a university at Toulouse for the defence of religious orthodoxy. Orthodoxy was to have other defenders than the academics whom the abbot of Grandselve was sent to recruit in Paris. The first articles of the treaty obliged Raymond to seek out and punish heretics in accordance with the instructions of the church, the germ of that Inquisition which was to find in Raymond such a resourceful adversary in the course of the next two decades. The papal legate was no doubt satisfied that the menacing proximity of the crown in Carcassonne would ensure that these promises were kept. To make the menace real, Raymond was virtually deprived of the capacity to defend his county against invasion. Toulouse and thirty other towns were to lose their walls and moats. Indeed, at Toulouse the demolitions began immediately, while twenty citizens were held hostage in Paris for the good behaviour of their neighbours.

There remained Raymond's personal humiliation, which had long been among the principal war aims of the church. On 12th April 1229, two days after signing the final draft of the treaty in Paris, Raymond appeared in his shirtsleeves in front of the half-completed façade of Notre-Dame cathedral, to beg for absolution from the legate. Among the spectators were the young king, Louis IX, the new archbishop of Narbonne (Arnald-Amaury was dead), and Folquet, bishop of Toulouse, the only participant who had lived through the storm from the first clap of thunder in 1207 to its gradual dispersal more than twenty years later. After the service of reconciliation, the count was temporarily imprisoned in the Louvre while royal officials took possession of eastern Languedoc and brought back the nine-year-old Joan of Toulouse from Carcassonne, perhaps the most important of all the crown's acquisitions in 1229. Through her the French kings were to lay hands on the last remaining possessions of her dynasty. Her betrothal to Alphonse of Poiters, which was celebrated at Moret in June, must have given considerable satisfaction to Romano Frangipani. He had long before concluded that Languedoc would only be catholic when it was in royal hands, and the future was to confirm his judgement. The Albigensian crusade was over, even though heresy had not been destroyed. That was to be the work of the Inquisition.

# ✢ XV ✢

## The Inquisition

'If thy brother entice thee secretly, saying Let us go and
serve . . . the Gods of the people which are round about
you . . . , then thou shalt surely kill him.'

DEUTERONOMY VIII.7,9

The crusade had outlived its founders. Raymond VI, Simon de Montfort, Innocent III, Arnald-Amaury were all dead, and among the other
authors of the crisis, only Folquet of Toulouse had lived to see its
final moments. A generation which had grown up with continual war
needed to be reminded that the crusade had once had other objects. In
proclaiming it in March 1208, Innocent had enjoined the southern
clergy to 'tend the seed which the martyred legate has sown and nourish
it with the preaching of the word'. The pope's optimistic words
remained the official policy of the church, as successive councils of the
southern bishops never ceased to declare. But in practice their declarations amounted to very little. At the outset of the war, the clerical
contingent threw themselves into a vigorous campaign of preaching.
Even Arnald-Amaury, who 'ardently desired to see the heretics die'
embarked, together with Folquet of Toulouse, on a preaching tour of
the Agenais in the early months of 1210. But his preaching was compared by the inhabitants to the droning of bees, and the attempt was
not repeated. After 1210 the preaching was abandoned by all but
Folquet, St. Dominic, and a handful of Cistercians. Of these, only
St. Dominic made a measurable impression on the Cathars. 'When he
preached,' one of his hearers remembered, 'his feelings were so intense
that he would break down in tears, communicating his emotions to the
whole audience; I have never heard a man whose words could draw so
many to repentance.' Dominic's followers had become a powerful band
by 1214, when Simon de Montfort presented them with the revenues of
the newly conquered town of Casseneuil. A year later a new recruit
offered them three small adjoining houses in Toulouse, under the
shadow of the Château Narbonnais in the southern quarter of the city.

Dominic himself left after less than six months, to find a greater role in Italy and northern France. But his followers continued his work, outgrowing the three small houses within a year of their arrival, and covering Languedoc with priories in a generation.

The early Dominicans enjoyed a few spectacular triumphs; yet it was apparent, even before the defeat of Amaury de Montfort, that their impact on the disciplined ranks of the Cathars had been small, far below the expectations of early optimists. In a less violent atmosphere the outcome might have been very different. But though Dominic himself was capable of learning from the missionary successes of the Cathars, his followers, for the most part, were not. They often fanned that uncompromising hatred of heresy which left no room for conciliation, and hardened the fluid frontiers of religious sects. It was the 'preachers' who, in the spring of 1211, persuaded the leaders of the crusade to reject everything that Raymond VI offered them, a policy which aroused grave misgivings among some of the northerners and prolonged the war by eighteen years.

The first Cathar Perfect had been summarily burned at Castres in September 1209 under the personal supervision of Simon de Montfort. Holocausts of unrepentant heretics had followed every victory: 140 at Minerve, 300 at Lavaur, 60 at Les Cassès, and countless others caught and burned in groups too small to be noticed by the contemporary historians of the crusade. The survivors fled before Simon's soldiers like field-mice before the reapers into an ever-dwindling corner of tall grass. Their first instinct was to make for the inaccessible hill-castles of the Corbières and the Montagne Noire. At Roquefort, three hundred heretics were reported to be hiding in 1209. But the old Trencavel dominions were thoroughly colonized and policed in the course of 1210 and 1211, and few of those who stayed there survived Some fled to the Toulousain, where Simon caught up with them in 1211. Those who went to Toulouse itself lasted longer, but the only safe refuge was to be found in constant movement. Thirty-five years after the launching of the crusade, Arnaude de Lamothe, a native of Montauban, recounted to the Inquisitor of Toulouse the story of her unsettled life, fleeing before a succession of catholic armies. In 1209, she was living in a house of Perfects at Villemur, a small town on the Tarn where she and her sister had recently received the *consolamentum*. Then, in June 1209, occurred the abortive expedition in Quercy, led by the archbishop of Bordeaux. The Cathars of Villemur were gripped by panic while the crusaders were still sixty miles away, and abandoned their town in flames. They went first to Roquemaure, then through pouring rain to Giroussens, and finally to Lavaur where they were shortly joined by a tidal flood of refugees from the valley of the Aude. Arnaude stayed in Lavaur until the autumn of 1210 when she fled to Rabastens, realizing earlier than her companions that the crusaders, who had already occupied most of the southern Albigeois, would strike next at the Toulousain. She spent a year at Rabastens, but in May 1211 Rabastens opened its gates to the crusaders. Arnaude had already left. After some months of wandering she returned to her native town of Montauban where, in 1212, she renounced her errors and was reconciled to the church by the bishop of Cahors. She lived quietly in Montauban until 1224 when, after the final defeat of Amaury de Montfort, she heard a sermon by a Cathar deacon and was persuaded to return to her old beliefs. When the deacon left Montauban he took Arnaude with him, together with her mother and sister. They spent a while in Linars and then passed on to Lavaur, where the three women again received the *consolamentum*. At the end of 1224, they resumed their wanderings, travelling by night for safety, escorted by sympathetic local guides. In the next two years they are found at Mauzac, Jul, Claret, Lanta, and Taravel, rarely staying in one place for more than a month. Finally, when Louis VIII arrived before Avignon in 1226, they fled to Toulouse where they settled in peace under the protection of a well-known Cathar nobleman, Alaman de Rouaix.

Arnaude had a better chance of escape than the leaders of her church, whose identities were well known and who had to rely on an elaborate network of unmarked paths and safe houses to protect them. Guilabert de Castres, who had made his first appearance in history as St. Dominic's antagonist at Montréal in 1207, survived throughout the war, administering the *consolamentum* and preaching to a widely scattered flock. In 1209 he had to abandon his base at Fanjeaux for the safer retreat of Montségur, but that did not prevent him from appearing on fleeting visits in most of the hill-towns of the Toulousain. During the long siege of Castelnaudary in 1220 he escaped unnoticed through Amaury de Montfort's lines to continue his mission in the surrounding region. Three years later, as Cathar bishop of Toulouse, he was able to hold a more or less public assembly of some hundred prominent Cathars at Pieusse, only twelve miles from Amaury's headquarters of Carcassonne. Even in the valley of the Aude, where the church had eradicated almost every trace of heresy, the Cathars returned with the *faidits* after Amaury's departure.

The catholic authorities began by instituting a primitive police system. In 1227 the council of Narbonne ordered bishops to appoint 'enquirers' in each parish to report on the doings of their neighbours. Against disciplined and resourceful communities of heretics, measures of this kind were predictably unsuccessful. The treaty of Paris marked an abrupt change of policy but made little impression on the Cathars. Raymond VII was required to make 'diligent enquiries' with a view to arresting and punishing heretics, and Romano Frangipani visited Toulouse in November 1229 to see to the enforcement of this provision. The result was a bulky collection of constitutions governing the persecution of heresy. An assembly of bishops agreed that lists would be drawn up of the entire adult population of each parish with a view to demanding oaths of orthodoxy and tracing the movements of absconders. But this ambitious scheme was probably beyond the administrative resources of the church and in any case added nothing to the panoply of powers which the bishops already enjoyed. The problem was that the bishops were not the best agents of a systematic campaign of repression. They had other cares, and were impotent beyond the boundaries of their own dioceses. They were given to sporadic outbursts of zeal, followed by long periods of neglect and they lacked the elaborate system of surveillance by which the Inquisition was to prevent 'penitent' heretics from relapsing. Raymond du Fauga, who succeeded Folquet as bishop of Toulouse in 1231, began his reign with a dramatic *chevauché* into the Toulousain, capturing nineteen heretics who had assembled to worship in a forest by night. All were burned. But the bishop's reign did not continue in this spirit. Although he was a Dominican, he was also a member of the comfortable establishment of Toulouse, a friend of Raymond VII and anxious to remain so. The contemporary who accused him of altering course with every change of wind had understood him well.

By 1233 the failure of Romani's constitutions was manifest. Those officials who attempted to enforce them often met with violent resistance, and one of them was murdered near Castelnaudary within a few days of the legate's departure. A Dominican teacher at the university of Toulouse who asserted from the pulpit that heretics could live in safety under the noses of the clergy was summarily expelled by the consuls. Yet there was much evidence to support his view. Cathar preachers were addressing large assemblies within a few miles of the gates, and one of their most influential protectors, Bernard-Oth de Niort, was still at large four years after being accused of a formidable catalogue of crimes against the faith. The latter case had become a humiliating *cause célèbre* for the southern church. Gregory IX personally intervened in March 1233 to command the arrest of Bernard-Oth and his two brothers; and Raymond, for fear that worse would follow, complied at once. Indeed Raymond so far overcame his indolent nature as to summon a new council of prelates and barons, at which he issued a series of severe edicts against heretics. But he was too late to prevent the pope from taking more radical measures. In Rome, on the same day, Gregory ordered a 'general inquisition' throughout southern France, and confided the task not to the bishops but to the Dominicans, acting as agents of the Holy See. Except for a brief interval in the middle of the century, the Inquisition was to remain in their hands until its work had been brought to a triumphant conclusion.

The first inquisitors, appointed in 1234, were Pierre Seilha, a former companion of St. Dominic, and Guillaume Arnaud, an ecclesiastical lawyer from Montpellier. They are obscure figures, these founding fathers of the papal Inquisition, whose personalities rarely emerge from the mass of arid legal documents that are now their principal monument. But their energy is beyond question. In the first five years of their mission, their movements can be traced in nearly every part of the vast tract of Languedoc under their supervision. On their first visit to Moissac, they burned 210 heretics. In Toulouse, a succession of prominent heretics went to the stake in the first few months after Gregory's decision and a few dramatic acts of savagery were enough to put the Cathars on the defensive for the first time since the death of Simon de Montfort. On the feast of St. Dominic in 1235 the bishop personally led a catholic mob from the Dominican convent to the mansion of an aged Cathar lady, who was dragged from her bed to be burned in the plain outside the city walls.

This sudden explosion of religious hatred aroused fierce resentment, not only among the victims and their protectors, those 'certain men of means' who were darkly mentioned by William of Puylaurens. Some inquisitorial practices were profoundly disturbing even to orthodox public opinion. The conviction of heretics who were already dead was particularly unpopular, since it involved parading their exhumed remains through the streets of the city, inflicting unmerited infamy on their descendants. In addition the inquisitors were often unduly impatient of treasured local privileges, particularly in the major towns. The citizens of Cordes lynched two inquisitors who were sent to examine them in 1233. Another inquisitor, Arnaud Català, only narrowly avoided the same fate when he attempted to exhume a heretic at Albi. But it was in Toulouse that the Inquisition faced the only sustained challenge to its authority. In the autumn of 1235, the inquisitor cited twelve prominent citizens to answer charges of heresy, an unheralded boldness which was treated as an insult to the city. The consuls replied by storming the Dominican convent and marching him physically out of Toulouse. When the citations were promptly repeated by his deputies, the convent was again attacked and its entire population carried by their hands and feet through the gates. In the orgy of anti-clerical violence which followed, the bishop was expelled, his palace sacked, and his horses stolen. Several clerks of the episcopal household were gravely injured.

Raymond VII's personal role in these events is obscure, as no doubt he intended it to be. Several of his closest associates were involved, and he had certainly done nothing to restrain them. This was enough for the inquisitor who, having found a safe refuge on royal territory at Carcassonne, duly excommunicated the count along with the consuls. Gregory IX was more circumspect. In 1236 he administered a magisterial rebuke to the count, but at the same time his legate in France discreetly invited the inquisitors to moderate their zeal. Raymond's position was a difficult one, for no more than his father could he destroy a sect which numbered among its protectors the greatest magnates of his principality. Yet at the same time, he had to placate the church and the French crown which were now, since the treaty of Paris, both powerful and close at hand. As for Gregory, he saw no advantage in needlessly alienating the count of Toulouse. He regarded Raymond, as he once explained to one of his legates, as a 'young plant to be watered with care and nourished with the milk of the church'. Moreover in all his dealings with France Gregory had one eye on Italy, where the emperor Frederick II's victories over the Lombard league once more threatened the political position of the papacy; Raymond, who was an imperial vassal for his Provençal lands, was still powerful enough to be worth befriending. Accordingly when the count delivered, in the summer of 1237, a petition in eighteen articles complaining that the church was making his position untenable, the pope was inclined to be sympathetic.

In September he suspended the Inquisition for three months while Raymond's complaints were investigated. The investigations proved to be lengthy. The three months became three years and it seemed likely, at one point, that the Inquisition had already seen its last days.

Raymond certainly hoped that the sole responsibility for persecuting heresy would be restored to the bishops, whose activities were likely to be less disruptive to the peace of his dominions. But his hopes were disappointed. He had his own hotheaded allies to blame. In April 1240, the twice dispossessed Trencavel heir attempted with great courage but little political skill to reconquer his inheritance from the occupying forces of the French crown. For a few weeks, much of western Languedoc was in his hands and Carcassonne itself was closely besieged. But Raymond VII failed to come to their assistance, and in October 1240 a fresh royal army arrived under Jean de Beaumont to crush the rebellion with brutal efficiency. Doubtless Raymond's refusal to intervene was wise, but the suppression of the rising added considerably to his difficulties, for the rising was attributed, with some justice, to the machinations of the Cathars. The persecuting instinct immediately gained a new lease of life. In 1241, Raymond was forced to accede to demands that the Inquisition of Toulouse be restored. The effect of the Inquisition's three-year hiatus had been noticeable, but it was certainly exaggerated by the council of bishops which later complained of 'irreparable damage ... from the success of the heretics, whose confidence has increased with every blow to the morale of the faithful'. The inquisitors amply made up in a few months for the three years that they had lost. In the course of ten weeks in 1241 and 1242, the inquisitor Pierre Seilha alone imposed penances on more than 732 convicted heretics in nine different places. In 1245 and 1246 the Inquisition of Toulouse dealt with cases involving more than six hundred villages and towns. An unparalleled burst of inquisitorial activity succeeded in less than a decade in depriving the Cathar church of its leadership and transforming it into an ineffective secret society.

The inquisitors had few powers that the bishops had not enjoyed before them. But their methods were a stark departure from tradition. The older accusatorial system left the detection and arrest of criminals to the complainant, usually the injured party, who then had to prove his case or pay a forfeit. The inquisitor, however, was at once detective, prosecutor, and judge. In the first ten years he and his colleagues travelled regularly about the province, conducting investigations on the spot.

Only later, after several inquisitors had been murdered on their travels, did they transact their business from a modest office in Toulouse, close to the Château Narbonnais, where a small corps of notaries and record clerks were permanently employed. To this crowded head-quarters, witnesses and suspects were summoned from every corner of the diocese of Toulouse. The procedure which was followed had evolved in the course of experience, but it changed very little after the definitive pronouncements of the four councils of Narbonne (1243), Béziers (1246), Valence (1248), and Albi (1254). Its object was always to secure a confession, more useful than a conviction on the evidence since it was likely to implicate other heretics whom the careful investigations of the inquisitors had failed to discover. An 'inquisition' began, there-fore, with a sermon, to which the local population was summoned. A period of grace was declared, within which any heretic might make a full confession and denounce his fellows with the promise of lenient treat-ment for himself. Only very rarely did this fail to produce the desired effect. On one of their first tours of the Toulousain, in 1235, the inquisi-tors encountered conspiracies of silence at Castelnaudary and St.-Felix; even ten years later the entire village of Cambiac agreed in advance to confuse the inquisitors by using assumed names. But these pacts were scarcely ever successful. It needed only one catholic to denounce his neighbour, for the conspiracy to collapse amid the mutual denunciations of frightened suspects.

At the end of the period of grace, those whose names had been denounced to the inquisitor were cited before the tribunal by announce-ments read on three successive Sundays from the pulpit of parish churches. There was nothing to prevent the suspect from escaping except the threat of excommunication. But excommunication involved the confiscation of property. Those who had wealth, and heirs to inherit it, generally appeared as they were bidden; and they included almost all the 'protectors' who were the principal targets of the inquisitors. The trial was undramatic. It was held in secret, in the presence of the accused, an inquisitor, and a notary. In theory, the inquisitor allowed the accused to be legally represented, but the councils of Valence and Albi had effectively excluded advocates by enacting that they were to be regarded as accomplices and punished with their clients. Consequently lawyers rarely attended, unless it were to persuade their client to confess. In the course of its work, the tribunal acquired considerable knowledge of the complexities of heretical dogma, and they were often able to trap suspects into admitting their errors, particularly as lying was abhorrent to both Cathars and Waldensians, even in the presence of the Inquisition. Torture could be used, but it was used sparingly, at any rate in the early years, and the torturers were specifically enjoined not to endanger life or limb. Only if none of those methods succeeded in eliciting a confession was recourse had to the evidence of witnesses. The names of the witnesses and the nature of their evidence were concealed from the accused, on the ground, said the council of Narbonne, that any other course would endanger their lives. The council instructed the inquisitors to examine the credit of witnesses with care before relying on them; but in principle, it declared, they might be perjurers, criminals, excommunicates or other heretics, subject only to the discretion of the tribunal. Only 'mortal' enemies, a list of which the accused was to draw up in advance, were definitely excluded. In practice the witnesses were often spies or *agents provocateurs* in the permanent employ of the Inquisition. More commonly, the evidence consisted of the confessions of other heretics. Raymond Gros, a Perfect of twenty-two years' standing who surrendered to the Inquisition of Toulouse in April 1236, was probably responsible for the greatest harvest of convictions that the tribunal ever reaped. His revelations, which took several days to reduce to writing, resulted in the death, or life imprisonment, of at least a score of prominent Toulousain Cathars, and the flight of many more. Where they could not be acted on immediately, such confessions were meticulously filed in the Inquisition's ever-expanding archive. It is not surprising that most of the more serious riots against the Inquisition had as their object the destruction of the tribunal's records. In 1246 a clerk and a messenger were set upon and killed while carrying the inquisitorial record-books through the streets of Narbonne, and the books were burned. Their experience was not unusual.

The proportion of convictions which such a system yielded was naturally high. There was no appeal from an inquisitor's verdict except, in rare and unusually gross cases, to the pope. After conviction, it remained only to impose a penance. The range of penances had been defined by Gregory IX in his bull *Excommunicamus* of 1231, but a broad discretion was left to individual inquisitors. Prominent heretics rarely escaped with less than life imprisonment, though this might be solitary confinement in irons on bread and water (known as *murus strictus*), or the so-called *murus largus* in which conditions were marginally less atrocious. The council of Narbonne was already complaining in

1243 of the small size and limited number of existing prisons, and of the shortage of stone and mortar to build new ones. Even so, the vast majority of convicts were not imprisoned but suffered lesser, if irksome, penalties. They paid fines, went on penitential pilgrimages which might last several months, or were made to wear saffron crosses on their backs. They lost all their civil rights, and might be required to live in any place appointed by the tribunal or the count of Toulouse. The greater penances were generally followed by the confiscation of the victim's property, the proceeds of which went, after deducting the inquisitors' expenses, to the state. In parts of Languedoc these confiscations resulted in a radical redistribution of land. The small town of St.-Felix, for example, saw 165 acres of its territory sold off in less than ten years for the profit of the state, and in countless other tight agricultural societies, the insecurity bred by rapid social change added to the alarming impact of religious persecution.

The punishments of the Inquisition were not, in theory, imposed but voluntarily accepted by the penitent heretic for his own spiritual benefit. The distinction was a fine one. Failure to undergo the prescribed penance was treated as evidence of relapse into heresy; and relapse, together with obdurate refusal to renounce error, was regarded as putting the heretic outside the protection of the church. He was excommunicated and 'relaxed' to the secular arm with a hypocritical prayer to spare him from death. Unless the victim recanted at the last moment, he was normally burned alive. This code, repellent for all its mannered coldness, was milder than the lynch law practised by Simon de Montfort, and its victims may well have been fewer. Bernard Gui, the fourteenth-century inquisitor who had a reputation for exceptional severity, 'relaxed' 139 of the 930 prisoners whom he condemned between 1207 and 1324. No estimate can be made of the number who died in the half century after the treaty of Paris. But it is unlikely to have exceeded five thousand.

It was the grinding persistence of the Inquisition, not its savage penalties, which broke the Cathar church in those fifty years. Its protectors, who were often prominent men tied by wealth and status to their homes, were more vulnerable than the heretics themselves. Few of them remained after the 1230s. Their disappearance made life difficult for humbler offenders, who were reduced to holding their meetings in forests by night and leading itinerant lives which must have reminded some of them of the worst phase of Simon de Montfort's crusade. Arnaude de Lamothe, whose flight from the crusaders we have already traced, was forced to resume her travels in 1229. Shortly after the treaty of Paris she fled from Toulouse with her sister and infirm mother and took refuge twelve miles away at Lanta, where her Toulousain protector Alaman de Rouaix had a house. By 1234, Alaman was already falling under the suspicion of the Inquisition, and Arnaude was wise to move into a small wooden hut some way from the town, where believers brought her food and fuel. After a fortnight she installed herself in the cellar of a nearby farmhouse. Here her sister died, probably of dysentery. Arnaude and her mother buried her in a copse, before abandoning the district altogether. For three years she lived in huts and caves, relying on sympathizers to bring her food, build shelters for her, and guide her by night from one refuge to the next. In 1237 she returned to the relative comfort of a succession of small towns and villages, but still changed her abode every few weeks and took elaborate precautions against detection. But in 1243 a service which she was attending in a wood near Lanta was surprised by officers of the count of Toulouse. Arnaude was arrested by the Inquisition. Her confession named well over a hundred heretics who had worshipped with her or had helped or sheltered her in thirty years of fugitive existence.

By 1240 almost the only safe refuge which remained to the Cathars was the hill-top fortress of Montségur, some twelve miles from Foix in the *pays de Sault*. Montségur crowns an almost sheer rock rising nearly five hundred feet out of the ground, surrounded by the peaks of the Pyrenean foothills. Its dramatic position has provoked a variety of improbable theories suggesting that it was a temple of the sun, a tabernacle of the Holy Grail, or the capital of an obscure cult of greater interest to twentieth-century mystics than to thirteenth-century heretics. But there is no substantial evidence that Montségur was anything other than an exceptionally powerful fortress which remained, alone among the many powerful fortresses of Languedoc, in Cathar hands throughout the crisis of the crusade. It had been built in 1204 for Ramon de Perella, a man of strong Cathar sympathies who had allowed a number of distinguished heretics, among them Esclarmonde de Foix and Guilabert de Castres, to make their homes there. Although the surrounding region was held by Simon de Montfort's marshal, Guy de Lévis, from September 1209, the castle itself remained unconquered. Yet it was not until after the treaty of Paris that Montségur became the capital of Languedoc's persecuted Cathar church. In 1232 Guilabert de

Castres convened an important assembly of Cathar dignitaries there, at which it seems to have been agreed to transform the fortress into a permanent refuge, a base from which the Perfects could conduct rapid tours of their frightened, scattered congregations. Substantial building works were undertaken to reinforce the west wall of the keep; and below the walls the rock was transformed into a hive of tiny cells which served as homes for a swelling population of Cathar refugees. Only the good-will of the local population enabled them to survive there for twelve years. During the exceptionally severe winter of 1233–4 collections of money and food were made on their behalf throughout western Languedoc and large stores of grain were still being accumulated for their benefit a few weeks before the fall of the castle. The fall of other refuges (Roquefeuil was captured in 1240) and the resumption of inquisitorial activity in 1241 drove fresh bands of refugees to the rock until, on the eve of the final disaster, there were probably more than five hundred inhabitants crammed into the narrow castle.

The existence of Montségur was a considerable embarrassment to Raymond VII, who was anxious to persuade the pope that Catharism was no longer a significant threat to the faith. In the autumn of 1241 the count, having reached an accommodation with the church, besieged the rock with a force which was large enough to frighten the defenders for all the strength of their position. But they had accumulated reserves of food against this eventuality. They also found a number of friends among the besieging army. Before the end of the year, Raymond had raised the siege, and life at Montségur resumed its normal course. The Inquisition looked on impotently.

In the following year the Cathars of Montségur overreached themselves. On 28th May 1242, four inquisitors from Toulouse arrived in the small town of Avignonet, on the Roman road south-east of Toulouse, to conduct an investigation. The governor of Avignonet was a figure from a past age, Hugh of Alfaro, the son-in-law of Raymond VI, who thirty years earlier had resisted Simon de Montfort for seven weeks in Penne d'Agenais. He sent a messenger to take the news to Montségur over fifty miles of rough road, and on the following night Pierre-Roger of Mirepoix, commander of the castle, arrived in Avignonet at the head of eighty-five knights armed with swords and axes. The gate of the citadel where the inquisitors were sleeping was opened for them by an accomplice who had introduced himself into the courtyard through an open window. The doors of the bedrooms were smashed open and the inquisitors, together with their staff, were hacked to death with the violence of eight years of accumulated hatred. The inquisitor Guillaume Arnaud, who died with the *Te Deum* on his lips, was run through several times with a sword and his head was crushed against the stone floor. His precious records were carried off and destroyed.

The news of the murder stunned the catholic clergy. Raymond VII was immediately excommunicated by Arnaud's successor as inquisitor of Toulouse, although no evidence whatever connected him with the crime. Indeed it was a serious embarrassment to him. A month earlier, Raymond had risen in rebellion against Louis IX, in alliance with the king of England and a formidable baronial caucus in the north. The murder of the inquisitors was naturally regarded as part of his plan, and the humiliating defeat of his English allies at Taillebourg in July left him to face accusations of heresy as well as treason. The active persecution of heresy was part of the price which the count had to pay for his restoration to royal favour and absolution from the stain of excommunication. No longer could the Cathars count on Raymond's indolent passiveness to blunt the weapons of the Inquisition. It was Raymond, not the Inquisition, who was to burn eighty heretics at Agen in 1246, one of the largest holocausts since the crusade. In the last six years of his reign, he spent as much as three hundred silver marks on rewards to the captors of excommunicated heretics.

Raymond did not, however, attend the final destruction of the Cathar citadel. It was probably at Béziers, at a church council held in April 1243, that the fate of Montségur was decided. A month after the council had ended, an army of several thousand royal troops encamped before the rock under the command of Hugh d'Arcis, the seneschal of Carcassonne. The garrison of Montségur was small, less than twenty knights with their squires, and perhaps a hundred sergeants. But they had advantages of which they made good use. The formidable natural strength of Montségur made it impossible for Hugh d'Arcis to encircle it, even with the considerable force at his disposal, and he was repeatedly embarrassed by the arrival of fresh troops to join the defenders of the castle. Shortly after the siege had begun Imbert de Salas, a native of Cordes who had been prominently involved in the murder of two inquisitors in 1233, fought his way through the French lines with substantial reinforcements. Until the last weeks of the siege, Cathar deacons freely came and went with small escorts, to raise help, carry messages, and visit the congregations of the plain. Letters of encouragement arrived from the Cathar community of Cremona, testimony to the importance which the fortress had for Cathars far beyond the confines of the *pays de Sault*.

The Cathars had accumulated enormous stocks of grain and water, and the besiegers, who were surprised by the tenacity of the resistance, waited in vain for them to surrender from starvation. Brief, indecisive skirmishes punctuated the long summer days, but went unrecorded except in the fragmentary reminiscences of those who later confessed to the Inquisition: women at the siege engines; robes torn and stained with blood; Cathars dressing the wounds of knights fallen from the wall; others administering the *consolamentum* amid deafening, unending noise; confused memories crammed with names and vivid unplaceable incidents. Having achieved almost nothing in five months, the besiegers took the difficult decision to continue the siege through the winter, and in November the tide changed in their favour. Durand, bishop of Albi, who had arrived with fresh troops from his diocese, was one of that incongruous class of clerical siege engineers who had already played a potent role in the conquest of Languedoc. He succeeded in installing a powerful trebuchet on the eastern side of the rock, where it was close enough to inflict severe damage on the east tower of the castle. The commander of the garrison, Pierre-Roger of Mirepoix, decided to withdraw his men from the outworks on the vulnerable eastern side, a measure which seemed safe enough in view of the steep escarpment which protected it. But it was a costly mistake. In early January a force of Basque volunteers who knew the slopes well climbed the rock, knifed the sentinels, and took possession of the eastern barbican before the alarm could be raised. The sight of the cliff path by which they had come horrified them when they looked down on it on the next morning. But their work had been done. Although their attempts on the main keep were successfully beaten off by the garrison, the castle was now as good as lost. Like all defeated armies, the defenders of Montségur began to clutch at straws and tales of relieving forces which never materialized. A Catalan mercenary captain called Corbario undertook, for the exorbitant sum of five hundred sous, to come to their assistance with twenty-five men, but he was unable to find any foolish enough to join him. For a while, the discontented officers of the garrison had to be persuaded to hold out by dishonest assurances that the count of Toulouse and even the emperor Frederick II were marching to their assistance. But Raymond was not even in Languedoc. He was in

Rome, negotiating his absolution from a sentence of excommunication which dated back to April 1242, the last occasion when he had been accused of clandestine sympathy for the Cathars of Montségur.

On 2nd March, after a determined attempt had failed to dislodge the Basques from the east barbican, Montségur capitulated. The decision seems to have been imposed on the Cathars by their own garrison, many of whom were not heretics, and valued their lives more than the survival of their paymasters. The relief of the besieging army can be measured by the generous terms accorded to a garrison which had resisted them for nine months. They were to be allowed to leave in peace, after accepting light penances from the Inquisition, an indulgence which included even the perpetrators of the Avignonet massacre. Only the obdurate who refused to abjure their errors would be punished. The castle itself was to be forfeited to the church and the king, but its defenders were allowed to remain in possession for fifteen days before it was actually surrendered; they delivered hostages for the performance of this curious stipulation. The reason for it is hard to discover, though it may conceivably have had some religious purpose which the records of the Inquisition, for all their thoroughness, fail to disclose. Certainly the last days of Montségur have all the tragedy and unreality of the closing scenes of *Götterdämmerung*. An atmosphere of mounting emotional intensity was fed by continual services and sermons. Several of the garrison came forward to mark their formal adhesion to the sect. Others received the *consolamentum* in groups of two or three throughout the last fortnight, although they knew that they were thereby condemning themselves to death. On the 16th March those who refused to abjure their errors (they included all the new Perfects) were chained and driven from the castle gate into the hands of the besiegers. They were begged to recant, but none did so. In the plain below the castle, the royal troops had lit a huge pyre of wood, surrounded by a stockade. On it more than two hundred Cathars died in the space of a few minutes. They included Ramon de Perella's daughter Escalarmonde, and Bertrand de Marty, the last bishop to preside over the Cathar communities of the Toulousain.

The garrison had another night to pass in the castle, and for Pierre–Roger of Mirepoix there remained a perplexing item of unfinished work. Two months earlier, after the fall of the east barbican, he had taken measures to safeguard the treasure of Montségur, 'gold, silver, and a great quantity of money', which had been entrusted to two deacons

from Toulouse. They had left the castle by night and been passed through
the lines by sympathizers among the besieging army, local levies whom
Hugh d'Arcis had unwisely posted at a vulnerable point of the blockade.
The treasure was still hidden in a cave in the Sabarthès. On 16th
March, the day before the final surrender, Pierre-Roger concealed three
or four heretics in his quarters. They were secretly let out of the castle
at night, and escaped down the steep rock-face to see to its disposal. Of
the nature of the hoard and the success of their venture, nothing more
is known beyond the fruitless speculations of romantic imaginations.
On the following morning Pierre-Roger and the remaining occupants of
the castle abandoned possession to the seneschal, accepted their
penances, and left.

Montségur was not the last Cathar refuge to fall to the catholics
(Quéribus held out on its cliff-top in the Fénouillèdes until 1255). But
its fall was a catastrophe for the declining Cathar church, for only
the defiance of Montségur had enabled the Perfects of southern
Languedoc to minister to their congregations once the local nobility had
deserted them. After 1244 the Cathars slowly ceased to be a church with
a coherent doctrine and a directing hierarchy. Many of its leaders were
dead, and their congregations had become isolated, autonomous cells.
No Cathar bishops are heard of in the Toulousain or the Albigeois after
1246, and the number of Perfects steadily dwindled. The *consolamentum*
was rarely administered in the second half of the thirteenth century.
There were believers still, but their beliefs, when they came before the
Inquisition, were increasingly muddled and some had not heard a
Perfect preach for many years before their arrest. Raymond VII's
submission to the church in 1243 was followed by a period of particularly
intense persecution in the course of which the Cathars lost such aristocratic protectors as they still had. By the time Alphonse of Poitiers took
possession of Languedoc on Raymond's death in 1249, the petty
nobility had come to accept that the victory of the church was irreversible. The throngs who assembled at Toulouse and Moissac to promise
their loyalty to the French commissioners included many whose ancestors
had sustained the Cathar church through the darkest years of Simon
de Montfort's war. Trencavel, having twice failed to recover his inheritance by force, announced his own submission to the crown in April 1247
in the church of St. Felix at Béziers. Louis IX allowed him a pension of
six hundred livres a year, and in the following year he was found among
the king's companions in Egypt. So was Oliver of Termes, who had

fought beside Trencavel at Carcassonne in 1240, but commanded Louis's crossbowmen in 1248 with a courage which was recognized by Joinville and Innocent IV; he died in 1275, having distributed the greater part of his wealth to the church. These abrupt conversions were telling symptoms of a larger movement of resignation and conformity among the grandsons of a turbulent generation of southern noblemen.

The minority who clung to their faith were compelled to profess it in caves, forests, and back rooms. The more enterprising fled to Catalonia, where the Inquisition had no more than an intermittent existence, or to Italy, where it was ineffective. Pierre Bauville, one of the conspirators of Avignonet, fled to Lombardy in 1245 and found colonies of exiled Cathars wherever he went. At Coni, a colony of heretics from Toulouse conducted services at the back of a tanner's shop; a former deacon of Toulouse presided over another community at Piacenza, and his former bishop lived quietly in Cremona. Bauville passed thirty years among these expatriates until, in 1277, he unwisely returned to visit his son at Toulouse, and was immediately arrested by the Inquisition. He had at least been spared the spectacle of the Cathar church paralysed by discouragement and decay, a condition to which the flight of its leaders abroad had largely contributed. There was much to be said for the opinion of a believer from Auriac who considered that the emigrants were cowards and deserters; 'how shall we be saved if we cannot receive the *consolamentum* at their hands?' 'Will it go on for ever, this hounding of Perfects?' another asked of his fellow worshippers in the back room of a shop in Sorrèze one of whom later repeated the remark to the Inquisition.

It did not need to continue for much longer. The Inquisition of Toulouse had more or less completed its work by the death of Alphonse of Poitiers in 1271, and in 1279 it unofficially suspended its activities. The other tribunals, those of Albi and Carcassonne, remained active, but by no means all their victims were Cathars. Some of them were merely political opponents of the Inquisition, whose existence was becoming an object in itself. Of the twenty-five eminent citizens arrested at Albi in 1299, it is unlikely that more than one was a Cathar. Bernard Délicieux, a Franciscan friar whose prolonged vendetta with the Inquisition cost him his liberty in 1319, was certainly entirely orthodox. True Cathars were still found in the southern highlands of Languedoc. Here the itinerant Perfect Pierre Authier eluded the inquisitors from 1298, when he arrived from Italy, until 1309, when he was captured near Castelnaudary. But no Prefect came into the hands of the Inquisition after William Bélibaste, who was burned by the inquisitor of Pamiers in 1321. He had taken refuge in Catalonia, but an *agent provocateur* had lured him to Tirvia, a Catalan property of the count of Foix where the inquisitor was waiting for him. Even he was found to hold a variety of eccentric beliefs which testify, even better than the circumstances of his arrest, to the decline of the religion whose last martyr he was. The inquisitors had already turned their attention elsewhere: to witchcraft, Waldensians, apostate Jews and spiritualist Franciscans, the eccentric fringe of Christian life which Languedoc had in common with every other part of Europe.

# ✠ XVI ✠

## Epilogue: France and Languedoc

'Thou hast made me the head of the heathen; a people
whom I have not known shall serve me.'

PSALMS XVIII.43

Raymond's reconciliation with the church spared him the miserable
end of his father. When he died at Millau in September 1249, he was
attended by five bishops, and his body was carried by a long train of
mourners and officials down the valley of the Tarn, across the Toulousain, and through the Agenais by barge to its temporary resting place in
the convent of Paravis. He was buried in the following spring in the
abbey of Fontevrault in the Loire valley, the mausoleum of the Plantagenets. For many years his effigy lay beside those of his grandfather
Henry II and his brother-in-law Richard Cœur-de-Lion, a reminder
that princes are the sons of their mothers as well as of their fathers.
Fontevrault, like Toulouse, had now passed into the hands of the French
royal family, and both were to be treated as the spoil of conquerors.
In 1638, the abbess Jeanne-Baptiste de Bourbon, daughter of another
French king, swept his remains away, to make space for building works
in the choir. As for Toulouse, it became a minor provincial capital,
never the most obscure of the king's cities, but rarely more than a
marginal factor in the political calculations of what has remained, to the
present day, a Parisian monarchy. Raymond's lands were inherited, in
accordance with the treaty of Paris, by his daughter Joan and her
husband, the king's brother Alphonse of Poitiers. They were in Egypt
when Raymond died, but commissioners were sent from Paris to take
possession of the principality in their name. In 1240, much of Languedoc had spontaneously risen in support of the disinherited Trencavel,
and the power of the crown in the Midi had come close to extinction.
But the year of Raymond's death passed uneventfully.

Alphonse of Poitiers was a stark contrast to his predecessor. Physically he was unimpressive, nineteen years old at his accession, rather

frail and short-sighted, and liable to occasional attacks of paralysis, the result of a disease contracted in Egypt. He did not enjoy travelling, and he did not often visit Languedoc. Apart from a rapid tour of his dominions in 1251, and another in 1269–70, he passed almost all his time in the immense mansion which he had built for himself in Paris, and on various country estates of the Ile-de-France. But his will was felt in the Midi, even if his presence was not. From Paris he addressed an unending stream of letters and instructions to his agents in the province, who applied them with a vigour that was unfamiliar and, in many cases obnoxious, to the local population. His officials, like the royal servants who had administered eastern Languedoc since 1226, did their work well, and their methods reflected the avarice and authoritarian instincts of their master. They were powerful enough to ignore the privileges and immunities which generations of southern townsmen had extracted from the enfeebled house of Toulouse. The consulate of Beaucaire, which Raymond VI had recognized in 1217, was at once abolished by the royal seneschal. Nîmes lost half its consuls, and the right to elect the other half. Both were directly ruled by the crown, but in his own sector of Languedoc, Alphonse of Poitiers was equally intolerant of communal self-government. He claimed the right to tax the citizens of Toulouse and appoint their consuls. His successor, Philip III, transformed the city which had defied Simon de Montfort into a passive oligarchy governed by consuls who were chosen by a mixture of co-option and royal appointment.

Unlike Simon de Montfort, Louis IX and his brother made no attempt to colonize the Midi with northerners. Many of the *faidits* were restored to their possessions, either under the treaty of 1229 or by royal grant afterwards. But a subtler transformation deprived them of much that they had recovered. The king frequently retained their castles and the authority that went with them. North-west of Nîmes on the edge of the highlands of Gevaudan lay the lordships of Anduze, Sauve, and Sommières, all possessions of a family which had ruled them for centuries. Pierre-Bernard of Sauve had married Raymond VI's daughter and had once nursed hopes of succeeding to his dominions. But his son lost the greater part of his lands after joining the ill-fated rebellion of Raymond VII in 1242. He was left with a pension from the crown of six hundred livres a year and the partially dismantled castle of Roquedur to live in. His income was probably as large as it had ever been, but his power had vanished. The swathe of low-lying land which joined Le Puy to Béziers and Carcassonne was too important to be left to a single untrustworthy southern baron. The royal seneschals of Beaucaire spent the remainder of the thirteenth century patiently accumulating legal rights in the area by a combination of luck, bullying and legal chicanery which was characteristic of their activity throughout Languedoc. The right to charge tolls, protect merchants, coin money, hear complaints in court, repair roads with local labour, all were lucrative privileges and a base for further encroachments on the surviving proprietors of the region. These were the substance of royal authority in the thirteenth century, not the grandiloquent formulae by which weaker monarchs announced themselves to their subjects.

If resistance was difficult for the lords of Sauve, it was impossible for poorer men. Estates which centuries of testamentary partition had divided into a mosaic of tiny family holdings were crushed by the burden of royal taxation which now descended on them. The family which ruled half the town of Alès had to witness the relentless erosion of their wealth and power by the officials who ruled the other half in the king's name. The family was represented in 1240, by the *châtelaine*, her mother, and an infant son. They found their jurisdiction infringed, their castles confiscated or demolished, their subjects taxed, and themselves repeatedly cited before various courts and finally expelled from their home. Their destruction had been completed in less than a quarter of a century. Elsewhere the process was slower, but the outcome was the same. The courts of Comminges and Foix, the lords of Les Baux, and their peers, may have survived. But the far larger class of small-town castellans and petty lords, the authors of the best and the worst features of Languedoc's vanished civilization, almost entirely disappeared, joining the ranks of those *déclassé* knights whom the count of Provence had forbidden to disgrace their status by sowing and reaping in their own fields.

Yet these men were not destroyed by Alphonse of Poitiers or Louis IX. They were allowed to destroy themselves, and prevented from recouping their losses by brigandage. The Midi's new rulers were more tolerant than Simon de Montfort of the peculiarities of southern society and, except where their political interests were threatened, they usually adopted the approach of their predecessors. Their officials were often, but not invariably, northerners, and enterprising natives like Sicard d'Alaman, could still make a fortune in royal service as they had done in Raymond's. The written law of the Midi survived intact until the

Revolution and even spread into neighbouring regions like the Agenais where its influence had been slight. Indeed the authoritarian overtones of Roman law commended it to some of Louis IX's successors, particularly Philip the Fair whose most influential counsellors included upstart jurists from Montpellier like Pierre Flote and William of Nogaret, a southern invasion of the north which was far from welcome to the snobbery and conservatism of an older governing class.

Louis IX and Alphonse of Poitiers both commissioned exhaustive enquiries into the misdeeds of their officials, and the fact that the reports have survived in such massive bulk has blackened their reputations more than they deserve. The *châtelaine* of Alès may or may not have been right in thinking that the seneschal persecuted her because she resisted his advances. How typical her experience was we cannot know. But the government of Alphonse of Poitiers was certainly better than that of the Raymonds, and it was probably better than any which followed it before the age of the eighteenth-century *Intendants*. The fact that the most turbulent of all French provinces submitted meekly to French domination suggests that some at least of its inhabitants thought a century of peace a just price for the loss of their political autonomy. The second half of the thirteenth century was a period of unparalleled prosperity in Languedoc. Narbonne cathedral, the fortress-church of Albi, and the Dominican convent of Toulouse were monuments of new wealth, as well as of the return to religious orthodoxy that went with it. A rapidly expanding population brought much marginal agricultural land into use, and created a rash of new towns that has few parallels in the history of urban planning. They can still be seen, and their names are bombastic reminders of the optimistic mood in which they were founded—Grenade, Cordes, Pavie, Bologne. In the long run, the future of Languedoc was to be a prolonged story of economic decline. But contemporaries can be forgiven for their failure to foresee it. The Black Death and the Hundred Years War proved to be far more destructive for them than the Albigensian crusade, and if Languedoc had become an impoverished backwater by the close of the middle ages, the freebooters of Edward III bear a greater responsibility than Simon de Montfort's crusaders.

The cultural impact of the crusade is a more elusive problem. It was certainly smaller than that of the Norman conquest of England in the eleventh century or even the Angevin conquest of Sicily in the thirteenth. But then the French had ruthlessly colonized England and they were thrown out of Sicily. Neither of these things happened in Languedoc. It remains true that the Midi on the eve of the crusade had a civilization which was recognizably its own. That civilization was already in decline, but its decline need not have been irreversible, nor was it inevitable that the fertility of the twelfth century should have been replaced by the barrenness of the fourteenth. The crusade and its aftermath destroyed the petty nobility which had paid the *troubadours*. It removed the seat of government to Paris. After it, such talent as there was followed the road to wealth and influence which led south to Catalonia and north to the Ile-de-France. The *troubadour* Pierre Cardenal earned his living at the court of James of Aragon. Guillaume Figuera, the tailor of Toulouse who had written songs of overpowering bitterness against the church of the crusade, ended his life in northern Italy among thieves, prostitutes, and publicans. Fortune-seekers went north, like William of Nogaret, the self-made lawyer from St.-Félix de Caraman who became the most powerful of Philip the Fair's ministers, in spite of the suspicion of heresy that had tainted his parents.

The Albigensian crusade was a landmark in the cultural unification of France. There were other landmarks, some of them more profound and more brutal in their effects than the violence of Simon de Montfort—the arrival of the printing press, the stultifying stagnation inflicted in the French provinces by Louis XIV's Versailles, the building of the railways, and the drab uniformity of modern building and enlightened agriculture. It was a slow, undramatic transformation, but its beginnings were nonetheless important for having passed largely unnoticed by contemporaries. The Languedoc of Alphonse of Poitiers was still quite unlike the France of Louis IX, but the process of assimilation had begun. The civilization of France was becoming the civilization of its northern provinces, and its regional peculiarities so many variations on a northern theme.

If the middle ages had not yet decided what it meant by a state, it knew, like the seventh-century encyclopaedist Isidore of Seville, that a nation was defined by a common origin and a common tongue. The Midi rightly thought of itself as a nation, for the *langue d'oc* was not a regional patois. It formed a group of its own in Dante's famous classification of languages, having retained closer links with Latin than languages, including Castilian and French, whose vocabulary was partly Germanic. Those who spoke it were commonly unable to understand French, like the royal bailiff's lieutenant at Albi who in 1228 referred to a seal as bearing an inscription in 'French or some other foreign language'; or like pope John XXII a century later, who was born in Cahors, educated at Orléans, and reigned at Avignon, but was nevertheless unable to read a letter which the king had addressed to him in French. Yet the *langue d'oc* is an almost extinct language, whose disappearance began long before the French government adopted a linguistic intolerance in the sixteenth century and retained it ever after. The bailiff's lieutenant who could not read French was for all that an official of the French king. Louis IX's brother Charles of Anjou might insist, as king of Sicily, that his Italian officials use French, but as count of Provence he was content to let them speak the *langue d'oc* and write Latin. Latin, indeed, remained the language of administration in the Midi even after the royal chancery in Paris had abandoned it in favour of French. But for all the linguistic tolerance of French rulers of the middle ages, their language naturally imposed itself on rival tongues which lacked literary patrons and verbose officials to give them importance and vitality. French was the language of influence and wealth. The majority who aspired to neither might ignore it but the ambitious could not. When Aldebert, bishop of Viviers, died in 1303 he expressed in his will the resentment of a conservative generation at the affectation of well-born youths who spoke French or Auvergnat among themselves; his heirs were to speak 'the language to which I was born and my father before me'. But his battle was already lost. At the other extremity of the Midi, Gaston Phébus, count of Foix, successfully resisted the French king's officials but succumbed to his language. He wrote prayers and hunting manuals in French, and according to Froissart, liked to speak '*non en son gascon, mais en bon et beau franchois*'. Snobbery was a sharper spur than politics.

The high Gothic architecture of the Ile-de-France made its appearance in the Midi with Clermont-Ferrand cathedral, begun in 1248 after the bishop had returned profoundly impressed from the dedication of the Sainte-Chapelle. Its architect, Jean Deschamps, went on to build the cathedral of Narbonne, and his son may have been responsible for that of Rodez. At Carcassonne, an unknown master began, some time after 1267, to draw the pure northern lines of St.-Nazaire, with a sculptural programme borrowed from the Sainte-Chapelle. Outside, the military science of a more orderly world added a new curtain wall to the old ramparts which had failed to keep out the crusaders of 1209. Doubtless French ecclesiastical architecture would have conquered

Languedoc in any case, just as it had conquered the rest of Europe without the aid of crusading armies. The Midi had always felt the influence of the north. Now it had little to contribute in return—some regional peculiarities, a preference for lateral chapels over aisles, and a dislike of flying buttresses, both reminders of an older Romanesque tradition. The one truly original masterpiece was the fortified cathedral of Albi, and that owed too much to the circumstances of its creation to have any influence in the north, where *routiers* did not terrorize cathedral cities and inquisitors did not need to be protected from murderous mobs. The sculpture of southern churches was either carved in a pure northern idiom, or followed with sterile faithfulness the Romanesque motifs which, in the eleventh and twelfth centuries, had been the finest contribution of the Midi to the artistic history of France. In the public gardens at Tarbes there is a reconstructed cloister with fourteenth-century capitals transported from the church of St.-Séver de Rustan. Their style is a century older than the Albigensian crusade. Beside such depressing monuments of lost vitality, the rare evidence of a fresh Mediterranean tradition amounts to very little.

It is too easy to regard the frontiers of nation-states as predestined and their political histories as a relentless march to find them. The 'natural' limits which Richelieu claimed for France in the seventeenth century have had the sanction of French armies, and of that sense of historical destiny which is peculiarly French. Yet in the twelfth century the Massif Central was a political and cultural frontier of greater importance than the Pyrenees. It is true that Languedoc was legally a fief of the French crown, but then so, at one point, had been the March of Spain which the house of Barcelona had transformed into a powerful and independent monarchy. The Pyrenees might have seemed a formidable natural barrier, but the coastal road and the Mediterranean were finer highways than any that connected Toulouse with Paris. Along it had travelled the money with which the Catalan dynasty had bought the homage of the Trencavels in 1067, and the architects who built at Tarragona a large-scale replica of the Cistercian cloister of Fontfroide. Southern France belonged to the same world as Catalonia, a world which was far removed from the France of Philip-Augustus and Louis IX. Much of it was already ruled by the house of Barcelona, and if social disintegration was to throw the rest into the hands of a foreign power, then it must have seemed likely, at the close of the twelfth century, that that power would be Catalonia.

# Epilogue: France and Languedoc

As it was, the Catalans lost the extensive lands that they had already acquired in the Midi, as well as the hope of acquiring more. The end of the house of Toulouse proved to be no more than a passing moment in the southern expansion of the French monarchy, a process which continued for more than a century after 1249. The last Catalan count of Provence was a cousin of the king of Aragon, but he ruled his dominions as an independent state, and when he died in 1245 his sole heiress was quickly betrothed to the French king's brother, Charles of Anjou. The Catalans went as far as they could to prevent this disastrous union, even attempting to kidnap the bride. But the attempt was a failure, and Charles occupied his new possessions with an army of lawyers to construct a centralized state out of the mass of obscure committal rights, in the efficient manner which the Capetians had made traditional in the north. Provence itself had a curious fate. Charles of Anjou's conquest of southern Italy, which was completed in 1268 on the battlefield of Tagliacozzo, transformed it into the French annexe of an Italian kingdom, whose connection with the French crown became increasingly distant with each new generation of its rulers. The French kings had to wait until the end of the fifteenth century for the final absorption of Provence into their dominions. In Languedoc they were more fortunate. Alphonse of Poitiers died in 1271 of an illness contracted on St. Louis's last crusade, and his wife followed him to the grave three days afterwards. Their marriage had been childless, and their heir was Philip III of France.

The Catalans had already recognized defeat. By the treaty of Corbeil in 1258 James of Aragon renounced all his claims in Languedoc and Provence, and Louis IX in turn recognized him as soveriegn of what had once been the March of Spain. Montpellier, Roussillon, and Cerdagne remained in the hands of the kings of Aragon, who added them to the Balearic Islands to form the curious dependency of Aragon known as the 'kingdom of Majorca'. Montpellier was purchased by France in 1349, but Roussillon remained a Spanish province until it was ceded by treaty to Louis XIV in the seventeenth century. If ambitious barons and Aragonese kings occasionally dreamed of restoring the alliances of the past, their efforts came to nothing. In 1275, the viscount of Narbonne plotted to throw out the French with Castilian help, and thirty years later Carcassonne thought to offer itself to an Infante of Majorca; but these gestures were regarded, even among southerners, as more ridiculous than dangerous. The Infante's father publicly boxed him on the ear.

# Epilogue: France and Languedoc

Conditions were very different when the Midi next fell under the sway of an austere and militant religion. The Calvinism of the sixteenth century took root in regions which had been Cathar strongholds in the thirteenth, but they did so after Languedoc had been governed for three centuries by one of the most centralized of all European monarchies. French protestantism was an essentially bourgeois phenomenon but, like Catharism, it had enough aristocratic support to field an army of petty nobles whom economic hardship had driven to rebellion. Small towns whose walls had been allowed to crumble since the Albigensian crusade and the Hundred Years War, and whose citadels were pierced by paths and hen-runs, were once again the battlegrounds of rival creeds. The sixteenth-century wars of religion were part of a wider conflict, the fruit of tensions that went far beyond the troubles of a single French province. They pose an intriguing problem of historical continuity. But if there was, as some thought, a link between the heresies of the thirteenth century and those of the sixteenth, then it was the Waldensians who provided it. The Cathars had long since vanished without trace.

# Notes

The primary sources for the history of the crusade are listed in the bibliography. These notes deal only with matters which are either controversial or particularly recondite.

(1) S. Stronski, *Le troubadour Elias de Barjols*, 1906, no. 1, 1. 20.

(2) Etienne de Bourbon, *Anecd. hist.*, no. 327, ed. A. Lecoy de la Marche, 1877, pp. 275–7.

(3) Indulgence often stated to have required forty days' service, but no mention of this in Innocent's correspondence, and that period seems to have been suggested by financial, not spiritual considerations. The legates laid down a minimum period in 1210 (see Peter of V.-de-C., 184).

(4) The chronology of these events is highly conjectural. Milo was appointed before 1st March 1209 (see Potthast, *Reg. Rom.* 3683) but almost certainly after 3rd February, when Innocent sent his plan of campaign to the legates. This would place the departure of Raymond's embassy in the second half of January. He would not have appealed to Rome if he had not already been rejected by Arnald-Amaury, so that November–December 1208 seems to be the most likely date for the encounter at Aubenas, and early January for the meeting with Raymond-Roger. Raymond's visit to Otto (mentioned only by Wm. of Puylaurens) is impossible to date but likely to have preceded his meeting with Arnald-Amaury.

(5) H. Leclercq, 'Embaumement', *Dict. d'arch. chrét. et de lit.*; C. G. Loomis, *White magic*, 1948, pp. 54–5, 171–2.

(6) On Gascon weapons, *Gérard de Roussillon*, ed. F. Michel, 1856, pp. 53, 144; *Hist. de la guerre de Navarre*, ed. F. Michel, 1856, pp. 365–8, 430–2.

(7) The date 10th July given by Vaissète, vol. vi, p. 286n[2] must be wrong as the crusaders did not leave Lyon until early July, see E. Petit, *Ducs de Bourgogne*, vol. iii, 1889, p. 167.

(8) Benjamin of Tudela, *Itin.*, ed. M. N. Adler, 1907, pp. 2–4. G. Saige, *Juifs de Languedoc*, 1881, on their economic activities; cf. J. Regné, *Etude sur la condition des juifs de Narbonne*, 1912, pp. 64–72, 188–91. G. Scholem, *Ursprung und Anfänge der Kabbala*, 1962, esp. pp. 9–15, deals brilliantly with Jewish mysticism.

(9) *Bullaire de Maguelone*, ed. J. Rouquette, vol. ii, 1912, pp. 446–7. And generally, G. Gualtier, 'Le vignoble et les vins dans le Languedoc oriental de la fin du xie siècle a la guerre de cent ans', *Etudes . . . à A. Fliche*, 1922, pp. 101–22; A. Dupont, 'L'exploitation du sel sur les étangs du Languedoc', *Annales du Midi*, vol. lxx, 1958, pp. 7–25.

(10) G. Sicard, *Moulins de Toulouse*, 1953, pp. 29–31, 38–41, 45, but floating mills would have survived for longer at Carcassonne where there was no navigation to obstruct.

(11) A. Wilmart, *Auteurs spirituels et textes dévots*, 1932, pp. 38–45.

(12) C. Du Cange, *Glossarium latinitatis*, 1883–7, s.v. 'sepeliri'.

(13) The chronology of these events is confused, see J. Miret y Sans, 'Itinerario del rey Pedro', *Bol. de la R. Acad. de buenas letras de Barcelona*, 1905–6, pp. 509–13; and *Chanson*, vol. i, p. 110n[2].

(14) *La Bible Guiot* analysed by C-V. Langlois, *La vie en France*, vol. ii (*d'après les moralistes*,), 1926–8, p. 62.

(15) Wm. of St.-Thierry, *Vita S. Bernardi* I. 1, Migne *Patr. Lat.* vol. clxxxv, col. 227. Fullest statement of the church's view in John of Salisbury, *Policraticus* VI, ed. C. C. J. Webb, 1909, pp. 8–58; cf. Stephen of Fougères, *Livre des Manières*, ed. J. Kremer, 1887, perhaps based on it.

(16) Vaissète, vol. vi, p. 872, vol. viii, cols. 604–7.

(17) A. Lecoy de la Marche, *Chaire française*, 2nd ed., 1886, pp. 53–9; T. F. Crane, *Exempla of Jacques de Vitry*, 1890, p. xxvii; P. Funk, *Jakob von Vitry*, 1909, is surely wrong to deny that he preached in 1211-12 (see Peter of V.-de-C., 285, 306) simply because the fact is not mentioned in his works.

(18) Caesarius of Heisterbach, *Dial. Mirac.* V.21, vol. i, p. 301, giving wrong date as appears from Rainer of Liège, *Chron.*, *M.G.H.SS.* xvi. 665, *Annales Marbacenses*, *M.G.H.SS.* xvii. 172, *Annales Colonienses*, *M.G.H.SS.* xvii. 826. For the poor, Peter of V.-de-C., 315, and cf. 339 on unaccompanied foot-soldiers.

(19) *Chanson*, vol. i, p. 210n[3]. Not the same as Martin of Olite (as Peter of V.-de-C., vol. i, p. 263n[2] asserts) since the latter was in command of Montferrand in 1222 (*Cart. Maguelone*, vol. ii, p. 217).

(20) Wm. of St.-Thierry, *Vita S. Bernardi*, I.5, Migne *Patr. Lat.*, vol. clxxxv, col. 241 ('loco horroris et vastae solitudinis'). On the landscape generally, M. Bloch, *Charactères originaux de l'histoire rurale française*, 1964–8, ch. 1 (on deforestation); E. Baratier, *Démographie Provençale*, 1961, pp. 75–80 (applicable to Languedoc too?); G. Duby, 'Les pauvres des campagnes', *Rev. d'hist. de l'Egl. de Fr.*, vol. lii, 1966, pp. 25–32; C. Higounet, 'L'occupation du sol du pays entre le Tarn et la Garonne', *Annales du Midi*, vol. lxv, 1953, pp. 301–30, and 'Les sauvetés de Moissac', *ibid.*, vol. lxxv, 1963, pp. 505–13.

(21) V. Fons, *Rec. de l'Acad. de Legislation de Toulouse*, 1871, p. 13.

(22) The size of armies at Muret is a problem. Peter of V.-de-C. gives 800 as Simon's strength and is almost certainly right, but his 100,000 for the enemy is absurd. Peter II brought 800 to 1,000 'homens a caval' from Spain (James of Aragon, p. 16), a term which surely embraces equerries and mounted sergeants as well as knights, so that Delpech, vol. i, p. 20 is wrong to multiply by three. No figures for his infantry (did he have any?); little doubt that Toulouse militia was principal infantry force in the army, but it was excluded from the battle. Southern princes had lost their lands and cannot have produced more than the knights they had with them in Toulouse plus volunteers mentioned by Peter of V.-de-C. (600?, 800?); of the southerners, ct. of Foix certainly fought in the battle (see Wm. of Puylaurens) but no mention of Raymond. Given conditions of Languedoc, a total southern strength (inc. Spaniards) of more than 10,000 fighting men is exceedingly unlikely, and of these perhaps 2,000 fought in the battle.

Armchair generals have been busy. The problem is that Wm. of P. states that Simon left Muret by the east, while *Chanson* states that he left by the Sales gate (which is on the west); no conflict because Sales gate gave onto passage leading E. to St.-Sernin bridge as well as onto Sales road (see plan).

# Notes

Nevertheless Delpech, followed by Oman, makes him leave by the W. and charge round town, across river, through Toulousain siege-works and into enemy ranks, a considerable feat; to do this they must dismiss Wm. of P. and place Toulousains and their camp on E. side of town although all sources agree that they were engaged in bombarding walls of lower town on W. side. Wm. of P., says Oman, 'obviously made the common error of writing east for west as we all do sometimes'; why read the sources at all? There is no reason to suppose that Toulousain camp was on Perramon hill (as Delpech, Dieulafoy, Belperron). Peter's camp was behind his lines (see Wm. of P., and *Chanson*), i.e. N. of plain since only Pesquiès is still a marsh in September. Dieulafoy's belief that Simon's first squadron charged W. into Toulousain besiegers and then E. into Spanish lines has no basis—improbable and dangerous and based on a misreading of Wm. of P.

(23) On Raymond and John, H. Cole, *Docs. illustr. of Engl. hist.*, 1844, pp. 242, 245-6, 249-50, 256-9, 262 (ambassadors, but what did they discuss?); T. D. Hardy, *Rot. lit. pat.*, vol. i, 1835, p. 108 (subsidies); Rymer, *Foedera*, vol. i (1), London, 1816, p. 123 (letter to R. Curzon); Hardy, *Rot. lit. claus.*, vol. i, 1833, p. 171 (letter to La Réole). John's orders to his Gascon officials (20th November) to persecute heretics 'lest we appear to be their allies and sympathizers' suggests that he had been accused of plotting against Simon (Rymer, vol. i(1), p. 126), hence copy to Peter of Benevento (*ibid.*). For John's movements in 1214 see itinerary in Hardy, *Rot. lit. pat.*, and P. of V.-de-C., 522; there is no reason to suppose, with Guébin (P. of V.-de-C., vol. ii, p. 215n[4]) that P. of V.-de-C. has confused Périgueux with Peyrouse, since John was certainly in Périgord in July and August: 19-25th July is most probable date. Ralph of Coggeshall, *Chron. Angl.*, ed. J. Stevenson, 1875, p. 168, says Raymond did homage for Toulouse to John, who paid him 10,000 marks 'ut dicebatur'; but this is hard to reconcile with Potthast, *Reg. Rom.* 4950 (Innocent pays for his journey to Rome) or with Hardy, *Rot. lit. pat.* pp. 106 108 (John does same).

(24) Pressutti, *Reg. Honorius* 304, 1122.

(25) Wm. of P., XXVII.

(26) Arch. Dep. Pyr. Atl. (Pau), E. 394 (report of papal commissioners).

(27) John of Garland, *De triumphis ecclesiae*, ed. T. Wright, 1856, p. 83.

(28) Oman, vol. ii, pp. 3-9.

(29) Roger of Wendover, vol. iii, p. 67 (Ganelon was the traitor who betrayed Roland).

(30) A *podestà* was a general, chief magistrate, and town clerk combined, who was appointed (usually for a year at a time) by Italian city republics to administer their affairs; he was usually a professional administrator chosen from another city, so that he would stand above factional conflicts. A *contado* was the rural district (usually corresponding to the diocese) which most Italian city republics had subordinated to themselves.

# Select bibliography

## SOURCES

### A. Religious treatises

All the THEORETICAL WRITINGS OF THE FRENCH CATHARS perished at the hands of the Inquisition. But there survive a ritual in Provençal (L. Clédat, *Le nouveau testament traduit au xiii^e siècle suivi d'un rituel cathare*, 1887); and a remarkable treatise, written in Italy, the *Livre des deux principes*, ed. C. Thouzellier, 1973. CATHOLIC WORKS OF REFUTATION are more common and are extremely revealing in spite of their obvious bias. The most important are Peter the Venerable, *Contra Petrobrusianos*, ed. J. Fearns, 1968; Alan of Lille, *De fide catholica contra hereticos*, Migne *Patr. Lat.*, vol. ccx; Durand of Huesca, *Lib. Contra Manichaeos*, ed. C. Thouzellier, 1964, and works by Italian writers based on their own (perhaps untypical) experience, Moneta of Cremona, *Adv. hereticos et Valdenses*, ed. T. A. Ricchini, 1743, Rainer Sacchoni, *Summa de Catharis*, ed. A. Dondaine in *Un traité neo-manichéen*, 1939, pp. 64–78, and Anselm of Alexandria, *Tractatus de hereticis*, ed. A. Dondaine, *Arch. Fratr. Praedic.*, xx. 1950. Bernard Gui, *Practica Inquisitionis*, ed. C. Douais, 1886, is the work of an experienced inquisitor, writing in 1321–2.

### B. Narrative sources

Chronicles rarely mention Languedoc before 1204. Apart from occasional (and suspect) references in English chroniclers, the only worthwhile source is GEOFFREY DE VIGEOIS, *Chron.*, ed. P. Labbe in *Nov. Bibl. Manuscr.*, vol. ii, 1657, pp. 279–342, a Gascon and an irrepressible gossip whose testimony should be used with caution. Some CONTEMPORARY LETTER WRITERS deal with the anarchy and the spread of Catharism, see particularly St. Bernard, Ep. 241, Migne *Patr. Lat.*, vol. clxxxii, cols. 454–6; Geoffrey of Auxerre in *ibid.* vol. clxxxv, col. 414; abp. of Narbonne in Bouquet, *Rec. Hist. Fr.*, vol. xvi, pp. 159–60; and Raymond V in *ibid.* vol. xiii, p. 140.

From 1204 the sources are full and extremely well informed. The 'official historian' of the crusade was PETER OF VAUX-DE-CERNAY, *Historia Albigensis*, ed. P. Guébin and E. Lyon, 3 vols., 1926–39. Peter was a Cistercian of Vaux-de-Cernay in the forest of Rambouillet, who came to Languedoc in 1212, when his uncle became bishop of Carcassonne, and remained there for most of the next seven years. Much of his chronicle is an eye-witness account and the rest is based on documents which he had inspected or the reminiscences of other participants whom he knew well. It is the work of an uncompromising fanatic, filled with slavish adulation of Simon de Montfort and hysterical abuse of Raymond VI. Peter occasionally draws a discreet veil over embarrassing truths. He was extremely sensitive to any suggestion that the church was divided in its attitude to the war, and he suppresses the doubts which Innocent III himself expressed on the matter. But Peter, who was not yet twenty when he came to the Midi, was too naïve to distort history. Fraud and violence became glorious when practised in the cause of the faith, and he made no attempt to conceal either. Whenever his account can be checked against documentary sources it is almost invariably found to be correct. The CHANSON DE LA CROISADE ALBIGEOISE, ed. E. Martin-Chabot, 3 vols., 1931–61, is an epic poem of 9,578 lines in Provençal. The first third of it is the work of WILLIAM OF TUDELA, a Navarrese priest who had lived in Montauban for many years and wrote under the patronage of Baldwyn of Toulouse. He was a mediocre poet but an honest and thorough historian, relatively free of bias. He was a firm catholic, but he resented the northern invasion and he believed that the church had cynically ill-treated Raymond VI. His ANONYMOUS CONTINUATOR, who continued the poem up to 1219, wrote poetry of a very high order but he lacked William's objectivity. What little he tells us about himself suggests that he was a layman from Toulouse, perhaps a lawyer, and probably in the service of the young Raymond. He was a passionate partisan of the south, and his account of events in the crusaders' camp cannot be relied upon. But he was present at the Lateran council and at the sieges of Beaucaire and Toulouse, and describes them with a vivacity and an eye for detail which are found in no other source. A fourteenth-century PROSE VERSION (Vaissète, vol. viii, cols. 1–206) supplies some lacunae in the only MS. of the *Chanson*, but otherwise adds little. WILLIAM OF PUYLAURENS, *Chronica*, ed. G. Beyssier in *Troisième mélange d'histoire du moyen âge*, Bibl. de la Fac. des Lettres de Paris fasc. 18, 1904, pp. 85–175, is brief, episodic, and late. He wrote the relevant part of his chronicle in extreme old age, some time after 1250, and his memory for dates and places is sometimes confused. But he had known many of the *dramatis personae*, having been secretary successively to Fulk of Toulouse and Raymond VII, and later an inquisitorial notary. Like William of Tudela he was a catholic but also a loyal supporter of the house of Toulouse. His work is filled with revealing anecdotes told to him by older friends who had taken part in the crusade.

WILLIAM PELHISSON, *Chronica*, ed. C. Douais in *Les sources de l'hist. de l'Inquisition*, 1881. The author was a Dominican of Toulouse who played a personal part in the establishment of the Inquisition in the 1230s and wrote a brief but vivid account of its tribulations.

Many European chroniclers mention the crusade and some of them add names and dates which are missing from the local historians. The most useful are the official chroniclers of Philip-Augustus RIGORD, *Chron.*, and WILLIAM THE BRETON, *Philippide*, both ed. H-F. Delaborde, 1882–5; ALBERIC OF TROIS-FONTAINES, *Chron.*, Mon. Germ. Hist., Scr. vol. xviii; ROBERT OF AUXERRE, *Chron.*, ibid. vol. xxvi. The memoirs of JAMES OF ARAGON (*Libre del feyts . . . del rey Jacme*, ed. Aquilo y Fuster, 1878) are late but the only reliable Spanish source for the Muret campaign. CAESARIUS OF HEISTERBACH, *Dialogus Miraculorum*, ed. J. Strange, 2 vols., 1851, contributes colourful but suspect anecdotes, including 'Kill them all'. HISTOIRE DES DUCS DE NORMANDIE (*c.* 1220?) ed. F. Michel, 1840, follows the doings of Savari de Mauléon. The best northern accounts of the crusade of Louis VIII are the CHRONICON TURONENSIS in Bouquet, *Rec. Hist. Fr.* vol. xviii; NICHOLAS DE BRAI, *Gesta Lodovici VIII* in *ibid.* (interesting but unreliable); and PHILIPPE MOUSKES, *Chronique Rimée*, ed. Reiffenberg, vol. ii, 1838 is an important echo of royalist propaganda. The English chronicler ROGER OF WENDOVER, *Flores Historiarum*, vol. ii, ed. H. Luard, 1887, is probably reliable on English policy but his account of the siege of Avignon is coloured by his outrageous francophobe instincts.

# Select bibliography

## C. Documentary sources

The RECORDS OF THE INQUISITION survive in part. They were compiled after 1234 but they deal with matters going back to the last years of the twelfth century, and they are the best account we have not only of the theology of the Cathar church but of its obscure existence during the persecutions which followed the crusade. They are to be found in manuscript copies of the eighteenth century in the Bibl. Nat. (Paris), Coll. Doat, vols xxi–xxxvii, and in Bibl. Mun. Toulouse MS. 609. Some extracts are printed in C. Douais, *Documents pour servir à l'histoire de l'Inquisition dans le Languedoc*, 2 vols,. 1900, and in G. Koch, *Frauenfrage und Ketzertum*, 1962, pp. 186–200. From time to time the bishops also exercised inquisitorial functions, but the only EPISCOPAL RECORDS which throw significant light on heresy in this period are those of Jacques Fournier, bishop of Pamiers (d. 1325), in *Le Registre d'Inquisition de Jacques Fournier*, ed. J. Duvernoy, 3 vols, 1965.

The OFFICIAL CORRESPONDENCE OF THE POPES, Innocent III (Migne *Patr. Lat.* vols. ccxiv–ccxvii), Honorius III (calendared by P. Pressutti, 2 vols., 1888–95), and Gregory IX (calendared and partly printed by L. Auvray, 2 vols., 1896–1910). The register of Innocent III includes some of the REPORTS OF THE LEGATES; others will be found in Vaissète, vol. viii, cols. 760, 765–6, 866–70, 817–19, 838–40, 893–4, 900–1, in *Gallia Christiana*, vol. vi, 1739, Instr. cols. 111–12, and in Bouquet, *Rec. Hist Fr* , vol. xix, p. 736.

OFFICIAL LETTERS AND CHARTERS of the counts of Toulouse (A. Molinier, *Cat. des actes de Raimond VI et de Raimond VII*, in Vaissète vol. viii, cols. 1940–2008), the Montforts (*ibid.*, *Cat. des actes de Simon et d'Amaury de Montfort*, 1874), and the kings of France (L. Delisle, *Cat. des actes de Philippe-Auguste*, 1856, and calendar appended to Petit-Dutaillis, *op. cit.*). ENGLISH DIPLOMATIC CORRESPONDENCE sheds some light on the years 1224–6, see particularly T. Rymer, *Foedera*, vol. i(1), London, 1816, 126, 174–6, 179, and W. W. Shirley, *Royal letters. Henry III*, vol. i, 1862, no. 209. MISCELLANEOUS DOCUMENTS in A. Magen and G. Tholin, *Archives Municipales d'Agen. Chartes*, vol. i, 1876; J. Rouquette and A. Villemagne, *Cartulaire de Maguelonne*, vol. ii, 1913–14; F. Galabert, *Album de Paléographie*, 1932; and the incomparable collection of contemporary documents in Vaissète, vol. viii. The best sources for the period after 1229 are the ADMINISTRATIVE INQUESTS of Louis IX and Alphonse of Poitiers, see Vaissète, vol. vii(2) and P. Guébin, *Les enquêtes administratives d'Alfonse de Poitiers*, 1959.

ACTS OF ECCLESIASTICAL COUNCILS in J. D. Mansi, *Sacrorum Conciliorum ... collectio*, 55 vols., 1759 etc. and, on the Carcassonne debate of 1204, P. Benoist, *Hist. des Albigeois et Vaudois*, vol. i, 1691, pp. 269–71.

## D. Literary sources

Contemporary biographies of the TROUBADOURS are collected in J. Boutière and A-H. Schutz, *Biographies des troubadours*, 1964. Many are mendacious, but see those of Guilhem Figuera, Folquet de Marseille, Perdigon, Pistoleta, and Raimon de Miraval. Jeanroy, *Poésie lyrique*, pp. 212–32, collects the main references to the crusade in their works.

## PRINCIPAL SECONDARY WORKS (1975)

BELPERRON, P. *La croisade contre les Albigeois*, 1945.
BORST, A. *Die Catharer*, 1953.

# Select bibliography

BOURILLY, V. L., BUSQUET, R., etc. *Les Bouches-du-Rhône. Encyclopédie departementale*, vol. ii (*Le moyen âge*), 1924.

BOYER, C. *Le siège de Minerve*, 1934.

BRUN, A. *Recherches historiques sur l'introduction du français dans les provinces du Midi*, 1923.

CANIVEZ, J-M. 'Conrad d'Urach', *Dict. d'hist. et de geog. eccl.*, vol. xiii, pp. 504–7.

DELPECH, H. *La tactique au xiii$^e$ siècle*, 2 vols. 1885.

DIEULAFOY, M. 'La bataille de Muret', *Mems de l'Acad. des Inscr. et B-L*, vol. xxxvi(2), 1901, pp. 97–134.

DOGNON, P. *Les institutions politiques et administratives du pays de Languedoc du xiii$^e$ siècle aux guerres de religion*, 1895.

DONDAINE, A. 'L'origine de l'hérésie médiévale', *Rivista di storia della chiesa in Italia*, vol. vi, 1952, pp. 47–78.

DOSSAT, Y. *Les crises de l'Inquisition Toulousaine au xiii$^e$ siècle (1233–73)*, 1959.

DUPONT, A. *Les cités de la Narbonnaise première depuis les invasions germaniques jusqu'à l'apparition du consolat*, 1942.

   'L'évolution des institutions municipales de Beaucaire', *Annales du Midi*, vol. lxxvii, 1965, pp. 257–74.

   *Les relations commerciales entre les cités maritimes du Languedoc et les cités Mediterranéennes d'Espagne et d'Italie du x$^e$ au xiii$^e$ siècle*, 1942.

FARAL, E. *Les jongleurs en France au moyen âge*, 1910.

FLICHE, A. 'L'état Toulousaine', in F. Lot and R. Fawtier, *Hist. des institutions françaises au moyen âge, Institutions seigneuriales*, 1957, pp. 71–99.

FOURNIER, P. *Le royaume d'Arles et de Vienne (1138–1378)*, 1891.

GOURON, A. 'Diffusion des consulats méridionaux et expansion du droit romain aux xii$^e$ et xiii$^e$ siècles', *Bibl. de l'Ecole des Chartes*, vol. cxxi, 1963, pp. 26–73.

GRIFFE, E. *Les débuts de l'aventure cathare en Languedoc (1140–1190)*, 1969.

   *Le Languedoc Cathare de 1190 à 1210*, 1971.

   *Le Languedoc Cathare au temps de la croisade (1209–1229)*, 1973.

GUIRAUD, J. *Cartulaire de N-D de Prouille*, vol. i, 1907.

   *Hist. de l'Inquisition au moyen âge*, 2 vols., 1935–8.

HELIOT, P. 'L'âge du château de Carcassonne', *Annales du Midi*, vol. lxxviii, 1966, pp. 7–21.

HIGOUNET, C. 'Un grand chapitre de l'histoire du xii$^e$ siècle. La rivalité des maisons de Toulouse et de Barcelone pour la préponderance meridionale', in *Mélanges . . . L. Halphen*, 1951, pp. 313–22.

HILL, J. H. and L. L. *Raimond de Saint-Gilles*, 1959.

JEANROY, A. *La poésie lyrique des troubadours*, 2 vols., 1934.

LACQUER, L. DE 'L'Albigeois pendant la crise de l'Albigéisme', *Rev. d'hist. eccl.*, vol. xxix, 1933, pp. 272–315, 586–633, 849–904.

LAHONDES, J. DE 'Les châteaux de Cabaret', *Bull. Soc. Archéol. du Midi*, 2$^e$ série, nos. 25–8, 1899–1901, pp. 121–39.

LEROY LADURIE, E. *Montaillou. Village occitan de 1294 à 1324*, 1975.

LEWIS, A. R. *The development of southern French and Catalan society*, 1965.

LIMOUZIN-LAMOTHE, R. *La commune de Toulouse et les sources de son historie (1120–1249)*, 1932.

LOT, F. *L'art militaire et les armées au moyen âge*, 1946.

LUCHAIRE, A. *Innocent III*, 6 vols., 1904–8.

MAGNOU-NORTIER, E. 'Fidélité et féodalité méridionales d'après les serments de fidèlité', *Annales du Midi*, vol. lxxx, 1968, pp. 457–77.

MAISONNEUVE, H. *Etudes sur les origines de l'Inquisition*, 1960.

# Select bibliography

MALAFOSSE, J. 'Le siège de Toulouse par Simon de Montfort', *Revue des Pyrénées*, vol. iv, 1892, pp. 497–522, 725–56.

MANSELLI, R. 'Il monaco Enrico e la sua eresia', *Bull. Ist. Stor. Ital. per il medio evo*, no. 65, 1953, pp. 1–63.

MARCA, P. DE *Hist. de Béarn*, 2nd ed., vol. ii, 1912.

MARROU, H. I. *Les troubadours*, 1971.

MUNDY, J. *Liberty and political power in Toulouse, 1050–1230*, 1954.

NELLI, R. *L'érotique des troubadours*, 1963.

*La vie quotidienne des Cathares du Languedoc au xiiie siècle*, 1969.

NIEL, F. *Montségur. Le site, son histoire*, 1962.

OMAN, C. *Hist. of the art of war in the middle ages*, 2nd ed., 2 vols., 1924.

PETIT-DUTAILLIS, E. *Etude sur la vie et le règne de Louis VIII*, 1894.

POUX, J. *La cité de Carcassonne. Histoire et description*, vol. ii, 1931.

ROQUEBERT, M. *L'épopée Cathare. 1198–1212: L'invasion*, 1970.

RUNCIMAN, S. *The mediaeval manichee*, 1947.

STRONSKI, S. *Le troubadour Folquet de Marseille*, 1910.

THOUZELLIER, C. 'Hérésie et croisade au xiie siècle', *Rev. d'hist. eccl.*, vol. xlix, 1954, pp. 855–72.

*Catharisme et Valdéisme en Languedoc*, 2nd ed., 1969.

THROOP, P. A. *Criticism of the crusade*, 1940.

VAISSETE, J. *Histoire générale de Languedoc*, 2nd ed. A. Molinier, vols. iii–viii, 1879.

VENTURA-SUBIRATS, J. *Pere el Catolic e Simon de Montfort*, 1960.

VICAIRE, M-H. *Hist. de St. Dominique. Un homme évangélique*, 1957.

WAKEFIELD, W. L. *Heresy, crusade, and Inquisition in southern France, 1100–1250*, 1974.

WOLFF, P. *Hist. de Toulouse*, 1958.

# Index

Abraham ben Issaac, 90
Adhémar de Poitiers, 86
Agde, 18, 20, 212
Agen, 17, 49, 85, 205–6, 238; bp. of,
66, 108, 175; Cathar bp. of, 147
Aimery de Montréal, 129
Alaman de Rouaix, 228, 236
Alan of Lille, 40, 48, 53
Alan de Roucy, 204
Alaric, 111
Alberic, cardinal bp. of Ostia, 44–5
Albi, 20, 45, 57, 222, 242, 248
Aldebert, bp. of Viviers, 249
Alès, 129, 246, 247
Alet, bp. of, 48, 61
Alexander III, pope, 46, 56
Alice de Montfort, *see* Alice de
Montmorency
Alice de Montmorency, 114, 146, 192,
196
Aliscamps, 221–2
Alphonse of Poitiers, 224, 225, 241,
244–5, 246–8, 251
Alphonse-Jourdain, count of Toulouse,
22, 45
Alphonso VIII, k. of Castile, 70, 144
Alzonne, 102, 106
Amaury Copeau, 219
Amaury de Montfort, 138, 205, 206,
209, 212; knighted, 161–2; marries
Beatrice of Burgundy, 174; elected
count of Toulouse, 199; campaign
of 1218–19, 202, 203; besieges
Marmande (1219), 203–4; offers
dominions to Philip Augustus, 207–
208; relieves Penne d'Agenais, 208;

bankruptcy, 210; leaves Languedoc,
210; opposes reconciliation of
Raymond VII, 213–14, 215; joins
Louis VIII's crusade, 216; subsequent career, 210–11
Anselm of Alexandria, 36
Antwerp, 37
Arles, 88; abp. of, 44, 158, 214
armour, 203
Arnald-Amaury, abt. of Cîteaux, abp.
of Narbonne, 71, 86, 88, 101–2, 103,
106, 113, 154, 178; character, 68;
visits Rome (1208), 77; recruits
crusaders, 77–8; refuses to accept
Raymond VI's submission, 81;
meeting with legates, 82; at royal
council of Villeneuve, 83; rejects
submission of Raymond-Roger
Trencavel, 89; at sack of Béziers,
93–4; at siege of Carcassonne, 99–
100; negotiates with Toulouse,
113–14; at siege of Minerve, 117–18;
at council of St.-Gilles (1210), 119–
120; and Las Navas campaign,
144–5; reproved by Innocent III,
159; becomes abp. of Narbonne,
175; quarrel with Simon de Montfort, 178–9, 181, 190–1; and
crusade of Louis VIII, 221; death
225, 226
Arnaud Català, inquisitor, 231
Arnaude de Lamothe, 227–8, 236
Arnold of Brescia, 37–8
Auch, abp. of, 116, 189
Auterive, 222
Autun, bp. of, 87

*261*

# Index

Auvergne, count of, 79, 85
Auxerre, 82; bp. of, 161
Avignon, 83, 89, 107, 182, 184, 206, 218–19, 221, 249; siege of, 217–20
Avignonet, 237–8, 240, 242

Baldwyn of Toulouse, 133–5, 141, 144, 147, 150, 173
*balistae*, 123
Bar, count of, 75, 137
Barcelona, bp. of, 160; county of, *see* Catalonia
Barravi (family), 25
Baziège, 202–3
Béarn, 23, 153, 157, 159
Beatrice of Béziers, 64
Beatrice of Burgundy, 174
Beaucaire, 15, 28, 90, 191, 221, 224, 245; siege of (1216), 182–6, 187
Beavais, bp. of, 122, 124
Benjamin of Tudela, 90
Bérenger, abp. of Narbonne, 68
Bérenger, viscount of Narbonne, 22
Berg, count of, 145
Bernard, St., 40, 44, 45–6, 55, 120
Bernard de Cazenac, 174, 197
Bernard IV, count of Comminges, 135–6, 157, 164, 171, 174, 188, 191, 202
Bernard V, count of Comminges, 220
Bernard Délicieux, 242
Bernard Gui, inquisitor, 48, 235
Bernard de Montaut, abp. of Auch, 82
Bernard de Ventadour, 29
Bernard-Raymond de Roquefort, bp. of Carcassonne, 111, 124, 174–5
Bertrand de Born, 28, 29
Bertrand de Marty, 240
Bertrand, cardinal of St. John and St. Paul, 190–1, 194, 195, 199, 206
Bertrand of Saissac, 28, 59
Bertrand, count of Toulouse, 22
Bertrand of Toulouse, 136
Béziers, 18, 20, 24, 57, 69, 72, 89, 90, 91, 96, 104, 137, 206, 208, 221, 246; cathedral, 24, 93; sack of, 90–3, 94; Madeleine, 93; St. Felix, 241; council of (1243) 238; bp. of, *see* William of Rocosels
Bigorre, 23, 189–90; *see* Petronilla
Biron, 149
Blanche of Castile, 222

Bogomil, 35–6
Bologne, 247
Boniface de Montferrand, 29
Bordeaux, 44, 148, 151; abp. of, 85, 137, 147, 227
Bouchard de Marly, 110, 118, 128–9, 139, 140, 167, 216
Boulbonne, abbey of, 201
Bourges, 215, 216, abp. of, 207; council of (1225), 215
Bouvines, 170, 177, 196, 203
Bram, 111
Brittany, count of, 216
Bruges, 37
Bruniquel, 134, 141, 144

Cabaret, 105, 109, 110, 128–9, 172
Cadouin, 149
Cahors, 249; bp. of, 139, 175, 197
Calixtus II, pope, 43
Cambiac, 233
Capdenier, Bernard, 25, 112; Pons, 25
Carcassonne, 19, 20, 21, 24, 49, 57, 70, 73, 89, 90, 92, 104, 109, 110, 111, 121, 125, 129, 132, 135, 137, 138, 139, 166, 169, 200, 207, 209, 210, 212, 220, 221, 223, 225, 231, 232, 242, 246, 251; bp. of, 61; Cathar bp. of, 72; siege of (1209), 94–7, 98–100; St. Nazaire, 249
Carpentras, bp. of, 66, 84
Casseneuil, 85, 177
Castelnaudary, 142, 161–2, 205, 221, 228, 229, 233, 243; siege of, 137–141, 167
Castelsarrasin, 152, 222
Castres, 102, 105, 111, 143, 211, 227
Catalonia, 22, 24, 97–8, 242, 250–1
Catharism, 42, 72, 73, 85, 92, 118, 230, 232, 238–9; name, 39; theology, 47–9; organization, 49–52; social life, 52–3; persecution by crusaders, 227–9; end of, 235–7, 241–3, 252
Celestine III, pope, 66
Centule d'Astarac, 204, 205
Cerdagne, 251
*Chanson de la Croisade Contre les Albigeois*, 260
*chansons de geste*, 85, 86, 141, 144, 170, 221–2
Charles of Anjou, 211, 249, 251
Charles the Bald, emperor, 41

262

# Index

Chartres, bp. of, 122, 123
Château Gaillard, 117
Châteauneuf, 191
Chinon, 78
Cistercian order, 54, 59, 72, 73, 79, 105, 226
Claret, 228
Clement, heretical preacher, 38
Clermont, bp. of, 88
Clermont-Ferrand, cathedral, 249
Cologne, 37, 39, 41, 42, 145
Comminges, 23, 157, 159, 246; bp. of, 153; see Bernard IV, Bernard V
Conrad of Urach, cardinal of Porto, 206–7, 208, 209, 213, 214
Constance of France, countess of Toulouse, 46, 63
Corbario, 239
Corbeil, viscount of, 166; treaty of (1258), 251
Cordes, 231, 238, 247
Cosmas the priest, 35
Couserans, bp. of, 153; count of, 191
Crest, 192

Dalon, 30
Dante, 17, 29, 112, 131, 132, 248
*dard*, 85
Diego, bp. of Osma, 70–3
Dominic, St., 54, 68, 70–3, 145, 226–7, 228
Dominican order, 25, 226–7, 230–1
Dreux, count of, 75, 122
Dulcia (Cathar), 50
Durand, bp. of Albi, 239
Durand of Huesca, 54, 73

Echbert of Schonau, 40
Eleanor of Aquitaine, 30
Elne, 18
Ermengarde, viscount of Narbonne, 20
Esclarmande of Foix, 60, 180, 236
Esclarmande de Perella, 240
Etienne de Servian, 71–2
Eugenius III, pope, 44

*faidits*, 172, 173, 175, 179, 180, 182
Fanjeaux 51, 57, 59, 60, 102, 138, 164, 228
Flanders, count of, 75
Foix, 20, 23, 102, 114, 153, 157, 159,

190, 246; abbey of St.-Volusien, 62; see Raymond-Roger, Roger-Bernard
Folquet de Marseille, bp. of Toulouse, 29, 30, 112–13, 114, 130, 135, 160, 167, 169, 180–1, 188–9, 195–6, 221, 225, 226
Fontevrault, 244
Fontfroide, 59, 68, 250
Foucaud de Berzy, 202, 205
Franquevaux, 73
Frederick II, Holy Roman Emperor, 208, 213, 231, 239

Gaston de Béarn, 137, 148, 157
Gaston Phébus, count of Foix, 249
Gaucher de Châtillon, count of St.-Pol, 100, 219, 222
Gent Esquieu, lord of Minerve, 28
Geoffrey of Auxerre, 45–6
Geoffrey Neville, 176
Gerhoh of Reichersburg, 40
Gervase of Tilbury, 18
Giraud de Pépieux, 110, 131, 152
Giraude de Laurac, 129, 131–2
Giroussens, 228
Godfrey, bp. of Chartres, 45
Grandselve, abbey, abt. of, 45, 59, 68, 223, 225
Gregory IX, pope, 223, 230, 231, 234
Gregory X, 91
Grenade, 247
Guilabert de Castres, 72, 228, 236–7
Guilelma, Cathar Perfect, 52
Guilhem de Moncada, 170
Guillaume Arnuad, 238
Guillaume Figuiera, 248
Guiot de Provins, 116
Guy, bp. of Carcassonne, 143, 145, 151, 173, 175
Guy de Levis, 210
Guy de Montfort (brother of Simon), 143–4, 146, 148, 160–1, 179, 189, 192, 198, 210, 211, 214, 216
Guy de Montfort (son of Simon), 210
Guy de Montfort (grandson of Simon), 211

Hautes-Bruyères, 210
Hautpoul, 146
Héloise of Ibelin, 143
Henry of Almain, 211
Henry I, k. of England, 170

# Index

Henry II, k. of England, 23, 54, 63 120, 244

Henry III, k. of England, 211, 216, 238

Henry of Lausanne, 43–4, 45, 46

Henry of Marcy, abt. of Clairvaux, 54–57

Hervé de Donzy, count of Nevers, 75, 78–9, 80, 86, 99, 100, 101–2

Holy Faith, order of, 206

Honorius III, pope, 201–2, 203, 204, 206, 210; character, 187; restores count of Foix, 190; urges Philip Augustus to invade Languedoc, 200–1; proclaims fresh crusade, 206–7; considers recognizing Raymond VII, 208–9, 213, 214

Hospitallers of St. John, order of, 65, 127, 150, 208

Hugh of Alfaro, 148, 237

Hugh d'Arcis, 238, 241

Hugh de Lacy, 138

Humbert of Beaujeu, 222, 223

Imbert de Salas, 238

Innocent III, pope, 15, 16, 60, 64, 70, 75, 76, 80, 82, 87, 93, 96, 104, 105, 106, 128, 147, 156, 171, 186, 190; character of, 66–7, 103; excommunicates Raymond VI (1207), 74; invites Philip Augustus to invade Languedoc, 75–6, 79; summons crusade, 77, 81–2; revokes powers of Arnald-Amaury, 108–9; safeguards interests of Raymond VI, 156; suspends crusade (1212), 159–60; restores Simon de Montfort, 162; deposes southern bishops, 174–5; condemns assault on Narbonne, 179; death, 186–7

Innocent IV, pope, 242

Inquisition, 40, 48, 53, 58, 68, 106, 225, 227, 230–5, 236, 240, 241, 242–3, 261

Jacques de Vitry, 145, 174, 186, 195–6

James I, k. of Aragon, 169, 189, 248, 251

Jean de Beaumont, 232

Jean Deschamps, 249

Jeanne-Baptiste de Bourbon, abbess of Fontevrault, 244

Jews, 40, 43, 73, 84, 89–90, 93, 95, 107, 112, 163, 217, 243

Joan Plantagenet, 147, 176

Joan of Toulouse, 224, 225, 244

John, k. of England, 74–5, 76, 81, 123, 129–30, 148, 156, 160, 176, 177, 179

John de Berzy, 202, 205

John XXII, pope, 249

John, cardinal of St. Priscus, 67–8

John, count of Soissons, 38

Joinville, 120, 242

Jordan of Cabaret, 220

Joris, 202

Jul, 228

Labécède, 222

Lacapelle, 150

Lagrasse, abt. of, 201

Lagrave, 140, 141

Laguepié, 146

*langue d'oc*, 30, 55, 142, 248, 249

Lanta, 228, 236

La Réole, 176

La Rochelle, 176, 216, 219

Las Navas de Tolosa, 68, 149, 156, 164

Lastours, 109

Lateran council (1179), 23, 56

Lateran council (1215), 173, 179–81

Laurac, 51, 57, 58, 59, 129, 217

Lausanne, 44

Lautrec, 57

Lavaur, 55, 56, 59, 129–32, 135, 137, 142, 221, 227, 228; council of (1212), 157–9

Lavelanet, 146

Le Mans, 44

Leopold VI, count of Austria, 145

Le Puy, 25, 246, bp. of, 85

Les Baux, 22, 246

Les Cassès, 133, 227

Lescure, 70, 201

Liège, 39, 41

Limoges, bp. of, 208

Limoux, 221

Lodève, 18, 24; bp. of, 47

Lolmie, 173

Lombers, 46–7, 57, 111

Lombez, 20

Louis VII, 19, 54, 133, 134

Louis VIII, 83, 160, 177; and campaign of 1215, 178–9; invasion of Languedoc (1219), 200–1, 203–5;

264

# Index

Louis VIII—*cont.*
accession, 209; character, 209;
undertakes new crusade, 212–13;
invades Languedoc, 215–22; death,
222
Louis IX, k. of France, 133, 222, 225,
241, 245, 246, 251
Lourdes, 189
Lucius III, pope, 42
Lunel, 90
Lyon, 83, 85, 87; archdeacon of, 181

Maguelonne, 18; bp. of, 69
Majorca, kingdom of, 251
Manichaean, 34
Marcabrun, 30
Marcion, 33, 34, 48
Mark, Cathar bp., 49
Marmande, 176, 177, 203–4
Marseille, 182, 183, 184
Martin Algai, 139, 140, 149
Mas d'Agenais, 176
Matilda de Garlande, 118
Maurand family, 25, 112
Maurand, Peter, 55
Mauzac, 228
Meaux, 223
Meilhan, 202
Melgueil, 82, 83
Mende, 25
mercenaries, 88, 120, 126, 139, 148,
149, 151, 152
Messalians, 36
Michel de Harnes, 196
Milan, 170
Millau, 244
Milo, papal legate, 82, 88, 107, 109
Minerve, 59, 105, 116, 133, 210, 227
Mirepoix, 20, 73, 102
Moissac, 149, 150, 151–2, 208, 230, 241
Montauban, 149, 150, 152, 157, 160,
227, 228; abt. of, 66
Montaudran, 136
Montégut, 141
Montferrand, 133, 137, 138
Montgey, 131, 133, 180
Montgiscard, 135, 188
Montgrenier, 190
Montlaur, 111
Montpellier, 23, 70–1, 89, 91, 92, 109,
110, 112, 126–7, 178, 214, 217, 247,
251

Montréal, 19, 57, 111, 114, 121, 138
Montségur, 50, 52, 180, 228, 236–41
Moret, 225
Muret, 22, 24, 153; battle of, 164–70,
202–3

Napoleon III, 116
Narbonne, 18, 20, 23, 25, 57, 90, 116,
126, 131, 137, 172, 175–6, 177,
178–9, 206, 209–10, 213, 234, 251;
council of (1227), 222, 229; council
of (1243), 234–5; cathedral, 247;
abp. of, 54, 225
Nevers, bp. of, 88
Nicholas de Brai, 221
Nîmes, 18, 20, 83, 107, 175, 185, 206,
220, 224, 245; cathedral, 63
Niquinta, Cathar abp., 49
Nissan, 94
Nuño Sanchez, 170, 189–90

Odo de l'Etoile, 38–9
Odo III, duke of Burgundy, 78–9, 88,
100, 102
Odo, count of Toulouse, 19
Oliver, Cathar preacher, 47
Oliver of Saissac, 28
Oliver of Termes, 223, 241
Oloron, 158
Orléans, 249; bp. of, 249
Otto, bp. of Carcassonne, 61
Otto IV, Holy Roman Emperor, 80–1,
83, 105, 128, 158, 176, 177

Pamiers, 72, 114, 142, 151, 153, 201,
212, 221, 243; abbey of St.-Antonin,
60; abt. of, 102, 175; statute of,
154–5
Paravis, 244
Paris, archdeacon of, 145, 148, 158–9,
173–4; customs of, 155; treaty of
(1229), 223–5, 229, 231, 236, 244
Paulicians, 35, 36
Pavie, 247
Pennautier, 121
Penne d'Agenais, 148–9, 208, 210
Perdigon, 30
Perpignan, 158; treaty of (1198), 23,
98
Peter of Aigrefeuille, bp. of Béziers,
61, 158, 175
Peter of Anduze, 86

265

Peter II, k. of Aragon, 69–70, 109, 131, 171, 178; at siege of Carcassonne, 97–9; visits Languedoc (1210), 114–115; conference at Narbonne, 126; conference at Montpellier, 127; visits Languedoc (1212), 157; sends ambassadors to Rome, 159; and Muret campaign, 163–4, 167–9

Peter of Benevento, papal legate, 171–172, 173, 177

Peter of Bruys, 44

Peter of Castelnau, legation of, 68–9, 70, 73, 74–5; murder of, 15–16, 75–6, 79; cult of, 81

Peter de Courtenay, 86, 130

Peter Damian, 38

Peter Garcia, Cathar, 48

Peter of Pavia, cardinal of St. Chrysogon, 55

Peter Valdès, 38

Peter of Vaux-de-Cernay, 58, 64, 93, 96, 99, 117, 151, 162, 179, 185, 259–260

Peter the Venerable, abt. of Cluny, 40

Petronilla, countess of Bigorre, 189

Pézenas, 111, 133

Philip Augustus, k. of France, 70, 74, 80, 86, 108, 120, 152, 161, 176–7, 181, 195, 203; refuses to invade Languedoc (1208), 75, 76; refuses to co-operate with crusade, 78; and Las Navas crusade, 144; unwilling to depose Raymond VI, 156; proposed invasion of England, 160; refuses to invade Languedoc (1223), 200–1, 207; and conference of Sens, 209

Philip III, k. of France, 245

Philip IV, the Fair, k. of France, 247, 248

Philip de Montfort, 211

Piacenza, 242

Pierre, *see also* Peter

Pierre Authier, 242

Pierre Bauville, 242

Pierre Cardenal, 248

Pierre Flote, 247

Pierre Seilha, inquisitor, 232

Pierre-Bernard of Sauve, lord of Anduze, 179, 245–6

Pierre-Roger of Cabaret, 28, 109, 121, 122, 128–9

Pierre-Roger of Mirepoix, 237, 241

Pieusse, 228

Pistoleta, 29

Poblet, 68

Poitiers, 44

Pont de l'Arche, 181

Pont-de-Sorgues, 217

Pont-St.-Esprit, 191

Ponthieu, count of, 122

Posquières, 90

Preixan, 102

Prouille, convent of, 73

Provence, 22

Puisserguier, 110

Pujol, 161

Puycelci, 161

Puylaroque, 85

Puylaurens, 52, 137, 138, 146, 205

Quéribus, 241

Rabastens, 228

Rainbaut de Vaqueiras, 29

Rainier da Ponza, 67

Rainier Sacchoni, inquisitor, 53

Ralph, monk of Fontfroide, 68, 73

Raymond du Fauga, bp. of Toulouse, 228

Raymond Gros, Cathar Perfect, 234

Raymond de Miraval, 29, 64, 109, 172

Raymond de Perella, 236

Raymond de Rabastens, bp. of Toulouse, 60, 69, 82, 113

Raymond de Roquefeuil, 180

Raymond de Salvagnac, 132–3

Raymond de Termes, 122, 124, 125

Raymond III Pons, count of Toulouse, 18

Raymond IV of St.-Gilles, count of Toulouse, 18, 22

Raymond V, count of Toulouse, 20, 22, 23, 28, 30, 54, 56, 61–2, 63, 183

Raymond VI, count of Toulouse, 29, 67, 70, 86, 97, 98, 125, 126, 131, 149, 152, 156, 158, 183–4; character, 63–5; dispute with abt. of St.-Gilles, 65–6; excommunicated (1207), 73–4; negotiates with Peter of Castelnau, 75; role in his murder, 15, 75–6, 77, 84, 108, 120; excommunicated (1208), 77; attempts to stave off crusade, 80–1, 82; penance at

Raymond VI—*cont.*
St.-Gilles, 83–4; joins crusade, 88–9; at siege of Carcassonne, 98–99; appeals against excommunication of Avignon, 107, 108; at conference of Montpellier, 126–7; and siege of Lavaur, 129–30; at siege of Castelnaudary, 137–41; shuts himself in Puylaurens, 146; at Bordeaux (1212), 148, 151; at battle of Muret, 167; absolution (1214), 172; condemns brother to death, 173; at 4th Lateran council, 179, 180, 181; invades Languedoc (1216), 182–4; in Spain, 187, 190; invades Languedoc from Spain (1217), 191–2; opinion of Simon de Montfort, 199; seal, 203; death, 208
Raymond VII, count of Toulouse, 74, 176, 187, 191, 195, 205–6, 208, 213; at 4th Lateran council, 179; besieges Beaucaire, 182, 184–5; reinforces Toulouse (1218), 197; victory at Baziège, 202; attacks Carcassonne, 209; at Council of Bourges, 215; excommunicated (1225), 215; and Louis VIII's invasion, 216, 217, 220, 221; captures Auterive, 222; surrender to Crown, 223–5; and Inquisition, 231–2; and revolt of Trencavel, 232; attacks Montségur, 237; excommunicated (1242), 238; submission to Church, 239–40, 241; death, 244
Raymond-Roger, count of Foix, 59, 72, 102, 104, 110–11, 115, 131, 135–6, 137, 139–40, 141, 142, 146, 157, 164, 171, 172, 173, 179, 180, 181, 190, 193, 195, 201, 202, 209, 212
Raymond-Roger Trencavel, viscount of Béziers, 84, 88–90, 96, 98, 99, 102–3, 172, 210
Raymond-Trencavel, viscount of Béziers, 24, 46
Raymonde Jougla, Cathar, 50
Rénaud of Boulogne, 170
Rheims, abp. of, 39, 151, 207; council of (1148), 38, 46
Richard of Cornwall, 216, 219
Richard I, k. of England, 117, 120, 147, 148, 149, 244

Richelieu, 17, 250
Robert of Arbrissel, 38
Robert de Courtenay, 86, 130
Robert Curzon, 160, 174, 177
Robert of Epernon, Cathar bp., 49
Robert Mauvoisin, 142
Robert, count of Montferrand, 47
Rocamadour, 137
Rochemaure, 88
Rodez, 21, 66; count of, 174; bp. of, 175
Roger II Trencavel, viscount of Béziers, 21, 56, 59, 90
Roger-Bernard, count of Foix, 152, 220–1, 222, 224
Romano Frangipani, cardinal of St. Angelo, 214–15, 216, 220, 222, 225, 229
Roquedur, 245
Roquefeuil, 237
Roquefort, 227
Roquemaure, 228
Roussillon, 23, 129, 251
Roussillon, fortress, 88

St.-André, abbey of, 220
St.-Antonin, 134, 141, 145, 146–7
St.-Félix de Camaran, 49, 54, 233, 235, 248
St.-Flour, 209
St.-Gilles, 15, 24, 44, 81, 83, 89, 119, 121, 185, 224; abt. of, 65–6
St.-Hilaire du Lanquet, abbey, 21, 61
St.-Marcel, 144, 146
St.-Martin la Lande, 139–40, 149
St.-Nicholas de la Grave, 150
St.-Papoul, abt. of, 62
St.-Paul-Cadajoux, 58
St.-Paul de Fénouillet, 48
St.-Pons de Thomières, abbey, 21
St.-Ruf, abt. of, 127, 129
St.-Séver de Rustan, 250
St.-Thibéry, abt. of, 190
Saissac, 139, 172
Savari de Mauléon, 129, 130, 137, 140, 148, 151, 216
Saverdun, 102, 153, 165
Séguin de Balenx, 85
Sens, 209; abp. of, 88, 207, 210
Servian, 71, 91–2, 205
Sévérac, 175
Sicard d'Alaman, 246

Sicard de Puylaurens, 220
Simon de Montfort (the elder), 86, 104, 115, 126, 142, 176, origins, 100–1; character, 101, 143; election as viscount of Béziers, 100, 101–2; burns heretics at Castres, 106, 227; besieges Minerve, 117–20; besieges Termes, 121–5; does homage to Peter II of Aragon, 126; besieges Lavaur, 129, 131–2; destroys Montgey, 133; besieges Toulouse (1211), 134–6; besieged in Castelnaudary, 137–41; campaign in Albigeois (1211–12), 144, 146–8; campaign in Agenais, 148–9; besieges Biron, 149; besieges Moissac, 151–2; government of Languedoc, 153–5, 174, 183–4; reproved by Innocent III, 159; arms his son, 161–2; at battle of Muret, 166–7, 169; elected provisional count of Toulouse, 178–9; fails to relieve Beaucaire, 184–6, punishment of Toulouse, 187–9; invades Bigorre, 189–90; attacks count of Foix, 190; invades Rhône valley, 190–1, 192; besieges Toulouse (1217–18), 192–8; death, 198; burial, 199, 210
Simon de Montfort (the younger), 100, 211
Soissons, 41; count of, 196, 200
Sorrèze, 242

Taillebourg, 238
Tanchelm, 37
Tarascon, 18, 87, 183, 184
Taravel, 228
Tarbes, 189, 250
Tarragona, 250
Templars, 127, 150, 178, 206
Termes, 105, 121–5, 175
Thedisius, 82, 107, 108, 109, 117, 119, 125, 158–9, 162, 175
Thibault IV, count of Champagne, 201, 211, 216, 219
Thomas Aquinas, 41
Thoronet (Le), 113
Thouars, 76
Tibald, count of Bar, 135
Tirvia, 243
Torves, 133
Toul, bp. of, 151

Toulouse, 25, 46, 49, 57, 87, 111–12, 113–14, 118, 130–1, 153, 158, 160, 161, 165–6, 169, 171, 172, 175, 178, 187, 206, 221, 227, 230, 231, 241, 242, 244, 245; council of (1056), 43; bp. of, 61; siege of (1211), 134–6, 137; destruction of fortifications (1215), 178–9; punishment of by Simon de Montfort, 187–9; siege of (1217–18), 65, 192–8, 200; siege of (1219), 204–5; siege of (1228), 223; destruction of walls (1229), 225; *bourg*, 112, 113, 189; *cité*, 112, 114, 189; Bazacle, 192; Place Montaigon, 130; Château Narbonnais, 136, 172, 173, 175, 178, 189, 191, 192, 194, 199, 226, 233; St.-Cyprien suburbs, 193, 196; Pont Neuf, 196–7; Daurade, 112; Dominican church, 25, 247; St.-Etienne, 56, 112, 188, 192; St. James, 56; St.-Pierre-de-Cuisines, 112; St.-Sernin, 55, 112, 192, 204 (abt. of, 69, 208); university of, 224–5, 229
Tours, council of (1163), 46
*trebuchets*, 116–17
Trencavel family, 20, 21, 23, 94, 97, 98, 224, 250; *see* Roger II Trencavel, Raymond-Roger Trencavel, Raymond-Trencavel, Trencavel
Trencavel (son of Raymond-Roger Trencavel), 210, 232, 241, 242
*troubadours*, 28–31, 64, 109, 129, 163, 172–3, 180, 207, 248, 261
Turenne, viscount of, 196

Uzès, bp. of, 126, 167

Vaison, bp. of, 66, 84
Valence, 83
Valentinois, count of, 174
Vareilles, 211
*Veni Creator Spiritus*, 151, 161, 179
*Veni Sancte Spiritus*, 96
Ventajou, 121
Verfeil, 45, 57
Vézélay, 41
Vienne, 178
Villemur, 85, 227
Villeneuve-lès-Toulouse, 188
Viviers, 191, bp. of, 69

# Index

Waldensians, 38, 40, 53–4, 70, 72, 234, 243, 252
Walter of Avesnes, 217–18
Walter Langton, 196
Waso, bp. of Liège, 40
William IX, duke of Aquitaine, 29
William Belibaste, 243
William the Breton, 24, 203
William Cat, 142
William of Contres, 121, 167
William de l'Ecureuil, 124

William, count of Julich, 145
William of Minerve, 117, 118
William of Nogaret, 247, 248
William Peire, bp. of Albi, 62, 201
William Porcelet, 88
William of Puylaurens, 61, 202, 204, 224, 230, 260
William of Rocosels, bp. of Béziers, 69
William of Tudela, 85, 87, 152, 260
Wireker, Nigel, 37

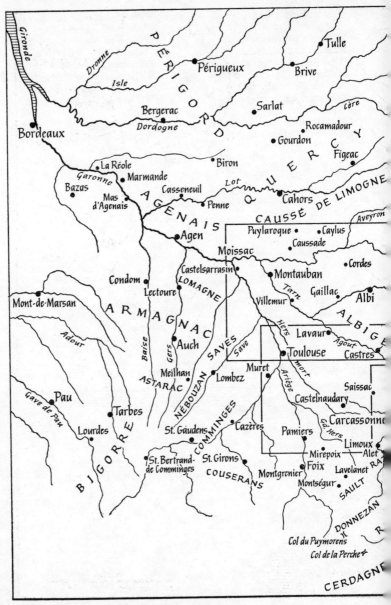

XI.  Languedoc in the time of the crusade